D1616776

English Folktales

# English Folktales

**Edited by Dan Keding and Amy Douglas**

World Folklore Series

**LIBRARIES**
UNLIMITED
A Member of the Greenwood Publishing Group

Westport, Connecticut • London

**Library of Congress Cataloging-in-Publication Data**

English folktales / edited by Dan Keding and Amy Douglas.
    p. cm. — (World folklore series)
    Includes bibliographical references and index.
    ISBN 1-59158-260-1 (alk. paper)
    1. Tales—England. 2. Folklore—England. I. Keding, Dan. II. Douglas, Amy. III. Series.
GR141.E57 2005
398.2'0942—dc22   2005016075

British Library Cataloguing in Publication Data is available.

Library of Congress Catalog Card Number: 2005016075
ISBN: 1-59158-260-1

First published in 2005

Libraries Unlimited, 88 Post Road West, Westport, CT 06881
A Member of Greenwood Publishing, Inc.
www.lu.com

Printed in the United States of America

The paper used in this book complies with the
Permanent Paper Standard issued by the National
Information Standards Organization  (Z39.48–1984).

10   9   8   7   6   5   4   3   2   1

The publisher has done its best to make sure the instructions and/or recipes in this book
are correct. However, users should apply judgment and experience when preparing recipes, especially parents and teachers working with young people. The publisher accepts
no responsibility for the outcome of any recipe included in this volume.

This book is dedicated to my parents who have always helped me to follow my heart and to Chris who holds my heart in trust.

Amy Douglas

I wish to dedicate the book to Tandy Lacy, my wife, who truly understands why I tell stories.

Dan Keding

Together we would like to dedicate this book to all the English storytellers who have shared their friendship and tales over the years. Especially to Mike Rust, Taffy Thomas, Helen East, Derek and Pippa Reid, and Richard Walker. The journey has been shorter because of you.

# Contents

Preface ...........................................................................................xi

Acknowledgments .......................................................................xiii

Introduction ...............................................................................xv

**A Brief History of England** ......................................................1

**The Fool in All His Glory** .........................................................15

Start and Finish ...........................................................................16

The Farmer and the Cheeses .......................................................18

The Pottle of Brains ....................................................................20

Jack Turnip ..................................................................................26

Lazy Jack ....................................................................................27

The Vinegars ...............................................................................35

The Old Woman Who Lived in a Vinegar Bottle ........................37

The Mare's Egg ...........................................................................40

The Most Unfortunate Man .........................................................43

**Wily Wagers and Tall Tales**.....................................................47

The Old Woman and Her Pig ......................................................48

The Dog That Talked ...................................................................50

The Horse Who Knew about Cars ................................................51

Old Lightowler..............................................................................53

The Hole Stone ............................................................................54

White Ram Night .........................................................................60

The Wrestlers of Carn Kenidjack ................................................62

**Dragons and Devils** ..............................................................65

The Lambton Worm ..............................................................66

The Laidly Worm ..............................................................71

Pollard and the Brawn ..............................................................75

    Recipe for Stotty Cake ..............................................................77

The Devil and the Coracle ..............................................................79

The Devil in Wem ..............................................................83

The Devil and the Stiperstones ..............................................................85

**Witches, Wonders, and Weddings** ..............................................................89

Lightening the Load ..............................................................90

A Story of Zennor ..............................................................92

The Stars in the Sky ..............................................................95

The Pixies' Bed ..............................................................98

The Old Woman and the Fairy Folk ..............................................................99

Wild Edric ..............................................................102

Tattercoats ..............................................................105

Kate Crackernuts ..............................................................108

    A Wedding Toast ..............................................................114

Molly Whuppie ..............................................................115

The Glass House ..............................................................120

The White Cow of Mitchell's Fold ..............................................................125

The Elder Tree Witch ..............................................................128

**Holy Days and Days of Heroes** ..............................................................131

The First Simnel Cake ..............................................................132

    Recipe for Shrewsbury Simnel Cake ..............................................................134

Golden Shoes ..............................................................137

    Oranges and Lemons ..............................................................141

The Great Bell of Bosham ..............................................................143

Brother Jucundus ..............................................................145

Little John and the Nottingham Fair ..............................................................151

Robin Hood and the Monk ..............................................................154

Sir Gawain and Dame Ragnall ..............................................................160

The Alderley Legend ..............................................................165

**Stories for When the Sun Sets** ...................................................169

    A Rhyme ...................................................170

    Teeny Tiny ...................................................171

    The Dead Moon ...................................................173

    The Golden Ball ...................................................177

    Jenny Greenteeth ...................................................182

    The Standing Stones ...................................................184

    The Girl and the Anorak ...................................................186

    Mr. Fox ...................................................188

    Gytha of the Mill ...................................................192

**Riddles** ...................................................199

**Answers to Riddles** ...................................................203

**A Parting Song** ...................................................205

    Notes on the Stories ...................................................207

    Glossary ...................................................213

    Index ...................................................217

    About the Editors ...................................................221

    About the Storytellers ...................................................223

# Preface

This book is the fruit of long friendship and a common love of story. Dan Keding and Amy Douglas first met more than ten years ago on the American side of the ocean. Amy was visiting the National Storytelling Festival in Tennessee as part of a year studying storytelling, and Dan was performing at the festival. Since then, a strong mutual respect for each other's stories, culture, and traditions has deepened into a long-lasting friendship.

Over the last decade, Dan has come to know and love England and its stories, while Amy has relished the opportunity to share her English stories with an American audience. They have both treasured the support and generosity of the English storytelling community.

# Acknowledgments

We would like to express our sincere appreciation to the many people who have helped in the creation of this collection.

Most of all, we thank all the storytellers who have contributed to the book. Their love of story and dedication to sharing, crafting, and caretaking of English folklore, myth, and tradition is the fuel that keeps the bright light of our heritage radiant. All the storytellers and details of their work are listed at the back of the book.

Thank you to all the photographers who have kindly given permission for their work to be included: Brian Douglas, Jackie Douglas, Janet Dowling, Helen East, Lynette Eldon, and Chris Lambart.

Our thanks go to The Association of British Counties (ABC) for their permission to use their map for the basis of the map of stories. ABC is a society dedicated to promoting awareness of the continuing importance of the eighty-six historic (or traditional) counties of Great Britain. To learn more about their work, please visit their Web site: www.abcounties.co.uk.

On the English side of the Atlantic, this book has very much been a family affair. Heartfelt gratitude is given to Chris Lambart, Amy's partner, for his enormous support in bringing cups of tea at just the right moment, his written to order synopsis of the history of England, and his technical help with the map. Thank you to Jackie and Brian Douglas, Amy's parents, for their time spent proofreading and to Jack and Molly Douglas, Amy's grandparents, for their rhymes and recipes. Thank you to both generations for inspiring their daughter/granddaughter with a deep love of language and tradition that has been a joy throughout her life.

On the American side, Dan thanks, as always, his wife, Tandy Lacy, for her never-ending support. Sadly no longer with us, he would also like to remember and acknowledge his maternal grandmother, who came to America in 1922 from Croatia and brought with her folktales and fairy tales that he learned from an early age. She gave those tales as a gift and in turn instilled in him his love of story and storytellers—those stories helped to shape Dan both as a man and as a storyteller, and that is where it all began.

# Introduction

Although England is a small country, it is amazingly diverse. As you travel through the country, every few miles the scenery, atmosphere and even the accent of the people change. There are modern built-up city centers, the wild windswept moors of Devon and Yorkshire, the domestic patchwork quilt of the rural middle England, mountains and meadows, forests and heath, babbling brooks and rushing rivers. The English history lies spread out across the land: ancient hill forts, ruined castles, black and white timbered manors, thatched cottages and the modern architectural feats of the Tate Modern and the Eden Project. And everywhere you go there are stories to be found. Every rock, mountain, field, and village has its own story. Some are well-known throughout the country, such as the stories of Robin Hood and King Arthur; some are almost forgotten, the memories of them lying in their place name or a mossed-over memorial—but they are all still here waiting to be discovered and brought to life on the tongue of a storyteller once more.

Passing on those tales from one person to another is part of the storytelling world and a tradition that is live and well in England. Every time that Dan visits England, he returns with a pocketful of stories, gifts to share with his audiences in America. Sometimes those tales are shared late at night after a performance or festival, sometimes on a journey, the places in the story being pointed out through the windows of the car.

There are storytelling clubs scattered all over England, some informal gatherings where like-minded people come together to swap stories, others where you can hear professional storytellers in concert. There are a number of storytelling festivals including Festival at the Edge in Shropshire, The Lakeland Storytelling Festival in the Lake District and the West Country Storytelling Festival in Devon. There is a Society for Storytelling (SfS), a national body promoting stories and storytelling throughout England and Wales and even a museum, Mythstories, dedicated to the art of storytelling. Wherever you go, it seems there is somewhere where you can sit back and listen to tellers as they weave their spell of words and take their audience on a wonderful, magical trip to faraway places. At Festival at the Edge, you can sit in the shadows near the campfires and watch as, one by one, tellers rise from the listening audience to take their place as links in an endless chain that stretches back through English history and celebrates the humor and joy, the sadness and grief, the struggle and hope that folktales keep alive for the people who have told them and for the people who have listened for countless generations.

These stories share a commonality with the folktales of all cultures. In these tales, we see the same struggles and hope that we encounter in stories of the peoples of the Americas or the Middle East, in the legends of Asia or Africa. As people read and hear the stories of another country, they not only gain a better understanding of its people, they also understand their own people and past as well. What better way to learn about another nation, another people, than through the folktales they have kept alive through countless generations. If bridges can be built in this world between nations, then the foundation of those bridges are the stories that people tell in their communities and around their kitchen tables, that they keep alive in their hearts.

Although a book like this can only scratch the surface of a country's folktales, it is our chance to celebrate the wealth and variety of traditional English stories and the talent of the many storytellers to be found here. Each storyteller has a different voice, style, and story to tell. We hope readers will enjoy these stories from England and hear the voices of the tellers as they read their words.

# A Brief History of England

## Christopher Lambart

England shares the island of Britain with Scotland and Wales. It occupies less than half the area of the island, but with the flattest and most productive land and the gentlest climate, it has by far the most people. Although before the Ice Age, Britain was joined to mainland Europe and has many of the same plants and animals, for thousands of years it has been an island.

The country's history goes back long before England ever existed as a country, and this history can be seen in England's landscape, its people, and the stories that are told there.

People first came to England in the Stone Age. For food, they hunted wild animals and gathered what they could from the land. They left behind few traces—stones, bones, and animal horns shaped as tools, as well as a few carved pictures. Later people began to settle, making clearings in the woodland that covered much of the country and establishing island villages in the marshes of the lowlands. They learned how to grow crops and tend animals. They also developed communities that raised the ancient standing stones and stone circles, such as Stonehenge and Mitchell's Fold, and the burial mounds known as barrows. They made primitive forts on hilltops by digging ditches and piling the earth into banks. Over time, they settled into tribes, each with its own area and its own chief or king.

Writing came to England with the Romans, and the first stories of England date from this time. After Julius Caesar conquered Gaul (modern-day France), he reached the English Channel and wanted to conquer the white-cliffed land he saw beyond. His two invasions, in 55 and 54 B.C. were both short-lived. He came. He saw. He did not conquer.

Roman conquest of the island came almost a century later, starting in A.D. 43. The emperor Claudius terrified the native tribes with his war elephants and defeated them with the organized might of his armored legions and the power of his catapults, which could shoot arrows and boulders over the defenses of their hill-forts. The last of the tribal chiefs to hold out against the Romans was Caractacus. He was captured and taken to Rome in chains. When he saw the city, he is said to have asked why they wanted his huts when they had all this grandeur. For that, he was given his freedom.

To retain their hold on the country, the Romans built stone forts and walled cities linked by roads—long, straight, stone roads that were well suited to marching and had mile posts showing the distance from Rome. Visitors can still walk on these roads in certain quiet places; elsewhere these ancient roads lie under modern ones of today. The Romans brought soldiers from all over the empire to England and used them to garrison the province. Land was given to the soldiers so that they could stay in England when they retired from the army. Over time, the retired soldiers and their families became part of the country.

Although they controlled England and Wales, the Romans did not conquer Scotland. To protect themselves from the Picts who lived in Scotland, the Romans built a wall across Britain in a place where it is only seventy-three miles from east coast to west. Hadrian's Wall, named after the emperor during whose reign it was built, still stands close to the present-day border between England and Scotland.

For four hundred years, the Roman legions stayed in England. Then the decay of the empire and the threat posed by tribes on mainland Europe led to the last of the legions being pulled back across the English Channel for the defense of Rome. England disappeared into the Dark Ages—so called because they are a time from which few records survive and so historians are often working in the dark when trying to understand what happened. During this time, the Picts crossed Hadrian's Wall, which had been left undefended, and raided England. It was also when the Saxons came in their long ships, first to plunder the coast and then to settle the land and conquer its people.

A few folktales come from this time. There are the tales of Vortigern (a Romanized king of southeastern England); his Saxon mercenaries, Hengist and Horsa; and Hengist's daughter, Rowena. But most of all, there are the beginnings of the story of Arthur, the Once and Future King, the king who was and will be. These stories are a light shining through the darkness of the period, but they are a light tinted and distorted by their telling and retelling over fifteen hundred years. No one can know exactly what spark of truth the stories contain. Maybe Arthur was a Roman soldier—or perhaps a man raised in Roman ways—fighting to defend his way of life from the invaders. All we know is that he is first named in writings that tell of this time.

The Saxons and the other tribes that came with them from northern Germany, the Jutes and the Angles, took the land and made their own kingdoms. Traditionally it is said that there came to be seven Anglo-Saxon kingdoms: Northumbria, Anglia, Mercia, Wessex, Essex, Sussex, and Kent. Like the Romans, the Saxons did not conquer all of Britain. The mountainous west of the island was held against them: Wales, Cornwall, and Cumbria were ruled by the old Celtic tribes with their memories of the glory of Rome. For many years, these areas, along with Ireland, were an outpost of Christianity beyond the pagan kingdoms of Anglo-Saxon England.

According to legend, in the sixth century, two hundred years after the fall of the Roman Empire, a young Christian man called Gregory was walking past a slave market in Rome. He saw two children with fair hair and blue eyes offered for sale. He asked, "Of what race are they?"

"They are Angles, from the kingdom of Anglia," came the reply.

"They are not Angles but Angels," was Gregory's answer.

Gregory became pope in A.D. 590. Remembering the slaves in the market, he sent Augustine to convert the Angles and the Saxons to Christianity. Augustine and others succeeded over time. By the eighth century, most of England was Christian. The church, with its bishops and its abbeys, acted as a unifying force between the English kingdoms and became a storehouse of knowledge and learning. Some Anglo-Saxon kings and princesses became great supporters of the church and are remembered as the founders of abbeys and cathedrals or were made saints for the miracles they performed or for dying for their faith.

Like the Romans, the Saxons built features that have survived in the landscape. Their great border barrier was not a wall but a 173-mile-long ditch and bank—a bank that in some places still reaches up to twenty-five feet high. The barrier—bank and ditch together—is known as Offa's Dyke, named after King Offa of Mercia, who is thought to have had it built in the eighth century. The border between England and Wales still runs close to its line.

England now had established what were to become its borders—the sea, the wall, and the dyke—but it still wasn't a single country. Instead, it was several kingdoms, some Anglo-Saxon, and some Romano-Celtic. These kingdoms were now troubled by new invaders from the sea. The Danes or Norsemen came to loot, plunder, and conquer.

Most famous of the Anglo-Saxons from this time is Alfred, king of Wessex. By 872, all the other Anglo-Saxon kings had either been defeated or fled, and their kingdoms had fallen to the Norsemen. Alfred defended Wessex in three ways. First, he created fortified towns called *burghs* (many English towns were founded in this way, and the word lives on in place-names both in England and America, such as Bamburgh and Pittsburgh). Second, he changed the way that people served in his army so that an army was always ready to fight the Danes. Third, he created his own navy to fight invaders at sea; now he could stop them before they could land on shore and keep them from setting up camps on the coast, where their raiding parties could find shelter and get supplies and reinforcements.

Having saved his kingdom, Alfred made peace with the Danes rather than seeking to conquer them. He then set about restoring his kingdom from the effects of the war and improving it through building and education. At that time, monks and priests were among the only people able to read and to write. Alfred learned these skills, as well as how to translate books from Latin, the language of the Romans and the Church, into Anglo-Saxon, the language from which English developed. He is also said to have ordered the writing of the *Anglo-Saxon Chronicle,* which was a history of England to that time and a contemporary record of events from then on. It was written in Anglo-Saxon and kept up to date for more than two hundred years. The *Chronicle* tells us that Alfred's grandson Athelstane expanded Wessex to encompass the whole of England and became the first king of England. His son Edgar was crowned in a ceremony that still forms the basis of the English coronation ritual.

The Danes returned, however, and gradually took over the northeast half of the country. Fighting continued until 1016, when an agreement was made between the English king, Edmund Ironside, and the Danish king, Canute: whoever lived longest would inherit the whole kingdom. Edmund died first, and Canute became king of England, Denmark, and, later, Norway. His twenty-four-year reign brought peace and reconciliation to the Danes and Anglo-Saxons. Canute regarded his Anglo-Saxon subjects as equals to his Danish subjects and agreed to uphold the laws of Edgar.

The crown passed back to an English king seven years after Canute's death, with the death of the last of his sons. Edmund's half-brother, Edward, was then declared king. He was a religious man—more like a priest than a warrior—and for this reason he was known as Edward the Confessor. He had been raised in an area of northern France that the Norsemen had conquered and later called Normandy. During his reign, links between Normandy and England grew stronger; William, the duke of Normandy, visited England, and members of the English court visited Normandy.

Edward ruled for more than twenty years. Although he was married, he had no children. When he died on 5 January 1066, his wife's brother, Harold, earl of Wessex, was made king of England. Because Edward had ruled for so long and had no children, however, others had been planning to become king.

Harold Hadrada, king of Norway, had decided that the English throne, which had belonged to Canute less than forty years before, should be his. Aided by Tostig, earl of Northumbria, who had been exiled to Norway even though he was the brother of England's former queen and the new king, he landed in the north of England with an army in September 1066. Led by King Harold, the English army marched north. On September 25, the two armies met near York at a place called Stamford Bridge. Tostig and Harold Hardrada were both killed. Their army was defeated. Their invasion was at an end.

But Harold Hardrada was not the only person who wanted to be king of England. When William, duke of Normandy, visited England, he had persuaded Edward to promise him the throne even though Edward had no right to do this. Also, when Harold has been stranded in Normandy by a shipwreck, he had been made to promise that he would help William become king. William had assembled an army and an invasion fleet. He had been waiting for a south wind so that he could sail across from Normandy. On September 27, two days after the battle of Stamford Bridge, William and his army landed on the south coast of England. Harold marched south.

The battle was fought on 12 October on a hill called Senlac near the town of Hastings in southern England. During the battle, Harold was struck in the eye by an arrow. Although they fought valiantly, his army was defeated, and Harold was killed. William the Conqueror became king of England following what became known as the Battle of Hastings.

This was not just a change of king. The barons and knights who had fought for William became the lords who controlled the country. In return for land and power, William's followers had to swear loyalty and promise to provide fighting men whenever the king wanted them.

New castles were built across England, first in wood and then in stone. Norman barons and knights replaced the Anglo-Saxon earls and thanes who had previously held power. Norman bishops and abbots were brought in to take control of the church. Some Anglo-Saxons, such as Hereward the Wake and Wild Edric, resisted and became part of the folklore of England, but twenty years after the Battle of Hastings, there were only two major English landowners, one English bishop, and three abbots left. The Normans controlled all other areas.

Although he changed the people in charge, William kept most of the laws and ways of running the country that had been established under the Anglo-Saxon kings. He kept the system of shire counties that had grown up under the Anglo-

Saxons, but in each shire, he created a sheriff, or *shire reeve,* to manage the royal estate, preside in the court, oversee the collection of taxes, and organize the militia. These improvements, along with the way he gave his barons land scattered around the country rather than gathered into a single area and made his knights swear loyalty to the king as well as to the baron whom they served, gave him control over his knights and barons. Even though there was a clear division between a Norman French-speaking aristocracy and an English-speaking majority, William made England the most united country in Europe.

If the Anglo-Saxons gave England its name and its language, its towns, its coronation ceremony, and its written history, the Normans gave it taxes and tax records. William wanted to know what he had conquered, how much land he had given to his knights, what he should expect from them in return, and how much his sheriffs should be collecting in taxes. He ordered a survey of every great house, village, town, farm, and mill in the country. This became known as the Domesday Book because, like the final day of judgment, there was no appeal against it.

The system set up by William continued largely unchanged under his successors. One of them, Henry I, married a Scottish princess who was descended from Athelstane and brought the ancient Anglo-Saxon line back into the ruling family.

In 1215, conflict between the barons and King John led to the writing of the Magna Carta or "Great Charter." The charter claimed to be a restatement of ancient laws and customs, but it was an answer to the wrongs that John had committed and showed that the king had to answer to his subjects. Among the rights the charter laid down were that no free man should be imprisoned or dispossessed without due process of the law and the judgment of his equals. King John was made to promise that he would neither sell, deny, or delay rights or justice to anyone. The Magna Carta also contained some recognition that the king could not impose taxes without the agreement of the people.

At that time, life for the poor was harsh and difficult: they had to serve their masters and grow their own food, and they had few rights in practice. Punishments for breaking the law were cruel and included execution and mutilation; one might also be declared an outlaw. Reasons a person might be considered an outlaw included failing to show up in court to face trial. Outlaws were not to be given food, shelter, or help of any other sort. Helping an outlaw was a crime, and killing one was not considered murder.

The towns grew in size and wealth and became havens for peasants, or "serfs," who ran away from their masters and wanted to live as freemen. Although they could still be arrested for having run away, they were able to hide in the towns. The towns were given, or sold, rights by the king—rights to hold markets, to establish councils to arrange local taxation and spending, and to make local laws. These rights were set out in written charters that are still part of the law of England.

In August 1348, a new illness that had spread across Europe reached England. The symptoms were paleness, retching, shivering, scarlet blotches, and black boils; often the result was death. The disease, the bubonic plague, became known as the Black Death. It ravaged England through the winter of 1348 and into 1349. It returned in 1361–2 and again in 1369. Within a year, the first outbreak killed at least a third—and possibly half—of the population.

The immediate result was chaos: crops could not be harvested, taxes could not be collected, goods could not be sold. Many who survived the disease starved in the aftermath. The longer-term effect was to give power to ordinary working people. At that time, all work depended on manual labor. The sudden shortage of people meant that the serfs could sell their labor rather than being forced to work for their overlord. Laws were passed to try and stop this, but the common people showed their power by disobeying the law, gathering together to riot and protest, and withdrawing their labor. They realized that by acting together, they could be stronger than their masters.

Throughout this time, England was fighting wars with France and Scotland, and money was needed to pay for the effort. In 1381, a tax was levied on every person over age fourteen. This was known as the head tax or "poll tax" ("poll" is an old word for "head"). Coming on top of the continuing unrest in the country, it resulted in riots and the killing of tax collectors across the country. The peasants of Kent and Essex marched on London. The people of London joined the protest.

The peasants' leaders were Wat Tyler, Jack Straw, and John Ball, a priest who had been jailed three times for preaching that all people were created equal. They asked to speak with the king, a boy of fourteen who had been king in name since he was eleven, even though his uncles held the real power. The royals agreed to the request. At a meeting in a field just outside London, King Richard II accepted their demands—for amnesty, the abolition of serfdom, and freedom to trade—if they would return quietly to their villages. This satisfied many of the peasants, but it was not enough for the leaders. They also wanted the death of the lords they held responsible. While the king was busy having amnesties written, the rebel leaders hurried to the Tower of London and led a mob inside, killing many people, including the archbishop of Canterbury. The rebels then took over London in a two-day riot of murder, looting, and arson.

King Richard asked for a second meeting. The rebels agreed. Again they met outside London, this time at Smithfield, the site of the livestock and butchers' market. Tyler's demands had increased, but the king said that they would have all that could be fairly granted. Then a quarrel broke out when one of the king's men recognized Tyler as a thief and a robber. William Walworth, mayor of London, tried to arrest Tyler. Tyler stabbed Walworth, but the dagger was stopped by Walworth's armor. Walworth struck back with his sword. He cut Tyler's neck and head. Tyler was stabbed again. He staggered back toward the peasants, but collapsed before he reached them.

Many of the peasants were trained archers, armed with six-foot-long English longbows. With this weapon, one archer could shoot twelve arrows in a minute and kill a man wearing the best armor from two hundred yards. With this weapon, English peasants had beaten the French in the battles of Crecy and Poitiers and would beat them again at Agincourt. They put arrows to their bows and started to pull back their bow strings.

Richard galloped toward them saying, "Sirs, will you shoot your king? I am your captain. I will be your leader. Let him who loves me follow me!"

The arrows never came. The rebels followed King Richard peacefully from the field. Although many were pardoned, many were later executed for their part in the revolt. Some were tried, but some were simply hunted down as outlaws. The demands to which the king had agreed were never put into practice, but the custom of forced service was nearly at an end. Within fifty years, tenant farming and paid labor had taken over serfdom.

With the increasing importance of towns as creators of wealth, kings had begun to summon representatives from every town to their "great council" since about 1340. The townsfolk sat with the representatives of the shires. Both sat separately from the lords but, uniquely in Europe, they met in a group that combined small landowners and townspeople as a common voice of the people. They were increasingly beginning to exercise power through their insistence that there should be no taxes without their agreement. They developed their own procedures—largely, it is said, because towns often chose lawyers as their representatives—and became established as the House of Commons of the English Parliament.

But the king still held real power. Between 1455 and 1485, there was an intense period of fighting for the crown. In thirty years, there were sixteen major battles and five kings died. The Wars of the Roses were fought between two branches, or "houses," of the royal family—the House of York, with a white rose as its emblem, and the House of Lancaster, with its red rose emblem. The Wars ended when Henry VII (Henry Tudor) beat Richard III at the battle of Bosworth Field.

Henry united the two halves of the royal family by marrying his cousin, Elizabeth of York, a marriage symbolically celebrated in the red and white Tudor Rose. Elizabeth is said to be the model for the picture of the queen on playing cards. Their son was Henry VIII. He had six wives, and split the church in England from the Roman Catholic Church. His daughter Mary tried to make the country Catholic again and burned people alive for beliefs that differed from her own. When Mary died, she was followed by her half-sister Elizabeth, who took the country further from the Catholic Church. Elizabeth I established a national church, the Church of England, with its Book of Common Prayer that established the prayers to be used on each day of the year, and had the Bible and church services translated from Latin into English.

When Elizabeth died in 1603, the crowns of England, Scotland, Ireland, and Wales became united under James Stuart, king of Scotland and Elizabeth's successor. Scotland and Ireland kept their own parliaments, however.

Although the Church of England had separated from the Roman Catholic Church, many people still felt it was too similar in its rituals and services. Some, known as Puritans, preferred worship without prayer books or hymns, churches without altars or statues, and religion without priests and churches. The new royal family had sympathy for the Catholic Church, and part of the realm, Ireland, was a Catholic country. At this time, the Pilgrim Fathers left England so that they could follow their religion in peace in a new England—America.

James was followed by his son Charles. Both believed that whatever the king did was right, no matter what anyone else said or what happened as a result. Because members of Parliament would not bend to his will, Charles ruled without one for several years, but eventually he had to call Parliament so that he could raise taxes. The quarrel between the king and Parliament grew worse. At its heart was the question of who ruled the country, but it was fueled by religious differences as well.

In 1642, civil war broke out. Charles lost the war and was tried as a tyrant, a traitor, a murderer, and a public enemy. He was found guilty and beheaded in January 1649. War continued. Ireland and Scotland rose up against the English Parliament and in support of the new king, Charles II. Oliver Cromwell, who had been a member of Parliament and had become a general in the Parliament's army, was sent to quell Ireland. He did this so ruthlessly that he is still an infamous and hated figure to the Irish. The Scots invaded England under Charles II. Cromwell beat them at Worcester on 3 September 1649. Charles II hid in an oak tree and escaped to Europe, leaving England without a king.

Now rid of the king, the English faced the problem of creating a viable new system of government. Various ideas were attempted, but England slipped into a dictatorship, with Cromwell—the Lord Protector—as king in all but name. Eleven regional militias were set up, each presided over by a major-general. The militias were there not only to maintain order but also to suppress vice and encourage virtue, as they saw it. Drinking, gambling, and horse racing were banned. The militias interfered with liberty and free speech.

After Oliver Cromwell's death, on 3 September 1659, people decided that instead of allowing his son Richard to take over, they would prefer to have a king again. Richard fled to France, and Charles II came to the throne in May 1660. Five years into his reign, in 1665, another plague hit England. It is still recalled in a schoolyard chant and game, "Ring-a-ring of roses. A pocket full of posies. Atishoo! Atishoo! We all fall down." The roses were the scarlet sores of the disease. The posies were flowers and herbs used to keep the disease away. The sneezing was another symptom. The falling down was death.

*In sixteen hundred and sixty-five, there was hardly anyone left alive,*
*In sixteen hundred and sixty-six, London burned like rotten sticks.*

The great fire of London is also remembered in a schoolyard song:

*London's burning. London's burning. Fetch the engines. Fetch the engines. Fire! Fire! Fire! Fire! Pour on water. Pour on water.*

The city burned for three days and nights. Much of it was destroyed and had to be rebuilt, and many of London's finest buildings, such as Saint Paul's Cathedral, date from this rebuilding.

Charles II was followed by his brother James II, who would be as unpopular as their father had been. In 1688, Parliament rebelled once more, but its members didn't want to risk a second Cromwell. They asked a Dutch prince, William of Orange, and his wife Mary, who was James's daughter, to take the throne. James ran away to France rather than fight. William and Mary were crowned, and a new relationship between the people and the monarchy was established, with the monarch as a figurehead but with the elected Parliament possessing the real power. This was formalized in the 1689 Bill of Rights.

Neither William and Mary nor Mary's sister Anne had children who outlived them. The problem of who would follow Queen Anne was decided by Parliament, now a united parliament of England, Wales, and Scotland, long before she died. In 1701, it passed a law declaring that the throne would pass to Sophia, granddaughter of James I and by marriage the princess of Hanover, and to her protestant heirs. No ruler of England could be a Catholic or marry a Catholic.

Sophia's son became King George I. He left the business of running the country to Parliament and the prime minister and rarely visited England. He was followed by George II; George III, who lost America in the Revolution and later went mad; George IV, who lived wildly as prince regent; and William IV.

In 1837, William's niece, Victoria, became queen at age eighteen. She was to rule for more than sixty years. Her reign is associated with England's industrial expansion and urbanization, but mechanization, new means of transport and mass production, were already leading to huge social changes by the time she became queen. In 1832, parliament passed the Great Reform Act, which created electoral divisions in the new industrial towns and cities and did away with the worst of the "rotten boroughs"—electoral divisions with tiny populations. It increased the number of people who could vote by reducing the amount of property that a man had to own to vote. After the act was passed, about one man in seven had the right to vote in elections for the House of Commons. (Women would not gain the right to vote until the twentieth century.)

In 1838, a People's Charter was published as a parliamentary bill. It contained six points: that every man should have the vote, that elections should be held using secret ballots rather than a show of hands, that members of Parliament should not have to be men of property, that members of Parliament should be paid, that electoral divisions should represent the same number of people therein, and that elections should be held annually. The Chartist movement that followed saw strikes, demonstrations, and mass petitions. In 1848, a petition signed by six million people was presented to parliament. The Chartists failed in the short term, but in the longer term, most of their demands were passed into law.

Although England had been ruled by women, only men were allowed to vote. In 1903, the Women's Social and Political Union was founded to campaign for votes for women. The campaigners, who became known as suffragettes, pursued their cause through political means and by direct action, including civil disobedience and hunger strikes. One woman, Emily Davison, died running in front of a racehorse owned by the king.

The suffragette campaign was suspended when the First World War broke out in 1914. During the war, a shortage of men to do essential work led women to take on many new roles. When the war ended, women over age thirty were given the right to vote. In 1928, women were given the vote on equal terms with men.

Even with almost all adults having the vote, could England be considered a democracy? Not only did it still have a monarch, but part of its Parliament was unelected: whereas the House of Commons was elected by the people, the House of Lords was not.

Since the fifteenth century, most members of the House of Lords had inherited their place in the Lords from their fathers. New peers could be created by the monarch, usually on the recommendation of the prime minister. Some bishops and senior judges were members of the House as part of their job. In 1911, the Parliament Act gave the House of Commons limited powers to make laws without the agreement of the House of Lords. The act was passed under the threat that enough new lords would be created to enable it to pass if it was blocked. Until then, the House of Lords had held power almost equal to that of the House of Commons. The only real difference had been that although it could block legislation in relation to money matters, it could not initiate it.

The power of the Parliament Act was extended in 1949. In 1958, the Life Peers Act enabled the creation of members of the House of Lords whose position would not be inherited. It also allowed women to be members of the House. Since 1958, only five hereditary peers have been created, but there are now more than 570 life peers. In 1963, hereditary peers were given the right to renounce their title and stand for election to the House of Commons.

In 1999, the latest process of reforming the House of Lords began. About nine-tenths of the hereditary members were removed. It was agreed that some should remain until the reform process was complete. Ninety hereditary peers were elected from and by the hereditary peers. Two hereditary royal appointments, the Earl Marshal and the Lord Great Chamberlain, were also retained because of their important ceremonial roles at coronations and at the annual state opening of Parliament. As of 2005, there were no agreed proposals for the new House and whether it should be elected or appointed

It is often said that history is written by the winners. Not only are the winners the ones who are there to write the history, but in telling the story, defeats are forgotten or seen as part of a path to victory. We also align ourselves with the victors and, in describing our history, often say more about ourselves than about what actually happened. Geoffrey of Monmouth finished writing *A History of the Kings of Britain* in about 1147, a few years before he was made bishop of Saint Asaph. It is said that in later years, a holy man was exorcising demons from a poor beggar. Holding the Bible in his hand, he drove demon after demon out of the beggar. A hundred demons were driven out, and at last the beggar was free from them. The priest, his work finished, put down the Bible and picked up Geoffrey's history, which he had been studying. Fifty demons that had hidden in the lies in the book leapt out and jumped back into the beggar. With its tales of Brutus, Arthur, and Merlin, Geoffrey's history wasn't history at all, but a foundation of English folklore that helped to create a common identity for the English people.

The Laidly Worm

Scotland

The Lambton Worm
Pollard and the Brawn

Northumberland

Old Lightowler
The Golden Ball
Gytha and the Gytrash
Brother Jucundus

Cumberland

County
Durham

Westmorland

The Farmer & the Cheeses
Robin Hood & the Monk
Little John and the
Nottingham Fair

Jenny Greenteeth

Lancashire

Yorkshire

The Alderley Legend

The Girl and the Anorak
The Old Woman and the Fairy Folk

Lancashire

The Pottle of Brains
The Dead Moon
Start and Finish

The Devil & The Coracle
The Devil in Wem
Lightening the Load
The Devil & The Stipestones
The Witch of Mitchell's Fold
The First Simnel Cake
Wild Edric

Cheshire

Derbyshire

Nottinghamshire

Lincolnshire

Staffordshire

Soke of
Peterborough

Norfolk

Shropshire

Leicestershire

Rutland

Isle
of
Ely

Wales

Warwick-
shire

Northamptonshire

Huntingdon-
shire

Cambridge-
shire

Suffolk

Herefordshire

Worcestershire

Bedford-
shire

Gloucestershire

Oxford-
shire

Buckinghamshire

Hertfordshire

Essex

The Mare's Egg
The Elder Tree Witch

Berkshire

Middlesex

Wiltshire

Surrey

Kent

Somerset

Hampshire

Sussex

Devon

Dorset

Golden Shoes

Cornwall

The Glass House

A Story of Zennor
The Standing Stones
The Wrestlers of Carn Kenidjack

The Great Bell of Bosham
The Hole Stone
White Ram Night

**Where the stories belong—a map of the traditional English counties.**

# The Fool in All
# His Glory

# Start and Finish

*A story from Lincolnshire retold by Viv Corringham*

A long time ago, two farmers were neighbors. Each had a son, and the boys were called Alpha and Omega. As they grew up, they were known as Start and Finish. After their fathers died, the two lads took over the farms and stayed good friends all their lives.

One day Start, now an old man, stopped to look what was in the swill tub outside Finish's kitchen door. As he leaned over it, an old billy goat saw a good target and charged, tipping him into the swill. Finish came out to see what all the noise was about and couldn't stop laughing when he saw Start's legs sticking out of the tub. Start, whose pride had been hurt, was furious and set about fighting his friend.

On the next market day, Start called on a lawyer and told him he wanted to bring Finish to court and claim damages for assault and battery. Later that day, Finish called in with the same complaint against Start. The lawyer explained that he couldn't represent both of them and gave Finish a letter for another lawyer.

Finish set off, but called into The Lamb, a pub he frequented, for a quick pint on the way and began to think what a silly old fool he was. By his third pint, he'd decided that life was too short to fall out with your neighbors. He looked at the envelope the lawyer had given him and saw that the heat from his hand had unstuck the flap. Pulling out the letter, he read:

 *Dear Fleecem,*
*Two old geese have come to market. You pluck one and I'll pluck the other.*

As Finish passed another pub, The Rising Sun, he saw Start's pony and trap outside. He went in and told him about their lawyers and read him the letter.

After hearing that, Start said, "Alright, let bygones be bygones. We'll shake hands and swallow a pint or two to soothe our ruffled feathers."

They drank until they were thrown out. As they left the yard, the innkeeper said, "Well, we've started them off, but only they know where they'll finish."

---

Next morning, Start's wife found the pony trying to get into his stable, still hitched to the trap where the two old men lay soundly sleeping.

A few days later, Start called on Finish.

"Would you like one of my fat geese for your Michaelmas dinner?"

"That I would," said Finish.

"Well you can have one if you promise to save the feathers."

"I'll do that. Will you come and fetch them?"

"Put them in a bag and bring them when we go to market next week," Start instructed.

So next market day, the old men came into town carrying two bags of feathers. They went to the first lawyer's office. On the way upstairs, they started shaking the bags and feathers flew all over the place. There was a butcher's shop beneath the office, and the butcher began to shout when he saw his best joints getting covered in goose down.

When the lawyer returned and saw all the feathers, he opened his windows to clear the room but the draught sent feathers swirling about in the street until it looked like a snowstorm. Some settled on the market stalls and got mixed up with the rock and cockles.

The poor fishmonger roared out, "Who do you think will buy fish covered with feathers instead of scales?"

Start and Finish watched through the windows of The Lamb and later drove home laughing so much that people said, "Those two old fools, drunk again!"

Well, the traders made such a fuss that the police were called and soon found out who had caused all the chaos. Start and Finish were brought before the magistrate and charged with a breach of the peace. The courtroom was packed as they both pleaded not guilty. It happened that the magistrate's clerk was Fleecem, the second lawyer. When asked what they had to say for themselves, the two men told the magistrate that they understood his clerk liked to do a bit of goose plucking in his spare time.

"What on earth do you mean by that?" asked the magistrate.

Finish handed him the letter. The magistrate read it out loud to the whole court. Everyone roared with laughter until he had to call for silence.

He told Start and Finish that the case was dismissed and they were free to go. Off they went and had a glorious celebration at every alehouse in town.

# The Farmer and the Cheeses

*A story from Nottinghamshire retold by Dan Keding*

Once a long time ago there was a farmer who made fine cheeses. One day as was his custom on market day, he set out to sell his cheeses in Nottingham. As he walked down the hill to cross over the River Trent into town, he stumbled and fell, and one of his cheeses flew from his pack and rolled down the hill. The farmer, who was not as clever a fellow as he was a fine cheese maker, saw what had happened and cried, "Well, if you can run to market alone so much the better. Why should I carry you? I'll send the others to keep you company and lighten my load at the same time."

And so the farmer took all the cheese out from his pack and rolled them down the hill toward the town. Some rolled into bushes, some went one way and some another until they were all out of sight.

"Keep going lads. I'll meet you in town," the farmer yelled after them. He walked down the hill and crossed the bridge that spanned the River Trent. As he made his way to market, he thought he might as well stop and have a drink. He stopped at an inn and drank his ale, all the time thinking how clever he was to send his cheeses on ahead to market.

It was late when he reached the market and he couldn't find his cheeses any-where. In fact, he saw few people at all selling their wares, for most had already had a profitable day, packed up, and gone home.

He stopped a man who lived near him and asked, "Have you seen my cheeses, neighbor? Did they come to market today?"

"Your cheeses? Who was bringing them to market today if not you?"

"Who?" cried the farmer. "Well they brought themselves, didn't they? They knew the way well enough, and they seemed to be in a hurry when last I saw them."

"Bringing themselves? To market? What are you talking about?" The neighbor was thoroughly perplexed by the farmer's story.

But the farmer wasn't listening to his friend.

---

"I think that they were running so fast that they ran right past Nottingham. If I'm not quick, they'll get all the way to York before I can catch them."

The farmer hired a horse and rode for York, but no one he asked had seen his cheeses that day either. The farmer rode back home without his cheeses nor the price they should have fetched, and though he asked for them on occasion, no word of them was ever heard.

# The Pottle of Brains

*A story from Lincolnshire retold by Hugh Lupton*

There was once an old woman, and she had a son whose name was Jack. Now, Jack was a pleasant enough strap of a lad, but lazy to a degree. All day and every day he would sit in the firelight warming the palms of his hands while his poor old mother was working her fingers to the bone and her bones to the marrow to keep the boy alive.

Years passed and years passed, and Jack grew—as sons will—until he was well beyond the age to earn a crust of his own.

Then one day, the old woman came home, lifted the latch, and opened the door. There was Jack stretched out on the floor in front of the fire, sleeping like a baby.

The old woman flew into a fury. She stamped her feet and wrung her hands: "Wake up, Jack, you lazy beggar!"

Jack sat up and rubbed his eyes.

"You're a waste of my time, Jack, you're a waste of your own time, what you need is a pottle of brains. Now you listen to me and do what I tell you. Go out of that door, along the road and up the hill to the hut where the Henwife lives, and you ask her—politely mind—if she's got such a thing as a pottle of brains to spare. Some call her a witch and some call her wise, Jack, but you speak to her civil enough, and she'll oblige. D'you understand?"

Jack pulled himself up to his feet and took his coat from the hook on the wall.

"Right enough, mother."

He made his way out of the door, along the road, and there, sure enough, was the green hill, and at the top of it a little hut with the smoke spiraling up from its chimney. He climbed and he climbed until he came to the yard outside. There were chickens everywhere, clucking and scratching. He stepped through them carefully and knocked at the door.

"Come in, Jack."

Jack opened the door and went inside. Through the smoke and shadows he could see the Henwife stirring a pot over the flames. One of her eyes was looking down into the pot, the other was looking up the chimney.

"What do you want Jack?"

"I was wondering whether you've got such a thing as a pottle of brains to spare?"

The Henwife's mouth widened into a gap-toothed grin.

"Well, maybe I have and maybe I haven't, Jack, but nothing comes from nothing in this world. If you want a pottle of brains then you must bring me the heart of the thing you love the best, then . . . perhaps. . . ."

Jack nodded and thanked the Henwife and made his way homeward.

As soon as he set foot over the threshold, his mother began her questioning: "Well then, Jack, have you got your pottle of brains yet?"

"Not yet, mother. She says I've got to bring her the heart of the thing I love the best."

"Well, what do you love best, Jack?"

"I reckon I love a nice plate of roast beef better than anything else in this world."

"Well then, Jack, there's only one thing for it, you'll have to go out into the field and kill the old cow."

So Jack went into the kitchen and sharpened up the carving knife. He went out into the field at the back of the cottage, and there was the old cow grazing quietly among the buttercups. He raised the knife above his shoulder and brought it down—schlaap!—and that was the end of the old cow. Jack slit her open, pulled out her heart, wrapped it up in brown paper, shoved it into his pocket, and made his way along the road and up the hill to the old Henwife's hut. He knocked.

"Come in, Jack."

He pushed open the door, reached into his pocket, pulled out the dripping package, and set it on the table.

"There's the heart of the thing I love the best, inside that brown paper package."

The Henwife grinned and raised one eyebrow.

"Well then, Jack, maybe you've got your pottle of brains and maybe you haven't; but there's only one way to find out! Riddle me this: What has four stiff standers, four dilly-danders, two lookers, two crookers, and a wig-wag—eh?"

Jack stood there in the smoke and shadows, scratching his head.

"Oh dear, oh dear, I don't know the answer to that one at all."

"Well then, Jack, you haven't got your pottle of brains yet. Off you go and bring me the heart of the thing you love the *best*."

So Jack turned and made his way down the hill. But as he was drawing close to his own cottage he saw his neighbors were gathered around his garden gate. Then he saw the doctor and the priest coming out of the door.

"Oh Jack, Jack, your old mother's been taken suddenly ill, and she looks as though she's about to die."

Jack ran inside and up the stairs, and there was his old mother lying on her bed. She lifted her head, smiled at him, and then fell back on her pillow—dead.

Jack buried his face in his hands and the hot tears trickled down between his fingers.

"My old mother, you brought me into this world, you suckled me at your breast, you looked after me all those years, I reckon I loved you the best in all this world . . . the best . . . in all this—" And once again Jack went down and into the kitchen, he sharpened up the carving knife and climbed the stairs to where his old mother lay. He raised the knife above his shoulder and . . . dropped it onto the ground.

"No, I can't do that."

Instead he bundled his old dead mother into a sack, swung it over his shoulder, and made his way along the road and up the hill. He knocked.

"Come in, Jack."

He pushed open the door and swung the sack down onto the table.

"There's the heart of the thing I love the best, inside that sack."

The Henwife grinned and raised both eyebrows.

"So, Jack, maybe you've got your pottle of brains and maybe you haven't; but there's only one way to find out! Riddle me this: What is greater than God, worse than the Devil, the Dead eat it, but if we eat it we die—eh?"

And poor Jack stood there in the smoke and shadows, shaking and scratching his head.

"Oh dear, oh dear, I don't know the answer to that one at all."

"Well then, Jack, you haven't got your pottle of brains yet, off you go and bring me the heart of the thing you love the *best of all*."

So Jack put his mother back in the sack, swung the sack over his shoulder and made his way down the hill. But when he reached the road he sat down on the soft grass at the edge of it and he began to sob, and the sobs turned to tears, and the tears to howls.

"The old cow's dead, my old mother's dead, and still I haven't got a pottle of brains . . . the old cow's dead, my old mother's dead, and still I haven't got a pottle of brains."

Well, it so happened that as Jack was sitting there a young woman was passing along the road—lovely she was, quick and fresh and warm as a spring wind.

She stopped and looked at Jack.

"What's the matter, Jack?"

"The old cow's dead, my old mother's dead, and still I haven't got a pottle of brains." And Jack told his story from the beginning to the end. She sat beside him on the grass and listened, and as she listened, she was thinking to herself, "I've always heard that a fool makes a good husband."

"And here am I," said Jack at last, "all alone in this world."

"Listen, Jack, I'll tell you what I'll do, I'll marry you, and I'll look after you, and you'll live happy ever after—just like the stories."

And Jack looked at her and he said, "Would you?"

"Yes, Jack."

She took Jack by the hand and pulled him up to his feet, and together they walked to the cottage.

No sooner was the funeral over than there was a wedding. The young woman became Jack's wife, and the west wind blew the confetti onto the fresh earth of the old mother's grave.

They lived in the cottage and the time passed.

Days became weeks and weeks became months, and one evening Jack and his wife were sitting in front of the fire. Jack's belly was full of roast beef, his clothes were all pressed and laundered, and he looked across at his wife, sitting lovely in the firelight, and he said, "You know, I reckon I love you the best in all this world . . . the best . . . in all this—"

And he got up to his feet, went through to the kitchen, and began to sharpen the carving knife.

But she smiled and called over her shoulder, "Jack, Jack, a heart that's beating is just as good as a heart that isn't. Let's go up there together." She took him by the hand and side by side they walked out of the door, along the road and up the hill. Jack knocked.

"Come in, Jack."

**The Pottle of Brains / 23**

He pushed open the door and lifted his wife up onto the table.

"There's the heart of the thing I love the best, underneath that lily white breast."

The Henwife grinned, raised both eyebrows, and stood up on her thin legs.

"So, Jack, maybe you've got your pottle of brains and maybe you haven't; but there's only one way to find out! Riddle me this: What is the golden box without a top or a bottom, it's filled with skin, flesh, blood, and bone and it can make two into one—eh?"

Poor Jack paced up and down in the smoke and shadows, shaking and scratching his head.

"Oh dear, oh dear, I don't know the answer to that at all."

But his wife, sitting on the table, leaned forward and whispered:

"Jack, say a ring, a *wedding ring*!"

"Oh!" said Jack, "Wait, I reckon that's a wedding ring!"

"Very good, Jack," cackled the Henwife, "Now riddle me this: What is greater than God, worse than the Devil, the Dead eat it, but if we eat it we die—eh?"

Jack closed his eyes.

"Oh dear, oh dear."

But his wife leaned forward and whispered again:

"Jack, say nothing."

"What, nothing at all?"

"No, say *nothing*!"

"Oh!" said Jack, "Now, there's an answer coming, now then, I reckon that's nothing."

The Henwife was dancing from foot to foot.

"Very good indeed, Jack. Now riddle me this: What has four stiff standers, four dilly-danders, two lookers, two crookers, and a wig-wag—eh?"

Jack wrinkled his forehead as though he was trying to wring an answer out of himself.

"Oh dear, oh dear."

But his wife leaned forward.

"Jack, say a *cow*!"

Jack turned to the Henwife then, smiling, triumphant.

"I reckon that's a cow."

"Oh, Jack, Jack," the Henwife skipped across toward him through the smoke and the shadows and planted a kiss firmly on his cheek, "Jack, you've got your pottle of brains at last!"

And Jack felt his head.

"Have I?"

It was the same size as it had always been before. He felt in his pockets, and there was nothing that hadn't been there for weeks since.

"Have I?"

The Henwife cackled and shrieked with laughter.

"Jack, Jack, there's only one cure for a fool, and that's to marry a woman with her wits about her. And Jack, that's just what you've done!"

Suddenly it was as though the sun had broken through the clouds, and Jack's face broke into a grin. He reached and lifted his wife down from the table, and arm in arm they walked out of the door, down the hill and home.

And from that day onward, Jack never had to worry about his pottle of brains, because he knew that his wife had enough for both of them.

*They lived happy*
*And so may we,*
*Let's put on the kettle*
*And have a cup of tea.*

# Jack Turnip

*A story retold by Taffy Thomas*

It was the iron winter. The snow was so deep that if you were out walking at night, you had to duck your head to walk under the moon.

Jack Turnip was walking down the lane with his axe over his shoulder. He trod on a frozen puddle. His feet slid from under him and he landed flat on his backside. He shook his fist at the icy patch, "So you think you're stronger than me? Or so it would seem." He stared pensively into space and thought, "Just a minute—the sun can melt the ice, so the sun must be the strongest . . . or so it would seem." Pensively, his thoughts continued in a strange but logical journey.

"Just a minute—a cloud can block out the sun, so a cloud must be the strongest . . . or so it would seem." His train of thought edged forward.

"Just a minute—the wind can break up the cloud, so the wind must be the strongest . . . or so it would seem." Logically, he dreamed on.

"Just a minute—the wind cannot blow away a mountain, so a mountain must be the strongest . . . or so it would seem." His mind game continued.

"Just a minute—a tree can grow on a mountain but a mountain can't grow on a tree, so a tree must be the strongest . . . or so it would seem."

He was moving to a triumphant crescendo. He walked toward the nearest tree, flexed his muscles, and swung his great axe. The tree crashed to the ground. He stood astride the tree, axe above his head in triumph.

"So I must be the strongest, or so it would seem." Tossing his axe to the ground, he leapt in the air.

"Whoopee!" But he landed back on that frozen puddle, his feet slid from under him and he landed flat on his backside . . . or so it would seem!

# Lazy Jack

*A story retold by Amy Douglas*

Long, long ago, there were a king and queen with a beautiful daughter, the princess. They loved their daughter so much, they gave her everything they could. She had bracelets and necklaces dripping with jewels, rich dresses embroidered with pearls, rooms filled with toys, a black puppy to play with, and a white pony to ride. She had servants to clean and tidy up after her and a cook to make her the finest, daintiest food.

But do you think the princess was happy?

No, she was not.

As she got older, her toys were left in the cupboards, the servants had to take her dog for walks, and the pony got fat in the stable. She was bored. There was nothing left for her to do. She spent each day in her room sighing and crying, and nothing interested her.

Her parents were beside themselves—they didn't know what to do. They tried everything they could think of to bring a smile to the princess' face. They brought in jugglers and acrobats, magicians and musicians, jesters and jokers, but the princess just sighed and cried and went back to her room.

They bought her new dresses, diamond tiaras and emerald earrings, teddy bears and tortoises, but the princess just sighed and cried and went back to her room.

What were they to do?

At last the king and queen sent out messengers to ride throughout the country telling the people that there would be a reward—a big bag of gold—for whoever could make the princess smile or laugh.

Lots of people came and tried to make the princess smile—they told jokes and pulled faces, they hopped on one leg and fell over, but nothing they could do made the princess smile. She just sighed and cried and went back to her room.

Not far from the town where the king, queen, and princess had their palace lived Jack. Now Jack was never bored. Jack was as happy as a lark as long as he was allowed to sit by the fire and do nothing. Well, almost nothing. First he would take the palms of his hands, and he'd warm them by the fire. And then, when they were warm enough on that side, he'd turn them over and he'd warm the backs of his hands. And when the backs of his hands were warm enough, he'd turn them over and he'd warm the palms again.

But while Jack was busy warming his hands by the fire, his mother had to do all the work. She did the washing, the drying, and the ironing; she did the cooking, laid the table, and washed up; she did the sweeping and the mopping; and she had to do the spinning and the sewing to make a bit of money for the two of them.

Do you think that was fair?

Neither did she!

One day, Jack's mother had had enough.

"Jack," she said, "Jack, I've had just about enough of you. Here's me, working my fingers to the bone, and all you do is sit there by the fireside. Get up, you lazy lump, you're off to get a job!"

"A job, mother?"

"Yes, a job! There's a farmer down the road who'd looking for a farmhand. So you get yourself up off that lazy behind of yours, out the door, and make sure you get that job. We've no money left at all and nothing to eat, and if you don't get that job, there'll be no tea for either of us tonight."

Jack looked at his mother and the way she was brandishing the broom and decided that perhaps getting a job wasn't such a bad idea. He picked himself up, dusted the ashes from his trousers, and made his way out of the door. He walked down the road, over the bridge by the town, and along down the road until he came to the farm. Sure enough, there was a sign on the gate that said, "Farmhand Wanted."

The farmer saw that Jack was a good, strong lad, and he set him to work straight away.

Jack had never done any work before, and after a while, he realized he was enjoying himself. He worked hard all day long so that when the farmer came up to him at the end of the day, he was delighted.

"Well done, Jack, you've worked so hard today, you've done the work not of one man, but two! Here's a gold coin for your wages, Jack, and I'll see you tomorrow."

"Thank you," said Jack. He took the gold coin with a smile and set off home. He gave the coin a rub to make it gleam, then he balanced it on his thumb and his forefinger, flicked his thumb, and sent it spinning up into the air, then caught it safe in his fist. All the way along the road he played with the coin, sending it spinning and dancing into the air and catching it. But half way across the bridge, he sent the coin spinning and dancing into the air and missed it. The coin went tumbling down, down, down until it landed in the river—*Splosh!* Jack leaned over the side of the bridge, but it was too late, there was nothing to be seen but the rippling water, and the coin was gone.

Jack arrived home, and there was his mother waiting on the doorstop.

"Oh Jack, Jack, you've been gone all day, so you must have got the job—did you get the job, Jack?"

"Yes, mother, I got the job."

"And did you get paid, Jack?"

"Yes, mother, I got a gold coin."

"A gold coin! Oh, well done, Jack! Give me the coin, Jack, and I'll go into town, buy some food, and cook you your favorite tea!"

Jack had to tell his mother what had happened to the coin. As she listened, her face grew pink, then red, then purple.

"Jack, you stupid boy! You dozy individual! You don't play with gold coins—they're too precious. Instead of throwing the coin into the river, you should have put it safe in your pocket. Will you promise me that whatever you get paid tomorrow, you'll put it safe in your pocket?"

Jack promised that he would.

The next day, Jack set off to work with a spring in his step and a whistle on his breath. He worked hard all day long so that when the farmer came up to him at the end of the day, he was delighted.

"Well done, Jack, you've worked so hard today, you've done the work not of two men, but three! Now Jack, the cows are doing well at the moment and giving us plenty of milk, so today for your wages I thought I'd give you a jug of cream and then you can have some cream on your porridge in the morning."

"Thank you," said Jack.

"See you tomorrow," said the farmer.

Jack took the jug of cream and remembered what he'd promised his mother. He opened up one of his trouser pockets and poured half the cream inside. Then he opened up his other pocket and poured the rest of the cream into that one. As Jack walked the cream dripped through the lining of his pockets and ran down his legs and into his boots. His feet squelched up and down in the cream until by the time he got home there was butter between his toes.

When he got home, there was his mother waiting on the doorstep for him.

"Jack, your trousers are all wet! Whatever happened to you?"

Jack told his mother all about the cream. As she listened, her face grew pink, then red, then purple.

"Jack, you stupid boy! You dozy individual! You don't carry cream in your pockets! You should have kept that cream in the jug. If it was too heavy to carry in your hands, you could have put it on your head and used your two hands to steady it. Whatever you get tomorrow, will you promise me that's what you'll do?!"

Jack promised.

The next day Jack set off to work with a spring in his step and a whistle on his breath. He worked hard all day long so that when the farmer came up to him at the end of the day he was delighted.

"Well done, Jack, you've worked so hard today, you've done the work not of three men, but four! Now Jack, we've been hard at work today in the dairy with all that cream making butter, so here's a big pat of butter for your wages."

"Thank you," said Jack.

"See you tomorrow," said the farmer.

Jack took the pat of butter and remembered what he'd promised his mother. He put the butter on his head, used his two hands to steady it, and started to walk home. It was a warm day. The sun beat down onto his head and melted the butter. Big drips of butter ran through his hair and down the back of his neck. Big drips of butter ran into his ears. A big drop of butter ran down his forehead and hung off from the end of his nose. Jack licked it.

By the time he got home, all the butter had melted and all he had to show for his day's work was a greasy head.

Jack's mother was waiting for him on the door step.

"Jack, your head's all greasy! Whatever happened to you?!"

Jack told his mother all about the butter. As she listened, her face grew pink, then red, then purple.

"Jack, you stupid boy! You dozy individual! You don't carry butter on your head! You should have taken some nice big green leaves and wrapped the butter up inside. As you walked home you could have dipped the butter in the river to keep it cool. Whatever you get tomorrow, will you promise me that's what you'll do?!"

Jack promised.

The next day Jack set off to work with a spring in his step and a whistle on his lips. He worked hard all day long so that when the farmer came up to him at the end of the day he was delighted.

"Well done, Jack, you've worked so hard today, you've done the work not of four men, but five! Now Jack, my terrier bitch is the best ratter in the county, and she gave birth to her pups six weeks ago. They're ready to go to their new homes now and I thought I'd give you one for your wages. She'll grow into a fine dog and keep all the rats and mice out of your larder.

"Thank you," said Jack.

"See you tomorrow," said the farmer.

Jack took the puppy and remembered what he'd promised his mother. He wrapped the puppy up in green leaves and started home. Every now and then he dipped the puppy into the river water. At first the puppy was still, but as she was dipped into the water she got cold and wet and started to struggle. She wriggled and scratched, then she sank her sharp teeth into Jack's finger. Jack dropped the puppy, and she ran back to the farm.

By the time he got home, all he had to show for his days work was a bleeding finger.

Jack's mother was waiting for him on the door step.

"Oh, Jack, your hand's bleeding! Whatever happened to you?!"

Jack told his mother all about the puppy. As she listened, her face grew pink, then red, then purple.

"Jack, you stupid boy! You dozy individual! You don't wrap a puppy up in leaves! You should have taken a bit of string from the farm, made a collar and a lead and walked her home on the lead. Whatever you get tomorrow, will you promise me that's what you'll do?!"

Jack promised.

The next day Jack set off to work with a spring in his step and a whistle on his lips. He worked hard all day long so that when the farmer came up to him at the end of the day he was delighted.

"Well done, Jack, you've worked so hard today, you've done the work not of five men, but six! Now Jack, with all this hard work, you'll need some good meat to keep your strength up so I thought you might like this big leg of mutton for your wages."

"Thank you," said Jack.

"See you tomorrow," said the farmer.

Jack took the leg of mutton and remembered what he'd promised his mother. He found a bit of string, made a collar and a lead, and tied it to the bone. He started for home, whistling as he walked and dragging the leg of mutton behind him through all the dust and dirt of the road. A stray dog sniffed the air as Jack went past and couldn't believe his luck when he saw the meat on the ground. His tail wagging he ran after Jack, tearing mouthfuls of meat from the bone. Soon there were two dogs following Jack, then three, then a whole pack of dogs, fighting over the meat, but Jack carried on walking and whistling and noticed nothing.

By the time he got home all he had to show for his days work was a bit of string—even the bone had gone.

Jack's mother was waiting for him on the door step. She saw Jack coming with the pack of dogs behind him.

"Good grief, Jack, what are you doing with all those dogs?"

Jack looked behind him, told her all about the leg of mutton and held up the empty piece of string.

Jack's mother's face grew pink, then red, then purple.

"Jack, you stupid boy! You dozy individual! You don't drag a piece of meat along the ground! Why didn't you just pick it up and carry it over your shoulder?! Whatever you get tomorrow, will you promise me that's what you'll do?!"

Jack promised.

The next day Jack set off to work with a spring in his step and a whistle on his lips. He worked hard all day long so that when the farmer came up to him at the end of the day he was delighted.

"Well done, Jack, you've worked so hard today, you've done the work not of six men, but seven! Now Jack, I've got something really special for your wages today. Do you see that donkey in the field?"

"Yes," said Jack.

"Well, he's too old to do the heavy work on the farm, but he'd be just perfect for your mother, she could ride him to the market and he'd carry her and her shopping all the way home."

"Thank you," said Jack.

"See you tomorrow," said the farmer.

Jack looked at the donkey and remembered what he'd promised his mother. Now it wasn't the biggest donkey that Jack had ever seen, but it was big enough. Jack put his head under the belly of the donkey, wrapped his right arm around its hind legs and his left arm around its forelegs. Jack took a deep breath, straightened his knees, straightened his back, and heaved the donkey into the air. Slowly, slowly, step by step, Jack began to stagger his way home.

At first the donkey was so surprised at being picked up that it sat still, staring around in disbelief. But as they came to the bridge over the river, the donkey had had enough. It wanted its four feet firmly back on the ground. It threw its head up into the air and began to bray.

"EEeee AAwww! EEeee AAwww!"

The donkey was struggling and squirming to be set free. Jack did his best to hold on to the four feet, but each of them seemed to be going in a different direction. One hoof kicked his jaw, another kicked his belly, soon Jack was staggering from one side of the bridge to the other and the donkey nearly fell into the river. No one could get past Jack with the donkey on his back and people started to queue on either side of the river.

"EEeee AAwww!" brayed the donkey.

"Stupid donkey!" said Jack.

And as they watched the donkey frantically trying to escape and Jack hanging on, the people started to laugh and point.

Well who should hear all the commotion down the street?

The princess. She heard the braying and the shouting and the laughing, and she wondered what on earth was going on. She went to the window, pulled the curtains aside, and there she saw Jack and the donkey. The princess couldn't believe her eyes! She'd seen lots of men riding donkeys over the bridge before, but she'd never seen a donkey riding a man!

A smile spread across the princess' face. The corners of her eyes crinkled. She put her hand to her mouth, but a giggle escaped through the fingers. Soon she was laughing so hard that her hands hugged her belly and tears streamed down her face.

Her mother, the queen, heard the strange sound from her daughter's room. She rushed inside and saw the princess.

"What is it, my love? Are you hurt? Do you have a stomach pain?"

The princess tried to reply, but all she could do was point at the window. The queen looked out, and there she saw Jack, red in the face, juggling the struggling donkey, desperately trying to keep it up in the air.

A smile spread across the queen's face, and soon she, too, was leaning against the wall, her legs weak with laughter.

It wasn't long before the king, wondering where his wife and daughter were, came looking for them. He heard the strange sound from the princess' room and opened the door. There were the queen and the princess, wiping their eyes, faces red and holding their stomachs.

"What on earth is the matter?"

The two women could only point at the window, and in a moment, the king, too, was laughing. In fact, soon there were servants, butlers, maids, cooks, boot boys, ladies in waiting all hanging out of the windows and laughing at poor Jack.

At last the king pulled himself together and hugged his daughter close.

"You're cured!" he said.

They sent a servant to fetch Jack, and he was brought into the throne room before the king, the queen, and the princess to be awarded his prize for curing the princess.

Jack was presented with the big bag of gold, but Jack wasn't looking at the gold. He was looking at the princess, who, now that she was smiling, was rather pretty. And as for the princess, well, the reason she was smiling was because she was looking at Jack.

The king and queen saw what was happening, and they smiled, too.

Soon the bells were ringing out across the land for the wedding of Jack and the princess. And, of course, once the two of them were married, Prince Jack came to live at the palace. But he didn't go there on his own. He brought his mother with him, too.

Jack's mother was given her own tower in the palace, a huge bedroom with a four-poster bed, and a rather cozy sitting room with a very comfortable rocking chair in front of the fire. She was also given all the servants she could ever need. There were servants to do the washing, the drying, and the ironing; servants to do the cooking, lay the table, and wash up; servants to do the sweeping and the mopping; there were servants to do *everything!* And so all Jack's mother had to do was sit in that comfortable rocking chair by the fire and warm the palms of her hands. And if she ever got bored of warming the palms of her hands, she'd turn them over and warm the backs of her hands. And if she ever got bored of warming the backs of her hands, she'd turn them over again and warm the palms of her hands . . .

# The Vinegars

*A story retold by Dan Keding*

Mr. and Mrs. Vinegar were very poor. They lived in a shabby little cottage that was always falling down around their heads. Whenever they fixed it, they used old boards and old pieces of twine and old bent rusty nails, and soon the house was falling down around their heads again. Eventually they had nothing left of their cottage but the rubbish that used to hold it together. One day while Mr. Vinegar was out, Mrs. Vinegar sneezed, and the whole house came down around her head.

When Mr. Vinegar returned, she cried, "Oh husband, look what I've done! I sneezed and the whole house came falling down."

"Well wife, there doesn't seem to be any place to drive a nail or put two boards together, but we still have the door. Let's go off and seek our fortune with our door!"

And so Mr. Vinegar took the door on his back, and off they went to seek their fortune. Of course, night came and they had not yet found their fortune, so they decided to sleep in the branches of a tree. They found an old oak, and Mrs. Vinegar climbed up and Mr. Vinegar pushed and shoved and finally they got their door up in the tree. They couldn't just leave it on the ground, could they?

In the middle of the night they heard voices below them. Robbers had stopped under their tree and were dividing up their stolen money. Mr. Vinegar was so frightened that he began to shake and shake and shake till he shook the door off the branch and it landed on the thieves. The thieves were so frightened, they dropped all their money and ran for their lives. The Vinegars just stayed in the tree till dawn.

When they finally came down, they picked up their door and carefully examined it and made sure it was not harmed in the fall. As they turned it over, Mr. Vinegar saw something under the door.

"Wife look! Our fortune has found us!" There in the dirt under the door were dozens of gold coins. They counted them over and over again, laughing at their good luck. They had over forty guineas.

"Husband, you must take this money to town and buy a good cow. With the milk we get from the cow, we will be able to keep some and sell some and never want for anything again."

Mr. Vinegar went to town, and he searched and searched and searched. He finally saw a cow for sale and he said, "If I had that cow I would be the happiest man the world." So he bought it.

As he led the cow away, he saw a piper playing in the streets, and all the children were following him and all the adults were throwing money at his feet.

"What a wonderful way to spend your day. If I had those pipes I would be the happiest man in the world." And so he traded his cow for the pipes.

He started to walk back to his wife and tried to play the pipes but nothing like music came out for him, and the people laughed and laughed and finally started to get annoyed. Poor Mr. Vinegar's fingers started to get sore and cold from trying to play the pipes. Then he saw a man wearing a warm pair of gloves.

"I would be the happiest man in the world if I had some warm gloves to keep my hands warm." So he traded his pipes for the gloves.

He walked and walked and soon was very weary from his journey. He saw a man walking toward him leaning on a stick.

"I would be the happiest man in the world if I had a straight stick like that to lean on while I walked." So he traded the gloves to the man for the walking stick.

As he walked through the woods an old owl who had seen all the foolish trades Mr. Vinegar had made hooted at him.

"What an old fool. You traded a cow for a set of pipes, the set of pipes for a pair of gloves, and now the gloves for an old walking stick. You are the most, most foolish man I have ever seen!"

Mr. Vinegar was so mad at that owl that he threw his stick at the old bird, but the owl flew away and the walking stick got stuck in the branches. The owl hooted and laughed.

But the owl's words were nothing next to the cries of Mrs. Vinegar when she heard the news of her husband's adventures!

# The Old Woman Who Lived in a Vinegar Bottle

*A story retold by Dan Keding*

Once upon a time there lived an old woman who lived in a vinegar bottle. One day as the woman sat alone in her house, a fairy passed by and heard her talking to herself.

"It is a shame, a shame, a shame," said the old woman. "I shouldn't live in a vinegar bottle. I should live in a nice little cottage with a thatched roof and a garden with roses. That's where I should live." And the old woman sighed.

The fairy whispered through the window, "Very well, when you go to bed tonight, turn around three times, shut your eyes and in the morning you will see what you will see."

So the old woman went to bed, turned around three times, and shut her eyes, and in the morning she woke inside a sweet little cottage with a thatched roof and a garden, and in the center of the garden there were roses. She was so surprised and so happy, but in her joy she forgot to thank the fairy.

Now the fairy traveled to the north, to the south, to the east, and to the west. Soon she was near the old woman's cottage and decided to stop in and see how she was enjoying her new home.

As she approached the front door, she heard the old woman talking to herself.

"It's a shame, a shame, a shame," said the old woman. I shouldn't be living in a cottage like this all by myself. I should live in a nice little house in a row of houses with lace at the windows, a brass knocker on my front door, and happy neighbors that call out 'hello' and 'how are you' every time we meet."

The fairy was a bit surprised. But she told the old woman, "When you go to bed turn around three times, shut your eyes and in the morning you shall see what you shall see."

So the old woman went to bed that night, and she turned around three times, shut her eyes, and in the morning she woke in a little house in a row of houses.

There were lace curtains, a brass knocker on the front door, and all her neighbors were happy and greeted her cheerfully when she went outside. She was very surprised and very happy, but again she forgot to thank the fairy.

Now the fairy traveled to the north, to the south, to the east, and to the west. Soon she was near the house of the old woman and decided to stop in and see how she was enjoying her new home. She was bound to be happy now.

When she got to the row of houses and stood outside the old woman's house, she heard her once more talking to herself.

"It's a shame, a shame, a shame," the old woman said. "I shouldn't live in a row of houses with common folk on all sides. I should live in a great mansion surrounded by a wonderful garden with servants to bring me this and bring me that and bring me what I need."

The fairy was surprised and a bit annoyed at this turn of events but once more she said, "Very well, go to bed tonight and turn around three times, shut your eyes, and in the morning you shall see what you shall see."

The next morning the old woman woke to find that she was in a great mansion with a wonderful garden. She had servants to do her bidding and to bring her what she needed and sometimes what she didn't need. She was very surprised and delighted, but she forgot to thank the fairy.

Now the fairy traveled to the north, to the south, to the east, and to the west. Soon she was near the great hall of the old woman and decided to stop in and see how she was enjoying her new position in life. She had to be happy now.

No sooner had the fairy reached the window of the mansion's drawing room than she heard the old woman talking to herself.

"It's a shame, a shame, a shame," she lamented. "I shouldn't be living here in this great house all alone. I should be a duchess or a countess and have my own coach. I should go to balls and parties with lords and ladies and even wait upon the queen."

The fairy was surprised once more by the woman's words, but she told her, "When you go to bed tonight turn around three times, shut your eyes, and in the morning you shall see what you shall see."

When the old woman woke, she was a duchess in a fine house in London with a coach and servants and a closet full of fancy gowns. On her desk was a pile of invitations to this party and that ball and an invitation to wait upon the queen. She was very surprised and very happy, but once again she forgot to thank the fairy.

Now the fairy traveled to the north, to the south, to the east, and to the west. Soon she was near London and the great house of the old woman and decided to stop in and see how she was enjoying her new position in life. She had to be happy now that she was a duchess.

When she neared the window to the great dining room, she heard the old woman talking to herself, "It's a shame, a shame, a shame," she cried. "Why should I have to bow to the queen? I should be queen and sit on a golden throne and the people should all bow to me."

The fairy was disappointed and a little angry, but she told the old woman, "When you go to sleep tonight turn around three times, shut your eyes, and in the morning you shall see what you shall see."

In the morning the old woman found herself on a golden throne with a golden crown and all the people of the kingdom bowed and called her their queen. She lived in a royal palace with all her noble ladies and gentlemen around her. She was delighted and began to order people from here to there and back again, but she forgot to thank the fairy.

Now the fairy traveled to the north, to the south, to the east, and to the west. Soon she was near the palace of the old woman and decided to stop in and see how she was enjoying her new position in life. She was the queen, what more could she ever want or need?

But when the fairy reached the window of the royal throne room, she heard the old woman talking to herself again.

"It's a shame, a shame, a shame," she cried. "I am only the queen of this little country. I should be ruling the whole world. Everyone should listen to my words and obey me. I should be the empress or maybe even the pope!"

The fairy had heard quite enough.

"Very well," she told the old woman. "Go to bed tonight, turn around three times and shut your eyes, and in the morning you shall see what you shall see."

So the old woman, eager to rule the world, went to bed that night. She turned around three times, she shut her eyes, and in the morning she was back in her vinegar bottle, just where she belonged.

# The Mare's Egg

*A story from Somerset retold by Helen East*

Some people just can't seem to settle—always looking for something new, somewhere better to be. Down where my mum lives in Somerset, it's the other way around. People like to stay put.

"Where you be to" is where you belong; where you were born, and your father, and father's father, too.

Take old Sid Gammon, for example. Sixty years scratching a living from the same bit of hillside his family had worked for generations. And in all that time he'd never been more than a day's walk from his village. Well, he hadn't had time for a start—he'd been that busy—but he hadn't had inclination either. Not, that is, until he won that ticket in one of those competition things: a day trip on a luxury coach, all the way to London it was!

Well he hadn't wanted to bother with it at first, but the family were on at him to give it a go, and he didn't want to waste good money, so in the end he agreed. And come the day, of course, he was as excited as could be, all stiff and smart in his Sunday best, and the whole family come to see him off—the Missus all anxious, the children wide-eyed, and all of them already dreaming of what he would bring back ("something sensible, now, Sid," "No! something really special!").

So away he went, and there was so much to look at, the journey just flew. And when he came to London Town—well! All sorts of buildings all higgledy-piggledy together, and so many people you wouldn't think they'd all fit in the one place! As for the shops, they were so smart, he didn't dare go inside, so he just kept walking and gawping, until he was quite tired out. But just as he was wondering where on earth he would find anything to buy for them back home, he turned a corner, and there was a market sprawling across the streets selling everything you could imagine for all tastes and all pockets.

Being the sort of man he was, Sid naturally headed for the fruit and vegetable stall—and there he stopped: Oooh! Ahh! The colors! The shapes! The smells! There was enough for a lifetime of looking. Food from all over the world. Things you'd think'd never come out of the earth (not Somerset earth anyways); things you'd think'd never go into the mouth (not Somerset mouths, not no how). And right in the middle was a simply enormous pumpkin, orange and bright as the sun.

Sid stared, as well he might, for pumpkins weren't things we used to get very often in England, and certainly not in Somerset. He stared so hard and so long the stall holder noticed, and he had time to take in Sid's Sunday best and country air, too.

"Got a right one 'ere," thought the man, and he rubbed his hands. "Alright mate?" he asked.

"Well," says Sid, "I be wondering . . . .What be that girt yellow 'un, then?"

"Oh that," says the man. "That's very rare, that is. It's an egg. Only got the one" (and he dropped a sack over the pile underneath the stall).

"Wunnerful," says Sid. "What manner o' beast be in that then?"

"Oh—a horse," says the stall holder, quick as a flash. "It's a mare's egg."

Now Sid was a pig farmer; he knew what was what.

"Mares don't lay no eggs," he said, shaking his head.

"Oh yes," said the man. "That's why it's so special, you know; comes from America. Bred them special to lay eggs over there. Hard work, of course."

Now Sid had heard that all sorts of strange things could be done over in that there Americeey, what with science and test tubes and that. Babies out of bits and now horses out of eggs, and there was the proof right in front of him. That was something special alright, and something sensible, too. The very present to suit everyone back home.

It took all his money, but it was worth it, and all the way home Sid sat with his egg in his lap, and dreamed of the horses to come.

Well of course, the family was as astonished as he was. They sat up nearly half the night, hearing his news, and gazing at the amazing egg. It wasn't until the children had gone to bed that the Missus started worrying again.

"How we going to hatch it then?" she wondered.

Well now that was a thought—he didn't have a horse, did he? And he wasn't sure he could get a horse to sit that long on that thing, even suppose he could borrow one. But he couldn't let on to the Missus, so he just gave her a knowing nod.

"Ah yes," he said, "we'll be hatching it ourselves."

Well, he took first turn, of course, seeing as he knew how it was done, and he settled himself, and he sat on that pumpkin the rest of the night, and all through the next day, too. Missus had to do his jobs for him. And bring his food to him and all. He sat and he sat, and he sat and he sat, but do you think that mare's egg hatched? It did not.

So by and by the Missus had to take over, seeing as she knew all about broody hens and so on, and she settled herself, and she sat and she sat. She sat for nearly a week. And all the children had to do her jobs. But do you think that egg hatched? No. It did not.

Well then the eldest girl had to have a go, and she settled herself, and she sat, and then the eldest lad, he sat, and then the little sister, and then the twins, and then even the baby had a go. But do you think that egg hatched? No. It did not.

And by now they'd been sitting for getting on for a month. And they were getting tired of having that great big pumpkin right in the middle of the kitchen, with everyone having to go round it all the time. And the pumpkin itself, what with the heat of the kitchen, and the warmth of all that sitting, it was getting riper and riper. And as it got riper, it got softer and softer, and what with all that sitting too, it started to squash, and squelch and split. And the ooze came out, and the smell rose up, and at long last the Missus, she put her foot down,

"Foal or no foal," she said, "that thing do smell foul, and I ain't going to have no more egg in this house."

So out they went, egg and all, looking for a new place to nest. But the pumpkin was so slippery and slimy that all of a sudden it slid right out of Sid's arms, and as the farm was right at the top of the hill, it started to roll away down. The hill being steep, it soon gathered speed, spun further and faster and further and faster, 'til far, far away it reached the bottom and disappeared deep in a gorse bush.

Now it so happened a hare was asleep in there, and as the pumpkin came to rest, it woke him up with a start. Up he jumped and out he ran, and off along the valley.

Up at the top, what did they see? Small and dark, two ears and four legs, galloping for all it was worth—"Tis a foal!" they cried. "It's hatched."

Alas, they were too late to catch it. And anyway, they all agreed that a foal that could run that fast would grow into a horse you never could hold.

"Like everything that comes from that there Americeey," they said, "It be in too much of a hurry for us."

So that was why, when the pumpkin seeds took root, and one little plant grew up out of that bush, no one braved the thorns to catch it. It's still there—so if you fancy a mare—why not go get it, and hatch it?

# The Most Unfortunate Man

*A story retold by Katrice Horsley*

There was once a man who believed himself to be the most unfortunate man in the world. He had no luck whatsoever. In fact, he just seemed to be followed by bad luck—he lost keys, lost jobs, lost girlfriends (that's whenever he found a girl who might go out with him, which was rare!). So he came to the conclusion that God must have forgotten to give him any good luck, and he decided he would go and ask God why.

He started on his journey toward the end of the world (yes those geography lessons have been wrong all these years . . . the world is FLAT!!).

As he traveled, he came to a wood, and in the wood he came upon a wolf. Well, I say "wolf," but it was more like a moth-eaten old fur rug. His ribs stuck out, his teeth were yellowed and loose and his ears . . . well they were the saddest, limpest ears that you could possibly imagine.

When the wolf saw the man, he raised (well tried to raise) one of those ears, and he let out such a sigh.

"What's wrong?" asked the man.

"Oh," whined the wolf, "I am just starving to death and I do not know why. Look at me, I should be in the prime of life and you would not even use me as a duster."

"Well," said the man, "I am off to see God, to find out where my luck is, if you like I could ask him why you are starving."

"I would be so grateful," said the wolf, and a slight hint of a smile hovered around his lips before he slipped into sleep.

So off went the man again, whistling through the wood and he hadn't been whistling long before he came to a tree. Well, I say tree . . . more like a branch really, with just two pallid green leaves trembling on it. As the man whistled past, his breath caused one of the leaves to loosen and spiral downward, and the tree let out a great sigh, right from its roots.

"What's wrong?" asked the man.

"Oh," sighed the tree again, "I just cannot grow, not at all. I fear I may die if I do not find out why."

"Well," said the man, "I am off to ask God where my luck is, and if you like I'll ask him why you are not growing."

"Oh thank you!" exclaimed the tree, taking care not to become too excited lest his other leaf might fall.

So the man continued on his journey, until he came to just near the end of the world . . . and there was a house, a lovely house, with a white picket fence, roses around the door, and leaning over the fence a rather gorgeous woman of ample proportions.

She called to the man and beckoned him over.

"Come inside, come inside. It's so rare I get visitors, me living so near to the end of the world." She led him inside and cooked a great meal, opened some homemade wine, and they laughed and joked and then she suddenly started to cry.

"Oh my," said the man, "what is the matter? I thought you were happy."

"Oh no," replied the woman, "I am so sad and lonely and I just don't know why."

"Well," said the man, putting an arm around her sobbing shoulders and comforting her. "I am off to see God to find out where my luck is. If you like I will ask him why you are so sad and lonely."

"Oh, thank you!" replied the woman, showering his face with kisses, "you are so kind."

So the man pulled himself away and walked to the end of the world.

God was there floating on a cloud, just above the edge of the world, and below him there was a huge drop into nothing.

"What do you want?" called out God.

"I want to know where my luck is," replied the man.

"It is right in front of your eyes," replied God, "You just have to recognize it."

"Oh right," smiled the man. "Sorted! Ta God."

He was just about to leave when he remembered the questions of his friends. He listened as God gave him the answers, and thus armed he headed back.

He arrived at the house of the woman and called out, hurrying past, "God said you need to find a husband to live with you."

"Oh," cried the luscious woman, "no one ever comes out here. You wouldn't want to be my husband would you? Live with me in this lovely little house while I cook for you and grow the vegetables and massage your feet."

"I'm sorry," replied the man, "But I'm off to search for my luck. God said it's right in front of me; I just have to recognize it . . . sorry!" And with that he continued searching for his luck.

He arrived in the forest and came to the tree.

"Oh please," called out the tree. "Did you find out what is wrong with me?"

"Yes," replied the man, "God said you have a chest of treasure buried under your roots and you need to get somebody to dig it up or else your roots will continue to wither."

"Oh," cried out the tree, "Could you do that? I have a spade just around the back of my trunk and you can keep the treasure."

"I'm sorry," replied the man, "I can't because I have to search for my luck. God said its right in front of me. I just have to open my eyes and see it. Sorry!" And off he went, continuing to search for his luck.

Before long he came to the wolf, still lying there, almost at death's door.

"Well," said the wolf, "Did you ask for me?"

"Yes," replied the man. "God said you are starving from lack of food so you have to eat the first stupid man who comes your way!"

And do you know . . . HE DID!

# Wily Wagers and Tall Tales

# The Old Woman and Her Pig

*A story retold by Dan Keding*

One day a long time ago, an old woman was cleaning her little cottage. As she swept the floor, she found a sixpence.

"What shall I do with this sixpence?" she wondered. "I know. I'll go to market and buy a little pig."

And so she went to the market and found herself a sweet little pig. She paid the price and started home with her pig. But when she came to the stile that crossed the farmer's fence, the pig refused to go over. She begged and she threatened, but the pig was stubborn and just sat down.

She went down the road till she found a dog.

"Dog, bite the pig so he'll go over stile, otherwise I won't get home tonight." But the dog refused.

She walked a little farther and saw a stick.

"Stick, hit the dog, for he won't bite the pig so the pig will go over the stile and I can get home tonight." But the stick refused.

She walked on and met a campfire.

"Fire, burn the stick, for it won't hit the dog who won't bite the pig so the pig will go over the stile and I can get home tonight." But the fire refused.

She walked on and found a stream.

"Water, quench the fire, for it won't burn the stick who won't hit the dog who won't bite the pig so the pig will go over the stile and I can get home tonight." But the water refused.

She came upon an ox.

"Ox, drink the water, for water won't quench the fire who won't burn the stick who won't hit the dog who won't bite the pig so the pig will go over the stile and I can get home tonight." But the ox refused.

---

She met a butcher as she walked down the road.

"Butcher, kill the ox who won't drink the water who won't quench the fire who won't burn the stick who won't hit the dog who won't bite the pig so the pig will go over the stile and I can get home tonight." The butcher also refused.

She went on and saw a rope.

"Rope, hang the butcher who won't kill the ox who won't drink the water who won't quench the fire who won't burn the stick who won't hit the dog who won't bite the pig so the pig will go over the stile and I can get home tonight." The rope refused.

She walked on and met a rat.

"Rat, gnaw the rope for rope won't hang the butcher who won't kill the ox who won't drink the water who won't quench the fire who won't burn the stick who won't hit the dog who won't bite the pig so pig will go over the stile and I can get home tonight." The rat said no.

She walked on and met a cat.

"Cat, chase the rat for rat won't gnaw the rope who won't hang the butcher who won't kill the ox who won't drink the water who won't quench the fire who won't burn the stick who won't hit the dog who won't bite the pig so pig will go over the stile and I can get home tonight."

Cat said to her, "If you will go to the cow and get me a saucer of milk, I will chase the rat."

So away went the old woman to the cow.

The cow said, "If you will get me some hay to eat, I will give you some milk."

The old woman went to the haystack and brought back an armful of sweet hay for the cow.

As soon as the cow had eaten, she gave the old woman some milk. The old woman raced back to the cat and gave her the milk.

As soon as the cat finished her milk, she started to chase the rat; the rat began to gnaw the rope; the rope began to hang the butcher; the butcher began to kill the ox; the ox began to drink the water; the water began to quench the fire; the fire began to burn the stick; the stick began to hit the dog; the dog began to bite the pig; the pig climbed over the stile; and the old woman got home that very night.

# The Dog That Talked

*A story retold by Dan Keding*

Once a long time ago there was a man traveling through the countryside. As he came to a village, there was a horse in a field next to the road. The horse slowly made his way to the fence and spoke to the traveler.

"Good morning, sir. Isn't it a great day to go walking through the country?"

The man looked at the horse and, though amazed, replied, "Indeed it is a lovely day."

When the man came to the village, he went to the pub and asked the landlord about the horse.

"Excuse me, but the horse in the field next to the road spoke to me."

"I don't think so, sir. We have no talking horses in these parts."

"I'm sure he spoke. He said 'good morning.' "

"Sir," replied the landlord, "was there a sheepdog lying nearby?"

"Why, yes. He was lying near the fence where the horse was standing."

"Oh, that's the answer, sir. You see, the horse doesn't talk at all, but the dog does, and he has been trying his hand at being a ventriloquist lately. I'll have a word with him about it."

# The Horse Who Knew about Cars

## A *story retold by Amy Douglas*

There was once a man driving along in the English countryside. On a narrow lane, he slowed down to take the corner, and the car stalled. He turned the key in the ignition, and the car growled. He tried again, the engine chugged and whirred, but wouldn't catch. He sighed, got out of the car, and opened the bonnet. He stood looking at the engine and scratching his head.

A voice came from behind him, saying, "Looks like your starter motor's jammed, mate."

The man spun 'round, but there was no one there.

He turned back to the look at the inside workings of his car, and the voice came again.

"Yep, of course there's a few other things it *could* be, but the starter motor looks like the best bet to me."

The man turned around again, but still no one was there. No one except the horse, his head hanging over a field gate, his eyes looking straight at the man.

"W-w-was that you?"

"Don't see anybody else here, do you?"

"No."

"Well then. Anyway, like I was saying, I reckon it's your starter motor. But if you give it a good thump with a hammer, that might just get it going."

"I haven't got a hammer."

"Well, there's a big stone lying just there, try that."

The man was dubious, but he didn't fancy being stuck in the middle of nowhere with a talking horse for the rest of the day, so he picked up the stone and gave the starter motor a hefty thump.

"Now try it."

This time when the man tried to start the car, the engine roared to life. He screeched down the road, and it wasn't long before he came to a village. He parked at the pub and made his way into the bar.

"Double whisky, please."

The barmaid handed the drink over and looked at him curiously.

"Are you alright, pet? You look as white as a sheet."

"Do you know, the strangest thing just happened to me. My car broke down, just along the road there and a horse leaned over the fence and told me what was wrong. I think I'm going mad!"

"Mmm . . .," said the barmaid, thoughtfully. "What colour was the horse?"

"Err . . . black."

"You were lucky," said the barmaid with conviction. "The white one knows nothing about cars."

# Old Lightowler

*A story from Goole retold by Jim Eldon*

Old Lightowler was selling a boat from Airmyn ferry landing. He had a buyer lined up, but it wasn't settled yet. The deal still had to be completed. The chap was coming to finish off the deal. He was coming to Airmyn where the boat was. The man turned up and hadn't been there two minutes before old Lightowler had brought the conversation round to step dancing—also called clog dancing. Old Lightowler was noted for his clog dancing, his stepping. And they hadn't been talking about stepping for two minutes before there was a bet on. The bet was whether old Lightowler could step dance on the deck of the boat all the way from Airmyn ferry landing, where he was selling the boat, 'round to Goole bottom steps where it was heading, where the chap was taking it.

So, they set off down the river, and old Lightowler was there, stepping away on the deck, stepping and clogging away; and they sailed down the river and past Howden Dyke, and there he was, stepping away and tapping away on the metal deck; and they went 'round past Hook village and round the corner down toward Goole dock entrance, and he was still there, stepping away and clogging away and stepping away and clogging away.

Anyway, when they came to the bottom end of Goole docks and they were coming along to Goole bottom steps, the chap, who was at the tiller, knocked her out of gear and turned the engine off to drift her alongside—as is the way of bringing one alongside at Goole bottom steps. And Old Lightowler, as is the way, jumped ashore to take the ropes. As he did this, the chap shouted, "That's it! You lost the bet, you stopped dancing before we reached bottom steps."

And that was it. Old Lightowler paid up, and the chap was real chuffed. The deal was completed, and he picked up his five-pound bet.

He wasn't nearly so pleased a couple of days later, though, when he worked out that he'd taken delivery of the boat with the noisiest tappets of any engine on the river!

# The Hole Stone

## A story from Sussex retold by Dave Arthur

 *In the days before the motorways,*
*When our horses had the time to graze,*
*There were Frankhams, Coopers, Lockes and Lees,*
*And no-one came to move us.*

The Frankhams were a Gypsy family who traveled the lanes and byways of the south of England in horse-drawn wagons, doing seasonal agricultural work, metal work, a bit of fortune-telling, and carving wooden clothes pegs and flowers. They could turn their hand to most things to make a living. There are still a lot of Frankhams about, but nowadays, they're settled in houses or on Traveller sites. But this story takes place in the old days before the motorways, when their horses had the time to graze, and life was conducted at a more gentle pace. It starts in an orchard where the whole Frankham family were camped out under the trees, picking the apples to sell at local markets and shops.

Jack Frankham looked across at his daughter Maria and noticed that she looked a bit thoughtful.

"Penny for 'em, gel," said Jack.

"Penny for what?"

"For your thoughts, you was miles away."

"Oh, yeh, I was thinking how nice it'd be to get married. But I don't s'pose you'd let me."

"How old are you now?" asked Jack, straightening up from the apple basket he was filling.

"Nearly nineteen," said Maria.

"Well, that's certainly old enough to get married," said Jack. "Your Mam was only eighteen when we got hitched. Is there anyone in particular?"

"Well, Billy Smith has been asking me if I fancied marrying him."

"Oh, has he indeed," said Jack. "Young Billy Smith, eh? He's a nice enough lad, and he's quick and clever with the horses. I reckon that'd be a good match. Shall I go and have a word with him and his dad?"

The Smiths were working another orchard just up the lane.

"Oh, would you, Dad?" said Maria, eyes bright, and a big smile on her lips.

"Yeh, course I will, gel."

Suddenly Jack stopped. "No, er . . . you can't marry Billy Smith."

"Why not?" asked Maria.

"Cos when Travellers gets married all the rest of the family and friends from all over Kent, Sussex, Suffolk, and Hampshire come to the wedding, and we haven't anywhere for 'em to camp. There's hardly enough room in this little old orchard for our lot."

Maria's lips started to quiver, and her eyes grew moist and shiny.

"Hang on, gel," said Jack, "let's not have the waterworks, I'll think of something."

He took off his cap, and scratched his head, and whistled through his teeth while he thought about what to do. Suddenly he had an idea. He looked up above the trees to where a large white house stood on top of a hill.

"I'll go up there and ask his lordship if we can borrow one of his fields for a wedding party."

Maria threw her arms round his neck.

"Thanks, Dad."

"Steady, gel," said Jack, "a rabbit's not food till it's in the pot, you know! But I'll give it a go. I'll have a word with the Smiths first, to see what we can come up with."

After a chat and a mug of tea with the Smiths, it was agreed that Billy and Maria were going to marry. So Jack set off up the hill to the manor house. When he got there he knocked on the door. The door was opened by the lord himself. It must have been the servants' day off.

"Hello, Jack," said the Lord, "what can I do for you?"

Jack was well known in the area.

"Well," said Jack, "it's like this, your lordship, my youngest gel, Maria, wants to marry young Billy Smith, and when us Travellers gets married all the other Travellers from Kent and Sussex and Suffolk and Hampshire, and Lord knows where else, all come to the wedding with their wagons and horses, and dogs, and grannies, and kids, the lot. And we haven't got anywhere for 'em all to stop. And I was wondering if you'd let us use one of your fields for the wedding party?"

"Of course you can, Jack," said the lord, "on one condition."

"And what's that?" asked Jack suspiciously.

"That I can come to the party. I love a good party."

" 'Course you can," said Jack, "and bring her ladyship. I'll send the lad up to let you know when it's on."

Word went out and was passed from Traveller to Traveller on the road and on the camping places.

"Maria Frankham's marrying young Billy Smith. There's going to be a big do, down near Paddock Wood."

Over the next two or three weeks bright painted wagons, pulled by fancy black and white Gypsy horses, started pulling onto the field behind the orchard. The horses were tied up along the hedge, the wagons were drawn up into a circle, a large fire was lit in the middle, and heavy iron cauldrons of stew and suet puddings bubbled over the hot logs, and steaming black kettles swung from the kettle-props. Dogs and kids ran about barking and shouting in excitement, and berry-brown, leathery-faced old grannies sat on the steps of their wagons, smoking their stubby little clay pipes and remembering their own wedding days, when they jumped the broom.

The day of the wedding arrived. The lord and lady came down and graced the proceedings with their presence, and, more important, their presents! There was food and drink, singing, storytelling, and laughter. Every one was having a great time. There was, of course, a musician there. He might have been a fiddler, he might have been a melodeon player or concertina player, I don't know. But whatever he was, he began to play "Haste to the Wedding" and followed it with a hornpipe, and Jack started to dance. Now Jack was a champion step dancer—he was known the length and breadth of Kent and Sussex for his dancing. He was almost magical, because when he started to dance everyone else just had to get up and shake a leg. You couldn't stop yourself. As Jack started to stamp out the rhythm to the music everyone started to dance—the men and women, the kids and teenagers, the grannies, the babies in their wicker baskets, the horses, the dogs, even the birds in the trees were dancing. You've never heard such a whooping and stamping and carrying on.

Suddenly the lord of the manor cried out, "Stop! Jack! Stop your dancing. I can't go on."

Jack stopped his dancing. And everyone else stopped. The lord of the manor was holding his sides, puffing and panting for breath, sweat pouring down his face.

"Phew!" he said.

"Jack," he said, "you're like a magician. When *you* dance, everyone has to dance. You can't stop yourself. It's fantastic. I just wish I could dance like you."

"Really?" said Jack, "You'd like to dance like me, an old Gypsy feller, and yet you've got all that money, and that great big house. Isn't it funny, we all want something we haven't got. You'd like to dance like me, and me, I'd like to have a big old house like you."

"You'd like to live in my manor house?" said the Lord.

"Yeh, that'd be just dandy, plenty of room there for the Frankhams and the Smiths, and our horses and dogs, and everything."

"Really?" said the lord, stroking his chin. "Are you a betting man, Jack?"

"Yeh, I have a bet now and again, on a horse or good dog," said Jack.

The lord looked around the field until his eyes fell on a large flat stone about three feet high just inside the circle of wagons.

"You're a great dancer, Jack, but I'll bet you couldn't dance on that stone from sunset to sunrise, and I'll bet you couldn't dance a hole right through the stone, so that I could see the ground underneath. You're a good dancer Jack, but I don't think you're that good."

"And what if I do it?" asked Jack.

"Then I'd give you my manor house."

"And what if I don't manage it?"

"Then I get your wagon. It'd look nice in the garden. A home for a home. What d'you say?"

"I'll have a go," said Jack.

Word went round the camp.

"Jack's gonna dance on that stone, and if he dances a hole through it he's gonna get the manor house."

They couldn't wait for the sun to go down.

What the Lord of the Manor didn't know was that Jack, amongst other things, was a blacksmith. The Travellers have always dealt in horses and metal-work. Jack nipped back to his wagon, and on the little portable anvil he took round to horse fairs, he beat himself up a pair of horseshoes, nailed them on the bottom of his boots, and clomped back to the party, climbed upon the stone and waited for the sun to go down.

As the sun sank behind the trees the musician started to play and Jack started to step it out.

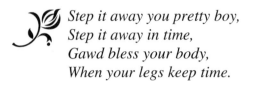

*Step it away you pretty boy,*
*Step it away in time,*
*Gawd bless your body,*
*When your legs keep time.*

Sparks flew up from his flying feet as the iron horseshoes chipped away at the stone.

Of course, as soon as Jack started dancing, everyone started dancing. It was chaos, bodies and animals hopping and whooping, waving arms, legs, hooves, paws, 'round and 'round the fire they went, while Jack stamped out the rhythms on the stone—hornpipes, jigs, reels, schottisches—he could dance anything. He was an all 'round dancer.

Nine o'clock and everyone was dancing, nine-thirty, ten o'clock, the babies in their cots fell back exhausted and sucked their thumbs and snored gently. Eleven o'clock, the old ladies fell into the ditches, legs up the air, fast asleep. The horses rolled over on their backs, birds fell out of the trees with exhaustion. By midnight people were falling like flies. The lord and lady were seen crawling under a wagon before collapsing.

By one o'clock in the morning the whole field was covered in snoring bodies, even the musician had slumped over his instrument, but Jack was still dancing. Sparks flew into the night air, as he shuffled and stamped, kicked and spun on the stone. Two, three, four, five, five-thirty, the cockerel on the farm down the lane started to crow. People started to wake up and stagger about bleary eyed, holding their heads. His lordship and his lady crawled out from under the wagon where they'd spent the night, and saw Jack standing by the stone.

"Good morning, Jack," said the lord, rubbing his eyes. "Phew, what a party. I don't suppose you've been dancing all night, have you?"

Jack just nodded.

"I don't suppose you danced a hole through that stone have you?"

"Come and have a look," said Jack.

So the lord of the manor went across, and, sure enough, Jack *had* danced a hole right through that stone, so that you could see ground underneath it.

"Right," said the Lord. "You've won the bet, Jack, you've got the manor house. But where am I going to live?"

"No problem," said Jack. "You can have my wagon."

And that's what happened. That's what they did. They hitched Jack's old mare up to the wagon, and the lord and lady climbed up, and they set off through the villages of Kent, telling fortunes, fixing pots and pans—and very good they got at it, too. They became familiar faces around the Kent villages for years and years.

Jack and the rest of his family moved up into the big house, with Billy Smith and their ponies and lurcher dogs and lived happily there for years until one day, the old yearning for the travelling life and the wood smoke smell of campfires, proved to strong to resist, and one fine spring morning they loaded up their wagons, left the house, and never returned. It slowly crumbled away and today it's just an ivy-and-weed-covered ruin. But the Travellers still point it out to their kids as they pass by on their way to the horse fair at Horsmonden, and sometimes late at night around a smoky campfire you might hear stories of Jack the legendary step dancer and the hole stone.

And that's why a lot of Travellers in Kent and Sussex say that to find a stone with a hole in it is lucky—after all a hole stone once won a travelling man a manor house. So if they find a pebble with a hole in it on the beach or on a country lane, they often pick it up and keep it in their pocket for luck. And I recommend that you do the same. We all need a bit of luck in this life.

# White Ram Night

*A story from Sussex retold by Jamie Crawford*

*This is an extract from a suite of shepherding stories I have concocted from various folktales. The county of Sussex was once known for the "age of the golden hoof" because of the prosperity generated by the huge flocks of sheep that grazed the coastal hills known as the South Downs. Sussex even has a shepherding saint, Saint Cuthman, who carted his old mother in a wheelbarrow from Cornwall all the way across southern England to the downland village of Steyning (where some of my forbears lived and there built a church). He could stop his sheep straying just by drawing a circle in the chalk around them with his crook. Saint Cuthman was so holy he could hang his gloves on a sunbeam. Most everyday shepherds were generally poor but skilled husbandmen who were respected for the stamina, reserve, and wisdom of their solitary way of life. The Jack in my story is in many ways far from typical!*

It's White Ram Night. That's when shepherds bring their flocks down to the farm for shearing in June and gather in the pub on the first evening to exchange stories and news.

"What noos?" asks one old shepherd of the rest.

"Sheep stealin', that's what!" says another greybeard, and there's a general murmur of agreement.

Old news, but all the same Jack says,

"Sheep stealin'?! Well, I always wondered what happened to the two of my lambs gone missing last spring. And that wasn' all."

The mutter of voices has stopped, everyone is listening. Jack continues, "I was up in my caravan for the lambing. Little after midnight and I'd just been round to check the sheep. All fine. Must have been dozing in my chair when Polly starts growlin' and then barkin' fit to waken the dead. I open the door and she's off into the night, yelpin' away. Take me crook and me horn lamp, put me chummy on me 'ed, and follow after. Walk and walk, callin' but she's gone. Swallowed up, like. Then I see a light ahead. Funny, I think, didn't know anyone was stayin' up here. I come to a house in the dark, all on its own. Door's open, light's comin' from a fire inside. Smell of cookin'. Someone sitting by the fire. A man. Knock, knock, 'Hello, I say, seen my dog, mister?' 'NO DOG 'ERE,' he snaps. I look around the room. Pot bubblin' over the fire, full of bones a-stewin' away. And there's a bed, or something like it, just a blanket and someone underneath, all I can see's a mop of woolly white hair showin. 'Oozat?' I say. 'That's . . . Granny,' he growls, 'asleep!' Then I hear a sound, a high whiney bleatin' sound in the room. Meeeeeeeahhh! 'That sounds like one of my lambs,' I say. 'That's the baby cryin',' he goes, 'now you come and waked her.' And there in the man's arms is a baby, or something like it, all wrapped up in a bundle it is. Strangest baby I ever seen. Long pink face and starin' wrinkly black eyes shinin' in the firelight. 'Well, oose baby zat then?' 'E looks at me then. 'Oose baby? Granny's baby!' He leers full in my face, 'She's just given birth and won't take too kindly to bein' woken by a stranger.' And that's enough for me. I leave that house and hotfoot it back to my caravan. Next morning dog turns up, all draggled she is. Been hit on the head. Polly is poorly! So I look after her a bit, pick her some herbs, and soon, well, Polly is jolly! But when I went back to that house, it was just a ruin, no sign of anyone . . . I reckon it were haunted, and those were ghosts I saw."

"Jack, Jack," says the first old shepherd. "You've had the wool pulled over yer eyes this time, m'boy. That Granny's hair was your own lamb's little fleece, that stew was made with her bones, and the baby, why, that was another of your lambs. And that man and his Granny were your sheep stealers!"

And everyone's laughing at Jack. Tickled pink.

But if you want to find out whether Jack got even with the sheep stealers, you'll have to wait till the shearing's done . . . you'll have to wait till Black Ram Night!

# The Wrestlers of Carn Kenidjack

*A story from Cornwall retold by Mike O'Connor*

*I was once having a cup of tea with old Ma Curgenven. I asked if she knew any tall stories.*

*"Listen to this," she said.*

In the days when kids worked in the mines, Jacky and Jan were two poor mining lads. They were so poor they didn't even have a belt between them to hold up their trousers. Instead their trousers were tied up with hairy string left over from bailing the hay. Now on a Friday, like anyone else, they looked forward to an evening in the kiddleywink. But the lads lived in Saint Just and then, unlike to-day, the people of Saint Just were so upright and virtuous, there was not a single pub in the town. To wet your whistle you had to walk all the way to Morvah.

One Friday evening Jacky and Jan were about to leave when their mother called them.

"Do you know what night it is?" she asked.

They shook their heads.

"Tonight is Hallowe'en, when you may see ghosts, ghouls, goblins, and even old Nick himself. You must be home by midnight."

The lads promised and set off to Morvah. Down the hill and across the stream at Nancherrow, then up past Botallack and Pendeen, apprehensively skirting the slopes of Carn Kenidjack. For on a dark night it is said that there you can see strange lights and hear wild hooting sounds—surely the work of ghosts, ghouls, goblins, and even old Nick himself.

Soon they reached the inn and soon they were singing songs and swapping stories. And because it was Halloween the songs and stories were all about ghosts, ghouls, goblins, and even old Nick himself.

They were so engrossed, they did not notice the passing of time. Suddenly there was the clock chiming midnight, and the lads knew they were in terrible trouble. As they ran down the road they thought, perhaps we could save time if we cut across the common just below Carn Kenidjack, and maybe we wouldn't be in quite as much trouble. So they left the road. They hadn't been off it for more than five minutes when they heard the sound of a horse being galloped through the night. They had to throw themselves off the path to avoid being ridden down.

Jacky called out to the rider,

"That's no way to ride at night!"

The horse stopped and turned. The rider wore a hooded cloak, but they could see his eyes glowing red in the darkness. He said, "I'm going up to Carn Kenidjack to watch the wrestling. Why don't you come too?"

Now there's no sport a Cornish lad likes more than wrestling, and suddenly it seemed the most natural thing in the world to follow the commanding stranger up Carn Kenidjack.

At the top of the carn the lads found a grassy bank. Beyond it was a wrestling ring, and there were two huge wrestlers, and seated all around were ghosts, ghouls, goblins, and old Nick himself sitting on a throne, with his eyes blazing red.

Then the wrestling began. It was like no match you or I have ever seen. The wrestlers were ten feet tall, and with every fall you could hear the crunch of breaking bones, the ripping of sinews, and the tearing of flesh. Every fall was applauded by the ghost, ghouls, goblins, and even old Nick himself.

Eventually one of the wrestlers lifted the other high into the air and smashed his opponent down onto a granite rock, and with all the watchers, went to the throne to receive his prize. But the loser lay motionless on the ground.

"We must help him," said Jacky. So Jacky and Jan scrambled down into the ring to where the poor giant lay.

"Is he alive?" said Jacky.

"Only just," said Jan.

"We must get a doctor," said Jacky.

"There isn't time," said Jan.

"Do you know any prayers?" said Jacky.

"I know one," said Jan, and he started. "Our Father, which art in heaven, hallowed be thy name. Thy will be done . . ."

And at that instant he stopped. On the back of his neck all the hairs were standing on end, and he knew he was being watched. He looked up and there were all the ghosts, ghouls, goblins, and even old Nick himself, his eyes blazing red.

They saw Old Nick raise his arm, they saw him point his finger, they saw him open his mouth. They didn't wait to hear what he said! They ran as fast as their legs could carry them down towards Saint Just. Behind them came all the ghosts, ghouls, goblins, and even old Nick himself.

Now Jacky and Jan remembered that ghosts dare not cross running water. If they could only get across the stream at Nancherrow, they would be safe. But with every pace the ghosts, ghouls, goblins, and even old Nick himself got closer.

Jacky was feeling tired, and Jan's laces were coming undone. They both had the stitch, and every second the ghosts, ghouls, goblins, and even old Nick himself got closer and closer.

They were one pace from the bridge when the biggest, ugliest, fiercest, hungriest goblin reached out and seized them both by the belt. With a snarl of triumph, he opened his jaws to reveal the sharpest teeth you can imagine and bite their heads off. But Jackie and Jan were just poor mining lads. Their trousers were only held up with old hairy string. The string broke with a twang, and so it was that Jackie and Jan crossed the bridge, but their trousers never did.

So that's the tale the lads told their mother to explain how they arrived home from the pub at one in the morning with no trousers on. Now that's what I call a tall story!

# Dragons and Devils

# The Lambton Worm

*A story from the North East, retold by Amy Douglas*

| | |
|---|---|
| *Whisht! lads, haad yor gobs,* | *Aa'll tell ye aall an aaful story,* |
| *Whisht! lads, haad yor gobs,* | *An' Aal tell ye 'bout the worm.* |
| *Whisht! Lads, hold your mouths,* | *And I'll tell you all an awful story,* |
| *Whisht! Lads, hold your mouths,* | *And I'll tell you about the worm.* |

Young John Lambton was a tearaway. The eldest son and heir to the castle of Lambton, near the River Wear in the county of Durham, he was breaking his father's heart with his reckless ways.

John was *supposed* to be learning the ways of being a lord, caring for the estate and setting a good example to the local people. Instead he had thoughts for nothing but pleasure. He spent his days hunting with his dogs raiding birds' nests and spent the evenings carousing. And he spent Sunday just like every other day. While his family, the castle residents, and all the villagers congregated to hear mass in Brugeford Chapel, John had better things to do.

One particular Sunday, despite his father's pleas to join them at the chapel, young Lambton went fishing. It was a beautiful day, and he sat with his line dangling in the River Wear waiting for the fish to take the bait.

At last his line dipped into the water and the rod was almost snatched out of John's hands. He caught it just in time and began to pull. There was something strong on the end of that line! Something big! An old salmon maybe, or a sea trout. The battle commenced, and all John's skill as a fisherman was put to the test. At last he heaved his catch onto the river bank.

It wasn't a fish.

He wasn't quite sure what it was. It was ugly, he knew that much. Glinting eyes stared at him and a mouthful of needlelike teeth gnashed at the ground. It was the length of his arm, all covered in dark, slimy scales, and there were nine holes on either side of its evil looking mouth. It smelt rotten.

"I wouldn't throw it back if I were you," came a voice over John's shoulder. John nearly jumped out of his skin and turned to look who was speaking. An old man stood there, a serious look on a kindly face.

"*You* caught it and it's *your* responsibility."

"Huh!" shrugged John. He picked up the squirming worm, turned his back on the old man and turned toward home. Not far from where he had been fishing was an old well. Out of sight of the old man, he threw the worm down the well and said no more about it.

But catching the worm had given John a bit of a turn. When the next Sunday came around, uncomplaining, he put on his Sunday best and went to the chapel with everyone else. Lord Lambton smiled and thought that at last his son had started to grow into his responsibilities. Indeed John turned over a new leaf, and it was only a few years later that he took up arms and made his way to the Holy Land to fight in the Crusades.

But at home, at the bottom of the well, the worm grew.

In the watery darkness, the coils multiplied until the well could no longer contain the monster.

One night it hauled itself up out of the well and began to explore the land. Its belly was empty and it smelt the sweet scent of cows in the field, of sheep grazing on the hillsides. It slithered through the land and, when it had eaten its fill, curled itself three times around a nearby hill.

The people woke the next morning to find their land devastated. Sheep and cattle were missing. Dark trails of black slime and withered grass curved through the fields. And then they saw the worm wrapped around the hill.

White and terrified, they made their way to Lambton Castle, demanding that the lord take action—*do* something.

The lord stood, listening to the tales, then went outside to look at the worm and wonder what to do. As they stood there watching, the lord standing at the front of the crowd, the castle residents and villagers cowering behind them, the worm began to uncurl. It left the hill and snaked its way across the fields and the meadows, straight toward them, the clamor of the people drawing it, the warm bodies all gathered so close together.

"Bring milk!" called the lord.

"What . . .?"

"Milk, bring all the milk that we have, pour it into the cattle trough. I've heard that worms like milk. Let it drink its fill and perhaps it will leave us and our cattle unmolested."

And that is what they did. The maids ran off to the dairy, the men following to help carry buckets and pails of milk to fill the trough. Once the trough was full and the worm nearly upon them, they took refuge inside, watching through the windows to see what would happen.

The worm sped up the drive, but it stopped by the trough. It sniffed the contents. The great head lifted, looked through the windows at the white faces within. Those watching saw the glint in its eyes, saw the needle sharp teeth as it smiled and the slime dripping from its jaws. Then it lowered its head to drink, and the watchers let out their breath.

From then on, only the occasional sheep or cow would go missing, for every day the worm would slither its way from the hill where it slept up the drive to Lambton. Each day the milk from nine cows would be set out for it and it would drink its fill. But the milk cost dear and few servants would stay at the house of Lambton.

Word spread about the worm, and heroes came to test their strength against the monster. But fight as they might, they could not defeat the worm, for whenever a piece of the worm was cut off, it would reattach itself and grow as though the worm had never been wounded. The knights did not have the same advantage.

And so the reign of the worm took hold. The old Lord Lambton and his steward fed the worm every day, and a pallor of gloom hung over the estate. The old lord grew haggard and more than once he prayed for his son and his safe return.

One day there was a clattering of hooves outside the castle. The lord looked out to see a great charger, and on his back a great knight, his armor shining, his skin tanned by sun and wind. Seasoned by battle, tempered by decisions hard made, Sir John Lambton had returned.

It was not the welcome he had hoped for. The land was barren. An air of defeat hung over the area. Only his father and his steward came out to meet his homecoming.

When Sir John heard the cause of the devastation, his heart sank, but he determined to at last put an end to the worm.

News of Sir John's return spread through the village, crofts, and homesteads. A glimmer of hope was lighted that perhaps *now* there was a worthy champion to rid them of the worm.

But John did not set out unaided. Instead of riding to meet the worm, he rode to see the wisewoman of Brugeford to seek her advice.

"You brought this curse upon the land and only you can defeat it," she said. "But do not go unprepared. You must go to the blacksmith and ask him to stud your armor with spearheads. Then you must go the River Wear, cross to the island in the middle of it, and taunt the worm until it attacks you. That is the only place where you have a chance to beat the worm. But even if you win the battle, there is still a price to be paid. When you return home, you must kill the first living being that comes toward you. If you do not, a curse will lie on your family, and for nine generations no Lambton will die in his bed."

So Sir John went to the blacksmith. He watched as his armor was studded with spearheads. He buckled on the armor, still warm from the forge and mounted his charger. He paused at his home and told his father all that the wisewoman had said.

"If I triumph, father, I will return and blow my bugle as a signal. Then let out the dogs and the first one to come to my feet I will slay to allay the curse."

Then Lambton rode away from the Hall, his worried father watching him grow smaller as the hooves thudded into the distance. Sir John rode past the well and along the river until he came to the island. He forded the river, dismounted his charger, and, thumping its rump, sent it flying back home. Sir John looked toward the dark spiral on Worm Hill and he began to shout and holler. The worm opened its eyes and looked toward the river. It saw the flash and gleam of the armor and sword. The worm unfurled itself from the hill and came sliding over the fields toward John. There was a splash as it dove into the river and then came up, water streaming from its head. It rushed at John, wrapping thick coils of its body around him and began to squeeze, tighter and tighter. Now John saw the wisdom of the old woman, for as the worm squeezed tighter, one by one the spearheads punctured the worm's hide and the blood came oozing out. The worm loosened its grip and instead bared its needle sharp teeth. The head of the worm danced from side to side, John parrying with his sword and managing to keep his footing on the wet rock. At last John saw his chance. The neck of the worm was undefended. John seized the opportunity and with all his strength sliced through the body of the worm. The waters took the body and carried it away down river. With one half swept away, the body of the worm could not join back together, and so, at last, the worm was defeated.

John pulled out his bugle and blew three long, sweet blasts, and across the countryside the people knew that at long last they were free. Inside Lambton Hall, Lord Lambton and his steward heard the bugle sound, and their faces lit up with joy. So delighted were they that John was alive, they forgot all his warnings and rushed out to greet him.

As John made his weary way back to the hall he couldn't believe it when he saw not the dogs bounding toward him, but his own father. He waved at him to go back and blew the bugle again. Now the servants let the dogs out and he killed the first that came to him, but it was too late. The curse lay on the family for nine generations, and indeed from Sir John Lambton himself until Henry Lambton, Esq. M.P., no Lambton did die in his bed. The first died in a hunting accident, the last on crossing the new bridge at Lambton on 26 June 1761, while many between were killed in battle. One General Lambton, who had survived battle and lived a long life, was at last confined to bed with a terrible illness. Though in great agony and though his doctors could not believe how he managed to keep breath in his body, he survived until after much pleading his servants lifted him out of his bed—and as soon as they did, he was released into death.

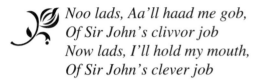

*Noo lads, Aa'll haad me gob,*
*Of Sir John's clivvor job*
*Now lads, I'll hold my mouth,*
*Of Sir John's clever job*

*That's aall Aa knaa aboot the story,*
*Wi' the aaful Lambton Worm.*
*That's all I know about the story,*
*With the awful Lambton Worm.*

# The Laidly Worm

*A story from North Yorkshire retold by Kelvin Hall*

Young Wynde, who lived in a castle far to the north of this land, was unnerved by his father's new wife, for her eyes, whenever they looked upon him, seemed full of venom, like a viper's fangs. Then, one evening, as he passed the closed door of her private chamber, he heard her voice chanting rhythmically, and the sound chilled his blood.

> *"Let it be for him as if shards of glass are wedged under his skin,*
> *As if the red-hot embers of the fire lay in his joints."*

And so he peered through the keyhole, and saw that as she sang, she also crouched over a tiny lead figure and the features of this figure were unmistakable his own. He knew that she had fashioned it, and was working black sorceries to bring him to a miserable death.

During these days, he had no one to turn to but his younger sister, Margaret. But his terror overwhelmed him, and he didn't even want to share with her what he'd seen and heard. Wynde decided that the only thing he could do for now was to get as far away from the woman as fast as he could. So he ran to his dead mother's old chamber and scooped up a handful of gems. And he ran to his father's chest and scooped up a handful of coins. And he ran down to the stable, took the fastest horse and rode through the gusty night, all the way to the coast. There he found a ship to carry him to foreign lands, and for many lonely years he stayed overseas.

He often regretted that he'd left his home so suddenly without a word to Margaret, but in the years that he traveled he grew stronger, braver, and wiser. One day he sat in an inn by the quayside filled with seafarers sheltering from the foul weather. As he chatted, he discovered that the ship's captain sitting opposite him came from his own land.

"What news from the north of Britain?" Wynde asked.

The captain looked hard at Wynde and spoke. "The whole country now lives in terror. A beast has arrived, from where no one knows. It devours men as easily as cattle and dogs. Its size is vast. Its skin is scaly. Its eyes bulge with fury as it slithers through the land. No one dares to fight it, but every day they leave seven cows tethered outside its cave, hoping thus to pacify it."

"I cannot leave my land and its people in such danger," thought Wynde to himself. And later that day he walked down to the shipyard. He wandered from ship to ship and from builder to builder till he found a man who looked unafraid of what Wynde would ask of him.

"Is it possible," he asked the master shipwright, "to build a ship that would somehow be protected from black enchantments and the curses of those that know them?"

"Yes," came the answer, "if I made it all of the wood of the rowan tree. But that would cost a pretty penny—"

"Then build it," said the young man.

The weeks went by as the ship was built, until the day he handed over to the shipwright the last of the jewels and coins he had brought from Britain. The master builder handed him a small spring of rowan to keep with him as a good luck charm. Then he led his horse aboard and set sail. But far off, in her turret room, his enemy saw that a crystal hanging from her wall had clouded over and knew by this sign that Wynde had set out to return. On the second day of his journey, Wynde saw a speck on the far horizon. As it came closer he recognized another ship. On its deck stood seven jabbering hags. They cackled, moaned, and danced, in this way calling up a wind against Wynde. It hurtled toward him so sharp that when a seagull flew between the ships it was instantly torn to shreds. But the moment the wind touched the outermost plank of rowan wood, it reversed upon itself. It swept toward the hags and tore them, screeching and screaming, to fragments which were swept away across the waves. Then a black ship approached, its hull bristling with long iron spikes that would split any vessel it touched. Its deck was filled with armored men, their gauntlets, helmets, shields, and clubs festooned in armored spikes like their ship. Each spike was tipped with poison. Wynde drew his sword, waiting ready with pounding heart. But as soon as the tip of the first spike touched the rowan wood, the whole black ship shriveled up like an insect in the flame and sank beneath the water. He knew all these things had been sent by his stepmother, and he knew something else: she was afraid.

Wynde landed on a deserted shore and set out across an empty heath. Suddenly he saw movement in the gorse as if a creature was wriggling through it. He drew his sword and sped toward it. But he found himself looking down on the cringing figure of a small ragged girl. He calmed her with his voice.

"What are you doing here?" he asked.

"I came out because I'm the smallest in the family and so the easiest to hide. I'm gathering sloe berries, for that's all we've got to eat."

"Do you know where the dragon is?"

Trembling, she pointed up to the hills, nearby.

And so, Wynde worked his way upward until he reached the mouth of a cave. Outside, a great heap of bones lay, the remains of the cows that had been offered daily to the beast. After only a few moments, he heard a slithering and a scraping. This was the sound of the dragon's sides and long tail against the stones, as it made for the entrance. Then Wynde's heart hammered against his chest and his mouth became parched with dread.

As the dragon pulled its monstrous body from the depths of the cave, he swung his great sword fiercely. The dragon instantly recoiled, and the blow missed. Wynde waited on guard for the creature to strike back. Then waited longer, for it scarcely moved. He saw a tear well up in the dragon's eye. Then another came, and they thudded to the ground like raindrops. Shocked, Wynde stared deep into those eyes. And a feeling came over him, as if he recognized them, as if he knew those eyes from long ago.

In that moment, a voice came from deep within the creature's bowels.

*O quit your sword and sheath your blade*
*And give me kisses three;*
*For though I am a poisonous worm,*
*No harm, I'll do to thee.*

His fear told him not to do as the dragon asked. His deepest heart told him to do it. Gingerly he leaned forward and placed his lips on the scales. The dragon didn't move. He did it again and again. The dragon's skin began to crack, then to peel away. First a human hand came out, then a shoulder, and then the flushed face of his sister, Margaret. The scaly skin fell to the ground, and there she stood, free of the weirding of her father's wife. For it was this that had her forced to take on the dragon's shape. Wynde gently placed his cloak around her, and they hugged each other tight. But then he helped her onto his horse, and they turned toward their father's castle.

"Now let us finish this matter," said he, and from his belt Wynde tugged the twig of rowan he had carried all this time.

Through the gate they went and up the stairs of the tallest tower toward the chamber where the sorceress followed her craft. When she turned and saw them at the door, she cringed. Then, as Wynde strode toward her, she began to mouth the words of an old and deadly enchantment. But before she finished it, he touched her shoulder with his twig of rowan wood. She gave a shriek and then slowly withered down into the shape of a bulging toad. It waddled out of the door, plummeted down the stairs, and hid itself from sight.

From that day, Wynde and his sister became the protectors of their land, and none were able to harm it while they lived. But it is said that now and again, people there who peer into dark, deep rocks and corners will see the eyes of the great toad, peering out at them, ever watchful, ever waiting.

# Pollard and the Brawn

*A story from Durham retold by Taffy Thomas*

If one travels to the northeast of England and enters County Durham, the boundary sign will read "County Durham—Land of the Prince Bishops." This is because, at the time of the Crusades, the bishop of Durham was given the status of prince as well as bishop. In those days, he lived in a town that is, to this day, still called Bishop Auckland.

At this time, the good people of County Durham were being terrorized by a brawn—a giant boar. This monster was terribly fierce, and it ate sheep, goats, pigs, and even little children. All the local folk went to the Prince Bishop to complain and seek help. The Prince Bishop ordered an announcement to be made in the market place to the effect that if any man was brave enough to track down the beast and slay it, he would receive a great reward. In the crowd at the market was Pollard, a knight freshly returned from the Crusades, his sword and his skill sharpened in battle. Not having much to occupy him at the time, Pollard decided he would be the hero to pursue the wild pig and slay it. However, sheltering behind Pollard was a rogue whose name is lost in the mists of time. The rogue, being cowardly and lazy, decided to follow the brave knight at a safe distance and cheat his way to the reward.

Following the trotter's prints, Pollard caught up with the beast in a narrow gully in a place which is to this day still called Brancepeth (the Brawn's Path). There was an hour-long fight between knight and beast. The two were well matched and took turns besting the other through most of the fight. The rogue observed this battle from the safety of a nearby bush. Pollard had just sufficient strength to force his spear through the heart of the beast, causing it to crash to the ground with a thud so loud they could feel the vibrations in Newcastle-upon-Tyne, more than thirty miles away.

The monster was so big, it took the knight half an hour to walk around its corpse. Pollard had a problem. He realized he could never carry the carcass back to claim his reward. Ingenuity prevailed, as Pollard realized part of the corpse would be sufficient to make his claim. He swung his double-edged sword, slicing through the neck of the beast. The monster's mouth opened, and its tongue flopped out, a pink tongue with three hairs on the tip of it. If there was one thing Pollard liked to eat, it was roast tongue. He thought if I could get half a stotty cake on each side of that tongue, it would be a sandwich to last a week. The knight cut off the tongue, tucking it in his back pocket. It was so long, the three hairs touched the ground. Bending down, Pollard grabbed the ears to take the severed head back to Bishop Auckland to claim his reward. However, exhausted from the battle, he was forced to lie under a tree and rest. He soon fell fast asleep. Peeping out from the bush, the rogue observed the sleeping knight and thought he could steal the head and claim the reward.

Pollard awoke and realized the head was missing. He knew what had happened and decided to race back to the Prince Bishop's palace to thwart the thief. He pushed open the heavy oak doors of the palace just in time to see the cheat holding up the severed head of the pig. Pollard shouted to the Prince Bishop, "Wait! It was not this man who slew the monster, but me."

The Prince Bishop protested, "But he has brought me the head as proof!"

Pollard informed the Prince Bishop that an examination of the head would reveal the tongue to be missing. He himself then produced the tongue from his pocket and advised the Prince Bishop that the only way he could have the tongue was if he had been the hero that had defeated the boar.

The Prince Bishop realized the rights of it and ordered that the rogue be hanged in chains. Congratulating Pollard for his bravery in slaying the brawn and his wit in thwarting the cheat, he rewarded him with as much land as he could ride around whilst the Prince Bishop ate his dinner. As the Prince Bishop called for his first course, the soup, Pollard mounted his horse and started his ride. Long before the Prince Bishop had reached his fifth and final course, the dessert, Pollard had reentered the place. The Prince Bishop informed him he could have covered more ground, but Pollard protested he had ridden as far as he needed, having ridden around the bishop's palace.

Theoretically, the palace and all its contents should have been the knight's reward. Sadly the Prince Bishop informed the knight that, as the palace and its contents had been bestowed upon him by King Richard himself, he was not at liberty to give it away. Pointing through a window, the Prince Bishop indicated a patch of land on the banks of the river Wear, the finest piece of agricultural land in County Durham. This land was for Pollard and his successors. Being a gracious knight, Pollard accepted this gift.

*If one visits Bishop Auckland to this day, one can still find the knight's land, for it is still known as Pollard's Land. In fact, there's a pub on it called The Pollard Arms, a place that Taffy Thomas, the storyteller, occasionally visits for refreshment.*

# Recipe for Stotty Cake

From Molly Douglas, Amy's Grandma

*A stotty cake is a kind of flat bread loaf peculiar to the North East of England.*

## Ingredients

### U.S. measures

- 2 cups white strong bread flour
- 1 oz lard
- ¼ cup fresh yeast
- 1 tsp sugar
- 1 tsp salt
- 4 cups (1 quart) warm water

### English measures

- 3 lb white strong bread flour
- 1 oz lard
- 2 oz fresh yeast
- 1 tsp sugar
- 1 tsp salt
- 1½ pints warm water

## Method

Mash the yeast and sugar with a fork and 2 tsp of warm water until a smooth paste is obtained. Sprinkle enough flour over the top to leave a thin covering.

Leave for about 10 minutes in a warm place until the yeast becomes frothy.

Put two handfuls of flour to one side to help with kneading later. Sieve the remaining flour with the salt into a bowl. Make a well in the center of the flour. Chop the lard into small pieces and place in the well. Pour yeast liquid into the well, followed by the remaining warm water (make sure it is still warm).

Knead the mixture until a smooth, elastic dough is achieved.

Put the dough into a warm bowl and cover it with a warm, damp tea towel. Leave in a warm place to rise until twice the size.

Divide mixture into four even pieces and knead each quarter separately. Shape each portion and roll out into a circle about one inch thick. Use a knife to score the dough with a cross so that the baked bread will divide easily into quarters. Put onto a greased baking tray and leave to rise in a warm place.

Preheat the oven to 425°F (220°C/gas mark 7).

When the stotties have risen, lightly dust the top with flour, put them into the oven, and bake for approximately 10 minutes until they are a light golden brown.

Take the stotties out of the oven and place them on to a cooling rack. Wait until they are just cool enough to be able to pick them up without burning fingers, break into quarters, cut each quarter in half, spread liberally with butter, and eat!

## Hints

Traditionally a stotty cake is always made with lard   and that's certainly the way my grandma makes them. However, I've been vegetarian for the past decade and have discovered that they taste just as good when butter is used instead. (Until my Grandma taught me how to make stotties this year I had no idea that they contained lard!)

Yeast likes to be warm, but anything warmer than 37°C (99°F) will kill it. Make sure your warm water isn't hot, and if baking on a cold day, retreat to the kitchen, and put the oven on low so that you *and* the dough are kept warm.

# The Devil and the Coracle

*A story from Shropshire retold by Mike Rust*

On the Stiperstones there is a rock called the Devil's Chair. They say that when the fog is down, then the Devil sits in this chair, but when the fog is up, we don't know where the Devil is, but he is somewhere in Shropshire. So it is always safer when the fog is there because at least we all know where he is.

Now the Devil he likes a bit of fishing, and he has this thing called the Devil's Coracle.* The Devil's Coracle is twice as big as everyone else's, and the rim of it flames with fire all the way round. He sits in there and he goes fishing from time to time, but because he is the Devil, he does not go fishing for fish—he goes fishing for souls.

Now we all live by the River Severn, and it was as true to say then as it is true to say now that the river is a dangerous place. It's got little gullies that go down, under the river for about a mile, then back up again. Every year, we know, there are a few people that perish in the water. The latest thing is for the kids to play *Titanic* in the floods of the river. They find the railings under the floodwater and stand on them and spread their arms out, but it's a dangerous game. So if you see them, tell them to get out of the flooded river or the Devil may catch their souls when he goes fishing.

Now one day the Devil was going fishing, and he chucked in his coracle somewhere about Montford Bridge. It floated down through Shrewsbury, and it floated down through Ironbridge, but he could not find any souls at all. And the Devil, he was aggrieved. He's a bad fellow, and when he expects something to happen, then he expects something to happen—and it didn't! He just wanted to catch something, anything at all, and it happened that he was just going past Jackfield, named after the Jack in this story who used to live there. It was about 4 o'clock, just as the sun was coming up in the morning.

Jack always was a cheeky lad, and he called out to the Devil, "Haven't you caught nothing then—nah—you can see by the look on your face you haven't!"

*A coracle is a small boat used in Britain since ancient times. It is made of a frame, usually covered with hide or tarpaulin.

The Devil turned round and spat. The spit was a fireball, and it just missed Jack's face as he ducked. The Devil said, "Well, what have *you* caught then? Let's have a look in *your* net."

The Devil looked down and Jack had not caught any fish at all.

"I'll tell you what I'll do, I'll make you a deal," said the Devil. "You go and get your coracle and we'll sit here and we'll put the net between us and we'll catch all the fish. You can keep all the fish and you can sell them down Bridgnorth market, and if there are any souls I will take them, but if at the end of a year and a day there's no souls been caught in our net, then I will take *you*, Jack, to Hell and you can stay all eternity."

And Jack thought to himself, *there's always someone dies in the river.* Besides, life was not too good . . . he thought of all the fish he could catch, so he made the deal and a bargain was struck.

It was a Thursday night, so the next Thursday night, Jack he got into his coracle, and he paddled into the river, and the Devil he got into his coracle and paddled down the river. They had a balloon net. Now a balloon net is shaped just like a balloon, but it has smaller holes at one side. The smaller holes go downstream, the larger holes go upstream, and the river runs through it. When the fish get in, they cannot get out, and the Devil and Jack just sat there with the net between the two of them. Jack was right-handed so he was holding the net with his right hand. The Devil was using his left hand, and they were just sitting side by side in the stream from the time the sun went down to the time the sun went up. The Devil, he looked in the net and thought, *there's not a soul in it at all.* And he threw it to Jack. After he went paddling downstream, Jack peered in, and there were some nice big fish. Jack, he took the fish down to Bridgnorth market, he sold them, and he made more money that day then he had done in seven weeks and fourteen days.

Well the next Thursday Jack was there, and the next, and from then they met once a week every Thursday evening. Sure enough the months turned, January, February, and then March and April, there was May and all the others, and nothing was happening at all.

Finally the Devil turned around and said, "There are only four left, Jack, only four weeks left and I still have not caught a soul and if I do not get a soul I am having *you*, remember the deal."

Jack remembered.

"You don't have to remind me, I always remember deals made with the Devil."

Sure enough they did not catch anything and there was only three Thursdays left, and Jack he did feel worried inside even though he tried not to look it outside.

Well the next Thursday came and went and sure enough there was nothing there and Jack took the fish, but as he went into Bridgnorth this time, he bought himself a new suit of clothes, and because it was the wintertime coming round, November and December time, he bought himself a big floppy hat.

On the second to last Thursday, he sat there and he had his big hat on and his new suit of clothes.

The Devil looked at him and said, "What's that?"

"Well, it's a nice, warm suit and since a third of your heat goes out of the top of the head this hat is going to keep me warm and I haven't got all those flames licking round me like some people have round here," says Jack.

They sat there fishing, but Jack, he was sweating a bit because of the woolen clothes he had just bought. The Devil, he cooled his tail in the water, and he was just steering the coracle by his tail because the river was up at this time.

That day they did not catch any souls at all, and the Devil he turned to Jack and said, "Now there is just one more time, and remember if I do not get a soul next time, I am taking you!"

"You don't have to remind me, I remember, I remember," and sure enough the last Thursday came around. But this time Jack took the new suit of clothes, and he stuffed it up with straw, and he put a broom handle up the back, see, and he made the straw man sit. He put the floppy hat over the top of the straw man and pinned the paddle on to the side of the coracle, then he extended the paddle up the side of the straw Jack's arm so that it would just wave as it moved in the water. Jack took off his clothes and laid them on the bank. Then he got into the water, pushing the coracle in front of him, and moved up into the current.

"Jack, catch the end then," said the Devil.

Jack just stuck his head out of the water.

"I'll just catch it."

The rope came over, he caught it, he tied it, and he ducked his head down under the side of the coracle and he stayed there all night, holding the coracle steady with his hands and his feet. It looked just as if he was holding it steady because the straw man's hand was moving with the paddle in the stream and everything was fine. Finally, finally, the sun came up, and the Devil he said, "Fine," he said, "Fine . . . you have had all the fish, I have not had any souls, so I am going to take *you* to Hell."

Now the Devil, he's a flashy bloke from time to time. There was a great big crack of lightning, there was a great big roll of thunder, and up into the air the coracle went and down into the water Jack went. He swam to the side, got his old clothes, and he went home to his wife. They got on their horse and cart, and they went all the way down to Gloucestershire and started a new farm down there—but that is a new story and for another time.

And the Devil? He went back to his chair. The fog was down, and he was muttering away because he hadn't got any souls, only Jack's. Finally, just as the sun was going down, he popped into Hell to have a pint, and there were all the imps, laughing away. Now one thing the Devil does not like is people laughing at him, and they were all chuckling *at him*.

"What's happening here?" said the Devil.

"All you have managed to get for a year's fishing is a coracle, a bale of straw, and an old floppy hat that someone's been playing cricket with because it's all sort of wide and sweaty. And the coracle has a big hole like someone burned it with a flash of lightning," they laughed.

*"What?!"* shouted the Devil. He realized that Jack had tricked him once again.

The Devil went down to his coracle and he went to Montford Bridge. This time, though, he wasn't sitting down in his coracle, but standing up. He put one foot one side, the other foot the other side, and he put his tail into the water as a rudder, and he went down the River Severn full pelt, forty miles an hour.

"THIS RIVER OWES ME A SOUL! THIS RIVER OWES ME A SOUL!" he roared. He went all the way past Bridgnorth, all the way past Bewdley, and they say he went all the way to Gloucester before he calmed down.

But to this day they say,

*If you go for a walk late at night,*
*And down by the river you see a strange sight,*
*A man in a coracle with a rod and line,*
*Do not stand there and tarry or take your time,*
*But run round as fast as ever you might,*
*Or your soul will be in Hell by the end of the night.*

# The Devil in Wem

*A story from Shropshire retold by Dez Quarréll*

Somewhere about the start of the 1700s, there was a motley group of lads in Wem in search of fun, but definitely not innocent fun. Anything with a thrill and a few pints of beer attached.

The lads had ranged Shropshire causing upsets wherever they went and found not one door was left open to them in all the other towns. So it was Friday night, and they were in their hometown local in New Street, looking for something apart from booze to fill their time. They tried skittles, dominoes, and cards, but nothing lifted their ennui. Then one bright spark came up with an idea.

"Let's conjure up the Devil," he said.

Not everyone knows how to make the Old Man appear. But that lad had got a friend who'd read a witchcraft book and he'd made a mental note of the recipe. It all seemed quite simple, too. They needed a great chalk circle on the floor, leaving enough room to move around between it and the walls and to give them easy access to the bar. Then it was only a matter of saying the magic words as they walked around that circle three times. No, I'm not going to tell you what words they were—you might try it, too. This is definitely a "don't try this at home, folks"; you'll ruin your lovely décor.

The third time around when their feet touched the point where they had begun, there was a blinding flash. The room filled with smoke, the floor cracked open and snapped shut, and there on the tiled floor was a big, black bull with an evil look in his eye and a bellow coming from deep in his throat. You've guessed it, it was old Jack Beelzebub, his snorting breath smelling of Old Man's Baccy and his horns glinting in the failing light.

It didn't take more than the blink of an eye and a screech from the barmaid before those lads regretted what they'd done. With Old Nick pawing at the chalk circle with his great big hoof, there was no time to waste—he'd escape that circle if they didn't get rid of him soon.

They tried the magic words backwards, while walking three times around widdershins (that's counterclockwise if you didn't know). It was no mean feat, especially after a drink or two, but it was all to no avail. The Devil, now he was there, albeit in the shape of a bull, was fixing to stay.

This needed the Captain of Hell's adversaries on the case, and luckily Wem is a holy place so there was no shortage of vicars, priests, and preachers ready to roll up their sleeves and do battle. One after another they came with bell, book, and candle, but as they tried to read the words from the good book, up came that devilish bull with a snort and put their candles out. Good men they might have been, but they couldn't read in the dark, so things were getting desperate. They weren't storytellers after all, and they couldn't remember the words. Those lads had recruited every holy man in town and found them all wanting.

They set off to Shrewsbury, some nine miles to the South. There was an Abbey there, and a Cathedral, too. Surely one of their extra holy men would be able to help. On their way they came upon a real fancy church, so fine it could have been a model for a wedding cake. It was called Battlefield, and there was a battle to fight now. So they decided to give that vicar a try.

A fine man was the Reverend Leonard Hotchkiss. He listened carefully to their pleas and a smile came to his face.

"I've just bought one of those everburn candles with a hundred-hour guarantee. A miracle of modern science, that's what they are."

It wasn't long before they reached the New Street pub and off went the Reverend Hotchkiss round that circle intoning the good book's words, as the big black bull got to work huffing and puffing to put his candle out. Third time around that bull looked pasty and pale and all blown out, which the candle flame definitely was not. Another blinding flash, again the room filled with smoke and that same floor cracked open and snapped shut. Then as the smoke cleared, there it was for all to see—or not to see, as the case may be, because there was nothing. That big black Devil bull had disappeared.

Hotchkiss was a hero, although he shunned any reward, his story lingered on. He got his prize some years later when the Shrewsbury School headmaster died. The governors said, "None of the masters are fit for the job—make Hotchkiss the new Head. If he can deal with the Devil in Wem, he can cope with some of the little devils we have in here."

It was done, delivered, and if you doubt this story's true, just read the role of honor at the school on the hill in Shrewsbury—Reverend Leonard Hotchkiss, Headmaster 1735.

# The Devil and the Stiperstones

*A story from Shropshire retold by Amy Douglas*

Of all the countries in all the world, the Devil is said to hate England the most, because it is the most beautiful and of course, since Shropshire is the most beautiful county in England, he hates Shropshire even more. In Shropshire, to the southwest of the county, is a range of hills called the Stiperstones. On these hills are five groups of rocks which jut out like spines on a dragon's back. There is a prophecy that if ever the Stiperstones sink into the Earth, England will be ruined.

It happened one day that news of this prophecy reached the ears of Old Nick himself, and a beaming smile spread across his face. He leapt up into the air and hotfooted it as quickly as he could to the Stiperstones. The Devil is a powerful being—he can build a bridge in an instant, castles overnight and fill a palace with gold in less time than it takes to say, "I'm rich!" Surely pushing some rocks into the ground would be easy!

He climbed to the top of the hill, triumphantly looked out across the county, and stamped his foot. Nothing happened. He jumped up in the air and came crashing down with both feet. Nothing happened. He took a deep breath, crouched down, leaped as high into the air as he could and came thundering down onto the ground. Still the ground withstood him. He jumped up and down and up and down for the best part of the day and still nothing happened. The Devil mopped his brow and collapsed onto the rocks on the top of the hill to catch his breath, and his hot body seared the rocks into the shape of a chair around his body. He couldn't understand it. With all his strength and power, the stones should slip into the earth like a hot knife into butter, but still they withstood him.

But the one thing that the Evil One has learnt since he was cast out is patience. The seven years he bribes a tempted soul with will pass for him like a breath on the wind. With as high a prize as the destruction of England at stake, he was prepared to wait, to plan, and to work. Every time he had a spare moment, he came back to the Stiperstones to sit in the chair he had made and to try to push it down with his huge mass and the weight of his malevolence.

Eventually, the Devil was down in Hell one day, and a terrible stench crept its way into his nostrils—a foul odor that made his demons begin to choke and retch—fresh air! He surveyed the roof of Hell, and there he saw it, a crack, a thin hairline crack, but a crack none the less. And when he saw where it was, he began to smile—for it was coming from Hell's Gutter, the long valley that lies between the Stiperstones and the Long Mynd.* Perhaps his stamping and enormous weight had had some effect after all and the hills were beginning to loosen!

Still, something was going to have to be done about the smell. He made his way up onto the Earth to see what could be done.

He inspected the crack and looked around to see if there was anything handy to plug the leak. There was nothing but heather and winberry** bushes, neither of which would stand up to the sulfurous fumes. Then he had an idea. The giants of Scotland and Ireland had formed a truce. They had stopped warring and creating havoc and instead were building a bridge of friendship, a causeway between the two lands—well, that was the last thing the Devil wanted! He would take the stones from the half built causeway and use those. He flew up into the air and made his way toward the Irish Sea. He gathered an armful of rocks, jumped up into the air, and made his way back to the Stiperstones. He let fall his load, and the rocks lay scattered on the ground—lonely pebbles in a sea of green grass. It was going to take him longer than he had first anticipated. He traipsed backwards and forwards, backwards and forwards, carrying armload after armload. At last on one trip, he noticed an orchard being harvested. The men were up in the trees throwing down the apples, while the women stood below, catching the apples in their aprons.

"That's it!" thought the Devil, "I need an apron."

He swooped down into the next field of cattle he came to, took four of the fattest and sleekest, skinned them, and made them into an apron. He tied the apron around his waist and went on his way. It was a brilliant idea. He was able to carry four times as many stones on that journey. The only problem was that carrying four times as many stones weighed four times as much. By the time he reached the Stiperstones, his face was even redder than usual, beads of sweat stood out on his forehead, and his arms were aching. But instead of dumping his load as soon as he got to the valley, he struggled up to the top of the hill and collapsed into his chair, hoping that the extra weight of the stones would help push the hills downward into the ground. Slowly he got his breath back and began to look around. The hills still hadn't moved. He tipped his weight forward and then forced it back down onto the stones. Still nothing. He raised himself a bit further and thumped back down. Still the hills withstood him. Finally his patience snapped. He jumped as far up into the air as he could and came hurtling back down onto the rock. It

*A nearby range of hills; the "y" in Mynd pronounced like "i" in win.
**Small bushes that cling to the ground and grow fruit like small blueberries.

wasn't just his patience that snapped. So did the apron strings. The stones inside the apron went scattering in all directions, littering the top of the hill. The Devil let out a howl of rage, threw what was left of the apron down onto the ground and stormed away in a cloud of dust—and I pity whoever met him next that day!

However, with such a great prize as the whole of England at stake, the Devil couldn't keep away for long. Whenever he's passing through Shropshire, he still returns to sit on his chair and try to force the hills downward. As he sits there, he sees the stones discarded on the ground, the smell of sulfur drifts upward from the unfilled leak and the memory of his failure returns to haunt him and cloud his mind. The clouds in his mind call to the clouds in the sky and the mist gathers round him and to this day whenever the tops of the Stiperstones are covered in mist then only a fool would venture there because everyone knows that the Devil is sitting on his chair, and he's not in a good mood!

But what the Devil doesn't understand is that he isn't just fighting the hill and the rocks. The people of Shropshire are a stubborn bunch—steadfast, sturdy, and true—and the land relies as much on them as they rely on the land. As long as there is one person with a love of the land, the hills and rocks, the moors and woods, one person with no room for the Devil in their heart, then the Stiperstones, Shropshire, and England will be safe, no matter how long the Devil sits on his chair and how hard he tries to defeat the hill.

# Witches, Wonders, and Weddings

# Lightening the Load

*A story from Shropshire retold by Dez Quarréll*

Now if you've ever been to Bridgnorth you'll know just how steep the hill is that leads from the low town to the high town. Walking up that hill is bad enough, pulling a weight up it is an awful task, and trying to drag a load up that hill when there's a witch trying to frustrate you, well, that's just too much.

In the old days, years and years ago, when carters came to make deliveries to the castle, they took one look at the hill and gulped. They drove their horses for all their worth up the hill past the caves, but no matter how hard they tried the horses would stop half way up the hill, right next to a cave where a little old lady lived.

Well you might think that was just a coincidence, but the carters didn't. This old lady was a funny old crone, a real loner. She dressed all in black and had a hooked nose and a croaky voice that sounded like a rusty hinge. Those carters started talking and tongues started wagging, word went around that the old lady was a witch and that she was hexing the horses, freezing their hooves and not letting them by.

What do you do when faced with a witch a'spelling you? Do you tie her to a ducking stool? Well, maybe not. Who knows what revenge she might exact. Do you give up and run away? Not if you want to make money on your load. It was cash on delivery after all. All that's left to you is to swallow hard and knock at the witch's door and try to make a bargain. And that's exactly what the carters did.

To start, they offered the old lady money, but no she said that wouldn't do.

"What do you want?" they asked, "We'll give you anything, just ask."

She didn't hesitate, and quick as a flash she said, "I want half your load."

She wouldn't be swayed, that's what she wanted, that's what she'd have. It didn't matter whether the load was gold and jewels or muck and dung, half the load was her demand and that's what she got.

So, dear reader, the carters went back to their carts and took half the load and gave it to the old lady and miraculously their horses began to move, albeit slowly, up the hill again. It was definitely magic, they thought, the old lady had lifted the hex. Now they knew she was really a witch and they'd not been mistaken.

There was never any quibbling; the old witch became a rich witch who always lightened every carter's load.

But before we end, there is a postscript to this tale that maybe we ought to tell. After a long happy old age, the old lady died, but her hexes obviously lived on. Those carters' carts still stopped half way up the hill next to her cave. The carters were amazed, but in the end they found a way around their problem, they left half of their load at home. After paying that fitting tribute to the grand old dame, she let them pass all the way up the hill to the castle. Honor was satisfied.

So if you are planning a visit to Bridgnorth, just you remember, travel light—leave half of your luggage at home.

# A Story of Zennor

*A story from Cornwall retold by Sally Tonge*

Further to the west of the busy town of Saint Ives along the rugged and wind-swept Cornish coast perches the village of Zennor.

Years ago, long, long before the arrival of the first artists and holiday makers, this was a humble little clutch of cottages and farms huddled round Zennor Church. These were the days before TV and video, computers and home entertainment systems. The villagers' greatest joy was to crowd into the church on a Sunday morning for a good sing-song, hear a sermon from the vicar and have a good gossip and chin wag at the end.

But most of all they loved their choir; it was said that Zennor church choir could sing the sky bluer and the daffodils more golden and lure dolphins to come and jump in the waters that sparkled beneath the cliffs. The finest singer in the choir was a young man called Matty Trewella. He was very handsome, and all the girls adored him, each hoping that he would ask one of them to walk home with him after the service.

So one Sunday, when the whole village was assembled in the church, the choir was singing away when the heavy oak door creaked open and a stranger dressed in a black cape that hung down to the floor snuck onto the back pew. The stranger sat and listened to the wonderful singing and before the end of the service got up and left the church without a sound but for the creak and click of the door.

This went on week in and week out. Every one in the village was intrigued as to the identity of the hooded stranger who came to listen to the singing of the choir, and none more than Matty, who vowed that next time he would follow the mysterious figure. So the next Sunday, as the figure slunk out of the front door of the church, Matty followed from a side door at the back of the choir's stalls. The stranger walked down the path, along the road that made its way through Zennor and onto a gorse-edged track that wound its way down to the sea. Matty kept up a stealthy pursuit, pressed up hard against walls, hiding behind rocks and bushes, lest the stranger should spot him.

At the water's edge, he crouched behind a rock and watched in wide-eyed amazement as the stranger let the cloak fall … to reveal … a mermaid. Her hair was braided with seashells and pearls, and her strong, silvery tail glistened in the sun. She stretched her pale arms up over her head and dove into the water. She swam out a little and then turned to beckon the incredulous Matty, who was standing in the shallows of the water. She called to him with a song:

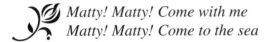 *Matty! Matty! Come with me*
*Matty! Matty! Come to the sea*

Her words floated over the water and into one of Matty's ears and out of the other and almost formed an invisible thread that pulled him into the water. Be-charmed and with his arms held out in front of him like a sleepwalker, he followed the singing and walked into the sea, up to his knees, his thighs, his belly, his neck, his mouth, his ears, his eyes, his forehead … till … he disappeared under the water. Gone.

When Matty didn't come back home for his lunch or his tea, his Mum raised the alarm and the villagers scoured the moors and the shores looking for him for three days and nights. At the end, they were forced to believe that Matty had been swallowed up and taken away from the village by the insatiable monster of the sea that still devours so many fine sons and daughters even to this day.

Now about twenty years later a fisherman was anchored off Zennor's coast, waiting for the tide to rise to steer his ship into nearby Saint Ives harbor. He'd dropped his anchor and was waiting for nature to take her course. After settling himself on deck to smoke a pipe, he suddenly heard a voice calling to him. When he looked over the edge of the boat, there was a mermaid sitting on a rock, her skin was pale and greenish, her hair blew about her in the breeze, jingling the shells and starfish woven into it, and in her arms she held a mer-baby.

"Oy, Mister, your anchor is blocking my front door and I can't get home, I've got to cook tea for my husband, Matty, and all our sixteen kids! Come on, move it, out of my way!" she shouted.

The amazed fisherman was not about to pick a fight with a mermaid and so, trembling, he promptly hoisted his anchor, and the mermaid dipped back into the sea, with barely a ripple.

When the channel was deep enough, he steered into the harbor and wasted no time in bustling along to The Sloop Inn, where he ordered a rum and maybe two and maybe three to steady his nerves. He stopped shaking long enough to jibber out what he'd just encountered on the sea: how the Mermaid had told him off for blocking her door and how she was in a rush to cook her husband Matty's dinner and how the fisherman was never setting foot on a boat again, the isolation had driven him crazy!

The locals nodded and smiled quietly, they soothed the fisherman, telling him that he wasn't crazy at all, but he was bringing good news of a local lad who'd disappeared years ago.

"We'd all given him up for dead, but your story tells us that Matty's alive and swimming at the bottom of the sea with a beautiful mer-wife and sixteen kids to his name! Good on him!" they said.

That story traveled up the rocky road from Saint Ives to Zennor, for a good story can travel in pretty much the same way as a good dose of flu! When the villagers heard this tale, it eased their lingering sadness. They decided to remember this event by carving a special pew end and setting it in the church. Now, if you go to Zennor Church you can go through the creaky door, and once your eyes get used to the dim light, you'll see a pew there with a carving of a mermaid on it, which the villagers made in memory of Matty. And now you know that story to tell to your friends and family.

# The Stars in the Sky

*A story retold by Dan Keding*

A long time ago there was a girl who wanted to touch the stars in the sky. Each night when the sky was clear, she would gaze out her window at the stars as they twinkled and glittered in the velvet blackness above her. The girl sometimes imagined them as diamonds, other times as tears of lost lovers, other times as the laughing eyes of a merry soul.

One summer evening when the sky was as clear as it could get, the young girl decided to seek the stars. She walked until she came to a millpond.

"Good evening," she said, "I am seeking the stars in the sky. Can you help me find them?"

"They're right here shining on my face," replied the pond. "They shine so brightly I can't sleep at night. Jump in and see if you can catch one."

The girl jumped into the pond and swam around and around, but try as she might she never caught a star.

She walked across the fields until she came to a woodland stream.

"Good evening. I am trying to find a way to reach the stars. Can you help me?"

"Yes of course," replied the stream, "the stars come down each night and dance on the stones and on the water. Come in and see if you can catch one."

The girl waded in but found no stars in that stream.

"I don't think the stars come down here at all," cried the young girl.

"It looks to me as if they do," replied the stream happily. "Isn't that just as good?"

"Not at all," said the girl wearily.

She walked on until she came to a clearing in the woods, and there, dancing in the moonlight, were a host of Little Folk, no taller than herself and elegant in their green and gold clothes.

"Good evening to you, Folk of the Hill," the young girl said respectfully. "I am looking for a way to reach the stars in the sky. Can you help me?"

The fairy folk laughed and almost sang out their answer.

"The stars shine on the grass here at night. Come join our dance if you want to find a star."

The girl joined their dance. She whirled and she twirled, but though the grass sparkled, not a star did she find as she danced.

She left the dance and sat down on a fallen tree.

"I have looked so hard and not found the stars in the pond or the stream nor in the dances of the fairy folk. Can't anyone tell me how to find the stars?"

They all kept dancing except one who walked over and smiled at her.

"You have indeed looked well, but now take this advice. Keep going and ask Four Feet to carry you to No Feet At All. Then ask No Feet At All to carry you to the Stairs Without Steps. If you can climb them, you might find what you are looking for this night."

"Will I be up among the stars?"

"You'll be somewhere, if not there," he replied.

She walked on until she came to a silver gray horse standing beneath a rowan tree.

"Excuse me, would you know the way to the stars?"

"I know little about the stars. I am here to do the bidding of the fairy folk," the horse replied.

The girl grew excited. "I've just been dancing with them and they told me to find Four Feet and that he would carry me to No Feet At All."

"I am Four Feet and I will take you where you need to go."

They rode on until the forest was far behind them and they had come to the shore. A wide path of silver ran out to the edge of the sea where an arch of brilliant color rose from the surface and climbed into the sky.

"This is as far as I can take you," said the horse.

As the girl climbed down, the horse bowed to her and ran off into the night. The girl looked out over the sea, and a huge fish swam up to the shore and spoke.

"What are you doing here, young lady?"

"The fairy folk sent me here on the back of Four Feet. I am looking for No Legs At All to carry me to the Stairs Without Steps."

"Well I am No Legs At All, and you can climb up on my back and hold on very tight."

The huge fish swam along the silver path that led to the arch of many colors. As they neared the arch, the girl saw that the stars glistened above the arch as it rose higher and higher into the sky.

"Here we are," said No Legs At All. "These are the Stairs Without Steps. Hold fast as you climb and walk carefully."

She started off on her journey. The way was very steep and the climb very hard, but she kept going. Whenever she thought about turning back, she just looked up and saw those beautiful stars, and it gave her heart new hope to keep climbing.

The air grew colder and colder and the stars became more and more brilliant. At last she reached the top of the Stairs Without Steps. All around her the stars twinkled and sparkled, racing across the heavens in dazzling streaks as if they were playing a game.

She had finally reached the stars, and now she stood there awed by their beauty.

After she had stood there a while admiring the beauty of the stars, she realized that it was very cold up there in the sky. She looked down but the colors of the Stairs Without Steps seemed to disappear in the darkness below.

In one last effort, she reached out to touch a shining star. She stretched and stretched and almost touched the star, her hand brushing up against it, when she lost her balance and down she tumbled. She fell and fell, faster and faster, down into the night. A bit sad she hadn't touched the star but very content that she had stood up in the sky and watched them dance around her in the heavens, she fell. And as she fell, she seemed to fall asleep.

When she opened her eyes, it was morning, and she was in her bed, the sun warm on her face. She wondered if it was a dream, when she suddenly remembered brushing her hand against that star. When she opened her fingers, her hand was full of twinkling stardust.

She told her story to her own daughter years later as they both watched the stars in the night.

# The Pixies' Bed

*A story from Dartmoor retold by Dan Keding*

Once a long time ago there lived an old woman. Now while others took their delight in weaving or knitting or baking, this woman took her pleasure in her garden. People would walk by her house and remark that her flowers were more colorful than those in other gardens. They noticed that her flowers were bigger and seemed to stand taller in her garden. They commented on how her flowers seemed to be more fragrant than any others they had ever sniffed at in all their days. The old woman delighted in hearing these compliments, and she would often give a flower to children as they passed by or bring flowers to someone who was sick or just needed a bit of cheering up.

The pride and joy of her garden were her tulips. It seemed that they lasted longer than most others, they stood even taller and were more colorful, and, strangest of all, they had the strongest scent. Their smell seemed to float across the garden. When they were in bloom, she would smell them first thing when she woke and last thing before she fell asleep.

The wise old woman had no idea why her tulips were so remarkable till one night just as she was about to slip away into sleep, she heard music coming from her garden. She quietly tiptoed to the window and looked out across her garden. There in the light of the full moon she saw all her tulips swaying in time to the music. Then she saw pixies—dozens and dozens of pixies—dancing and singing. Once in a while a pixy would dance over to a tulip and look inside. Then the old woman understood why her tulips were so special. The pixies used them as beds for their babies. The little pixies were cradled in the tulips while their parents sang and danced in the field on the other side of her fence.

After that night the woman would often stay awake and listen to the music and watch her dancers as they whirled and twirled in the moonlight. It gave her great joy to know that the little people loved her garden as much as she loved it.

When the old woman passed away, the man who bought her cottage planted vegetables and got rid of all her beautiful flowers. The Little Folk were so angry that they made sure the weeds grew taller in his garden than in any other. But they never forgot the old woman. Although no human hand had ever planted a flower on her grave, the most beautiful bed of flowers always covering her resting spot.

---

# The Old Woman and the Fairy Folk

*A story from the Black Country retold by Peter Chand*

In the West Midlands region of England, there is an area known as the Black Country. This area lies within the boundaries of the two cities of Birmingham and Wolverhampton and the town of Dudley. The Black Country got its name because it was heavily involved in industry, and factories and furnaces sprang up all over the region. Along with this industry came huge chimneys, from where heavy black smoke would billow for miles and darken everything it touched with a coating of soot.

This legend comes from the area and tells of a time before the factories had arrived when most of the region was still open land.

There was once an old woman, kind and fair, who was liked by all of her neighbors. She was always willing to help anybody in trouble, whether with kind word or deed. Even though she was very poor, the old woman would still share her food with someone less fortunate than herself.

One warm Sunday afternoon she was returning from church to her rundown cottage, when she stopped under an elm tree to rest. After only a few moments she looked around thinking she had heard something, but put it down to her old ears playing tricks on her. Barely another moment had passed when she heard the noise again, and this time it was unmistakable. The woman turned around and started fumbling in the hedge behind her. She followed the sound, and there in the warm sun under a thornbush, she saw the most beautiful baby she had seen in her whole life, gently gurgling, with not a care in the world. The baby was not even as long as her forearm, and her heart went out to it, for even though she had given birth to children of her own, none had survived. Once she had got the child home she warmed some milk for it, and watched its beautiful face as it drank. It was a face that was intelligent and wise, unlike any infant's she had seen before.

It didn't take the old woman long to realize that she had found a fairy child. Many a time she had seen small circles in the grass that locals said were fairy rings, where the little people would dance under the light of a full round moon, but like most folk she had not believed it. She believed now, as right under her nose was a living, breathing fairy slurping at the bottle as if it had not eaten in days. The woman sang a nursery rhyme until the fairy's bright eyes shut and then placed her in an old crate lined with her nightdress, wishing she had enough money to afford a proper cot and blankets.

In the morning, the old woman was sad, because the baby had gone, but where it had lain, there was a gold coin as payment for her kindness. With this money the woman could buy enough groceries to last her the whole year and fix the leaking roof of her cottage. A few years passed, and every once in a while there would be a gold coin left for her in the crate, which was now lined with a fine blanket that the woman had knitted by the light of a new oil lamp she had bought. Sometimes the fairy itself would appear, always leaving before morning, and, even though it had grown, it was much smaller than a human child of its own age. It would tell the old woman how you were supposed to leave pieces of cake out for fairies, so that if one passed and was hungry, it would be able to eat and carry on with its journey. The fairy also warned the old woman, "You must not tell a soul how you got this money. People can get jealous and mean. The jingling, jangling of money does strange things to folk—not all folk, just some."

The woman promised not to tell, and the coins continued to appear. The fairy child would appear out of nowhere and tell the old woman stories that would make her howl with laughter. Stories of how mischievous fairies would change themselves into logs, and before some poor soul had thrown them onto their fire they turned back into a fairy, danced around the room, then disappeared, leaving the householder goggle-eyed and stuck to the spot with fear. Before leaving the fairy would always repeat the same warning, "You must not tell a soul how you got this money. People can get jealous and mean. The jingling, jangling of money does strange things to folk—not all folk, just some."

By this time the woman had enough money to buy some fields around her house, which was now no longer a rundown cottage, but a beautiful home with a large neat garden full of parsley and other lovely herbs, and many beautiful flowers that would attract butterflies and bees. Soon people in the surrounding farms started whispering to each other, "How has she got all this money all of a sudden?" Or gossips would say bitterly, "She must be a witch or something."

Soon the woman, who had originally been a friend to all, was now looked upon with suspicion and jealousy. One day the woman was baking in her kitchen when a particularly nosey neighbor entered and asked bluntly, "Making tasties for a friend?"

Without even thinking the old woman replied, "Oh just for the fairy folk in case they pass."

As soon as she had said it, the old woman regretted opening her mouth, and the gossip ran out of her home as fast as her legs would take her, to spread the gossip to all who would listen. The old woman was heartbroken, because after that day the fairy never ever returned. Some people say, however, that the fairy child who was rescued from beneath a thornbush never forgot the kindness the old woman had shown him. They say that since that day, the fairy has made it so that whenever there are coins in your pocket and greedy or jealous people are nearby, they will rattle even louder than normal, as a sign to keep them safely tucked away. For as we all now know, people can get jealous and mean. The jingling, jangling of money does strange things to folk—not all folk, just some.

# Wild Edric

*A story from Shropshire, retold by Amy Douglas*

Edric wasn't always wild—strong, powerful, a little rough, but not wild. Edric was one of the greatest nobles in Shropshire, the only one of all the Saxon nobles to keep independence from William the Conqueror. Edric was a true noble of his time: proud, strong, with three great loves in his life: the chase, the fight, and, of course, the tankard.

One day he was hunting in the forest of Clun with a group of his friends and they started a white hart. Immediately Edric was on its tail, and the other hunters were not far behind. But the hart was swift and cunning. It turned this way and that, through brambles and bushes and soon only the fastest and most daring were left in the chase. At last, the horses tiring, the hart with one last spurt disappeared, and they were left in the gloomy half light of evening. Edric slowed his horse and looked around. Of all his hunting companions only one was left. In the thrill of the chase, neither had paid any attention to the direction they had taken or the sun slowly sinking, and they decided the best thing that they could do was to make themselves as comfortable as they could where they were and make their way home the next day.

As they dismounted and went to slacken the horses' girths, they caught a faint sound of music on the wind. Leading their horse they were led on by the lovely and mysterious sound, entranced by its beauty until at last the trees thinned and they saw a cottage. More important, they saw what was within the cottage: beautiful women, whirling, spinning, and laughing as they danced to the strange music that had brought them there. But Edric had eyes for only one of those maidens, the one in the center with flashing eyes, the light bouncing off her long golden hair as it span and twirled about her.

The law of the land gave Edric the right to choose his bride, and finally he had found the one he wanted.

Edric could stand it no more. Despite the shouted warning of his friend, he ran into the cottage and grabbed the center woman around the waist. Immediately the music stopped. All the women turned upon Edric, scratching and clawing, but Edric swept them out of his way, charging toward the waiting horse. Edric and his companion galloped off into the woods, heedless of the dark and the unknown route until they realized that there was no one in pursuit and their pace slowed.

They carried on through the dark and at last found their feet on a familiar track and made their way back to the manor.

For three days and three nights, Edric's captive said not a single word, despite whatever kind words and persuasions Edric used. She sat and watched people come and go from the hall, she listened, but she said nothing. Finally, on the fourth day, she looked at him and she smiled.

"Good luck to you, Edric. I have watched you these three days and I have seen that you are a good man. I will marry you—and you will be lucky, enjoying health and peace and plenty. But there is one condition. If ever you reproach me with my background—with my sisters, the place you snatched me away from or anything to do with that night, I will be gone and you will lose both your bride and your luck."

Edric's face broke into a broad grin to hear her speak, and his heart leapt to see her smile. He willingly promised that he would never reproach her with anything.

But such promises are easily made and easily broken.

Preparations were made for a grand wedding with nobles present from all over the country, Edric desperate to give his new bride the best and to show her off to all and sundry.

The news of the wedding even reached the ears of William, the king and conqueror, and he requested that Edric should bring his new wife, the Lady Godda as she was known, to court so that he could see the truth of the rumors of her beauty and her strange appearance.

Edric accepted the invitation and William declared that the lady must in truth be fey, for such beauty could not be bestowed upon a mortal. Neither could he deprive such a beautiful lady of her husband, and so he and Edric made peace.

The years passed happily until one day, Edric had been hunting—a long day of rain and mud and nothing, not even a rabbit to show for it. He came into the hall and asked for Godda, but she was nowhere to be found. Normally he would have waited patiently, for there was something different about Godda and he had always resisted the temptation to question her too closely about her comings and goings.

This, however, was not a normal day. He was tired, he was cold, he was hungry, the state of his people was weighing upon him, and he longed for the comfort of her company. But hour after hour went by and still there was no sign of his wife.

When at last she did appear, she looked so calm and unruffled that Edric's moodiness flared up into anger, and he shouted at her

"And where have you been!? Leaving your duties, leaving your husband! I suppose you've been off gallivanting in the woods, laughing with your sisters at my expense!"

As soon as the words were out of his mouth he regretted them, but it was too late. They were gone, never to be called back, and so was Godda.

Edric ran crying for her from room to room, but for nothing. The house was empty, the light of her presence lost forever.

Everything happened as Godda had foretold. Edric was so consumed with grief that he forgot all else. He spent each day riding through the woods calling and calling, trying to find the cottage in the woods, straining his ears for a strain of that unearthly music.

Edric did not reply to William's messengers, and their friendship broke apart. William declared Edric an outlaw. Edric lost his land and manors and was reduced to wandering the forest searching for his beloved Godda.

Now Edric sits in a cave rather than a grave, and not yet is he allowed to die.

Underneath the Stiperstones he waits to help a true Englishman back onto the throne. He lies there sleeping and only awakes to warn of danger to England. Whenever there is to be war, he rides forth through the forest to give warning. But somehow, somewhere along the way, he must have been forgiven, for when he rides forth he is at the head of the hunt, with flushed cheeks and tousled black hair, while only a step behind, on a white mare, sits a beautiful lady, her golden hair streaming out behind her.

Edric Silvaticus, Edric the Wild, was the only Saxon noble in all of the west to hold out against William the Conqueror. Together with King Bleddyn and King Rhiwallon, he fought for independence. One of his residences was Middleton in Chirbury Manor, in the village beneath Stapeley Hill. At the bottom of Bomere Pool, a huge fish still swims with Edric's sword buckled to its back, waiting for the time when Edric's heir will reclaim it.

Musician from Mepal Molly playing accordion in a pub session after a day of dancing. Mepal Molly dance only once a year on Plough Monday, the Monday after twelfth night. Traditionally the ploughmen would tour the area, dancing in return for food, beer, and tobacco. It became a form of ritualized charity for the ploughmen who were unable to work while the earth was frozen. The ploughmen would dress in rags and rub soot over the faces to disguise their identity while begging. These days the dancers are local men from all sorts of professions and backgrounds, but the tradition continues. Photograph by Chris Lambart.

Dave Arthur sat on the steps of a traditional gypsy caravan.

**Dancer from Ducklington Morris Men
in front of Ely Cathedral.
Photograph by Christopher Lambart**

**Amb Tro Mummer's smoke-breathing
dragon at Festival at the Edge, 2003.
Photograph by Amy Douglas**

**Morris dancers on the promenade at the annual festival in Sidmouth.
Photograph by Dan Keding.**

Straw Bear and his keeper, Wittlesea Straw Bear Festival. Straw Bear Day is the Tuesday after Plough Monday, and the festival takes place on the nearest Saturday. The Straw Bear is led through the town, accompanied by dancers and musicians. It dances outside big houses and pubs in return for refreshments, until at the end of the festival, when the Bear is burned. The tradition of the Straw Bear is thought to have its roots in a fertility rite to bless the land before the sowing of the crops. Photograph by Chris Lambart.

Morris teams, Littleport Riot, and Little Egypt dance in the procession at Whitby Folk Festival. Photograph by Chris Lambart.

A street in Pinner. Note the sign proclaiming the pub,
The Queen's Head. Photograph by Dan Keding.

Fishing boats pull ashore on the beach in Sidmouth. Photograph by Dan Keding.

**The well-known English bus. Photograph by Dan Keding.**

**An example of a traditional English pub, The George and Dragon, in Much Wenlock, Shropshire. Photograph by Brian Douglas.**

Storyteller Peter Chand performing at Festival at the Edge, 2004.

Jim Eldon, "The Brid Fiddler," playing the fiddle on a boat trip.

A pair of step dancing clogs, complete with irons. Photograph by Janet Dowling. See "The Hole Store" (p. 54) for the story

Traditional jig doll, played here by Michelle O'Connor. Photograph by Chris Lambart.

Shrewsbury Simnel Cake. See pages 134–136 for the recipe.
Made and photographed by Amy Douglas.

Canal boats like these carried freight along the rivers and canals of England. Today they are often enjoyed by people on holiday. Photograph by Dan Keding.

Mitchell's Fold at dawn on the midwinter solstice, 1998. See "The White Cow of Mitchell's Fold" (p. 125) for the story. Photograph by Jackie Douglas.

# Tattercoats

*A story retold by Dan Keding*

Once a long time ago there lived an old lord in a castle by the sea. His wife and children were not living, and his only relative was his little granddaughter, whose face he had never seen. He hated his granddaughter because at her birth her mother, his favorite daughter, had died. He swore that the child could live or die, but he would never look at her. He turned his face to the window, and each day he cried till the tears had worn away the stone and had flowed in little rivers into the sea. He sat there as his hair turned white and grew down past his shoulders to the floor and wove around his chair and out the door into the hall. All this time there was only the old nurse to care for the young child. She gave her scraps from the table and old clothes to wear. The other servants, knowing that the old lord hated her, treated the girl badly and called her Tattercoats because she wore a dress that was patched together from the rags that the old nurse had given her. When they teased and mocked her, she would run into the fields and woods and cry till the pain of their words finally went away.

The girl grew up with harsh words and little affection from anyone at the castle besides the old nurse. The only friend she had was the gooseherd boy who would play his pipes to cheer her. He played so beautifully that even though she might be sad or hungry or cold, his music helped her forget all her troubles, and soon she would begin to dance with his flock of geese dancing and singing right beside her.

One day all the folk in the castle and in the countryside around were talking about the king. It seemed he was traveling through the land with his court trying to find a young woman to become his son's bride. In the nearby town, he was giving a great ball, and all the nobles in the countryside around were invited.

An invitation came to the lord by the sea, and when the old man read it, he called for his servants to cut his hair and beard. He sent for his best clothes and rings for his fingers. He had his white horse saddled with gold and silver and silk so that he might ride to meet his king.

Tattercoats wept in a corner of the kitchen. She cried because she would never be allowed to see the king or to sit at a fancy table and eat with the lords and ladies of the land. No one knew she was a lady. When her old nurse heard her weeping, she went to the lord and begged him to take his granddaughter with him to the king's ball. The old lord glared at the nurse and told her to be silent. The girl would stay behind. She had no place at his side or at the king's table.

The other servants heard this and taunted the nurse. "Tattercoats loves to dress in rags and dance with the geese. She could never be a fine lady."

The old nurse begged again and again, but the old lord grew angrier and angrier, and finally he had the servants drive her from the room with blows and curses. The old nurse went to look for the young woman, but Tattercoats had gone off to the fields to find the gooseherd boy and tell him of her sorrow.

The gooseherd boy listened carefully as Tattercoats told him her story. He told her that they should go to see the king on their own. Tattercoats just looked down at her bare feet and her dress of patches and sighed. The gooseherd boy started to play on his pipes, and soon she forgot all about her bare feet, her ragged clothes, and her tears—all she wanted to do was dance. And so they danced toward the hall where the king was to have his great ball. The geese led the way with Tattercoats dancing behind and the gooseherd boy playing his pipes. It was a grand but unusual parade.

They had not traveled too far down the road when a handsome young man rode up on a magnificent horse. The young man was dressed as fine as any prince and asked the members of this unlikely troop if they knew where the king might be staying this night. When he learned that they were also going to visit the king, he dismounted and leading his horse, he walked along beside Tattercoats.

As the unlikely trio walked along, the gooseherd boy played a low soft tune on his pipes. The young man smiled at Tattercoats as she continued her dance. Each time he looked at her, she seemed lovelier than the time before. As they walked along, the young man was awed not just by her beauty but also by her good nature. Finally he blurted out that she was the most wonderful woman in the world, and he wanted to marry her. She shook her head and laughed.

"What would your family and friends say if you came home with a ragged girl for a wife? You had better ask one of the ladies who will be at the dance tonight for her hand and forget about the girl in the tattered, patched dress."

The gooseherd boy played a new tune on his pipes, one that was sweet and high and floated on the air like a cloud on a summer's day. With every note the young man's love grew for Tattercoats. Again he begged her to marry him.

"Do not tease me," she scolded. "I have been abused enough by those who should love me."

"If you do not believe me, let me prove I love you and wish to marry you," the young noble begged. "Tonight come to the ball at the stroke of midnight just as you are with your bare feet and tattered dress and your friend the gooseherd boy and his geese. I will dance with you before the king and all his lords and ladies and present you to them as the woman I love and my bride to be."

Tattercoats heard the sincerity in his voice and saw the affection in his eyes, and she agreed to be there at the stroke of twelve.

The castle hall was filled with the lords and ladies of the land. All were in their best finery as they danced to the tunes of the king's own musicians. As the clock struck twelve, in danced Tattercoats to the music of the gooseherd boy's pipes followed by his flock of dancing geese. The nobles stared in disbelief, and then they pointed and laughed at the odd parade. Tattercoats paid them no attention as she dreamily danced into the center of the great hall. As they came before the throne of the king the young noble who had fallen in love with her left his seat next to the king and began to dance with her. When the music stopped, he took her hand and kissed it. Turning to the king, he declared his love.

"Father," he said, for indeed he was the prince and the king was his father, "this is the woman I have decided to marry, she will be my bride for she is the loveliest and kindest of woman."

As the prince spoke, the gooseherd boy began to play his pipes. At first it sounded like the song of the birds in the woods, then as a brook dancing over rocks, then like the first rays of dawn. As he played, the rags that Tattercoats wore turned into the finest of silks, shining with jewels, a crown upon her head. The geese all turned into pages that held her train and spread rose petals at her feet.

The king rose to meet his son's bride and swore to all that indeed she was the sweetest and loveliest girl in the realm. The prince and Tattercoats were wed, and they lived as happily as ever a couple lived. And one day when the prince became king and she queen, they ruled in harmony and fairness.

As for the gooseherd boy, he was never seen again, though the memory of his songs lingered on in the hearts of all who had heard them. The old lord went back to his castle and kept his strange promise never to set eyes on his granddaughter, a promise that caused him more tears. If you pass that way, you may see him in the window crying for what might have been.

# Kate Crackernuts

*A story retold by Katy Cawkwell*

*There lived a woman,*
*There lived a man,*
*But they married a little too late.*
*For the father already had a daughter, Anne,*
*And the mother, a daughter, Kate.*

Anne, well she was as bonny as the blossom on the trees, but Kate was plain as nuts. Anne had golden hair and sky blue eyes, but Kate's hair was mousy, and freckles covered her snub nose. It didn't matter to the girls one bit—they were as close as true sisters, but it mattered to the mother. It mattered and it minded and it worried away inside of her that her own daughter Kate wasn't pretty like her stepdaughter Anne. In the end, it mattered so much that she had to do something about it. She went up the hill to see the Henwife and she told her what was wrong. The Henwife listened.

"Send me the bonny one, pretty and sweet, send her early with nothing to eat!" the Henwife said.

So the mother went back down the hill, and she told Anne to go and see the Henwife early the next morning before breakfast. Anne woke early, she rubbed the sleep out of her beautiful blue eyes and went downstairs. But as she was going out of the kitchen door, she saw a bite of bread on the table and she was that hungry, so she took it and munched on it as she went up the hill to see the Henwife.

The Henwife was waiting for her, "Come in my pretty, don't stand there looking, go to the pot and see what's cooking!"

Anne saw that there was a great black pot hanging over the fire and so she went across and looked inside, but she couldn't see anything, except her own pretty face reflected in the pot. The Henwife flew into a rage, "You go home and tell your mother to keep her larder door better locked!"

Anne was afraid. She ran back down the hill and told her mother what the Henwife had said. The mother took a bunch of keys from her pocket, and she locked the kitchen door.

"Go again to see the Henwife, early next morning before breakfast!" she said.

So Anne woke early and she went downstairs, but the kitchen door was locked so she went out the front and up the hill. As she was going up the hill, she saw some women out in the fields picking peas and she was that hungry, so she begged a handful of the fresh green peas and she crunched them as she went up the hill to see the Henwife.

The Henwife was standing at the door.

"Come in my dear, pretty one, go to the pot and see if it's done!"

Anne went over to the great black pot and looked inside.

"I can't see anything," she said. The Henwife stamped her foot and cried, "You go home and tell your mother that the pot won't boil if the fire's not watched!"

Anne didn't understand, but she ran back down the hill and told her mother what the Henwife said. So early the next morning, the mother woke Anne and took her by the arm and led her out the house and up the hill and Anne had nothing to eat.

The Henwife grinned a toothy grin when she saw them.

"Come in, my pretty, look in the pot, see if it's ready, see if it's hot!"

And when Anne bent over the great black pot, well, the pot began to boil and the pot began to bubble and her own pretty head fell off her shoulders into the pot and a sheep's head jumped back on! The Henwife laughed so hard her teeth fell out, and the mother smiled and took Anne by the elbow and led her back down the hill to the house.

When Kate saw what had happened to her sister, she took a soft white cloth and she wound it around Anne's head so that no one could see the horrid sheep's head. Then she whispered to her, "We're going away. We're going to leave this place and go out into the world to seek our fortunes."

Kate took her sister by the hand, and the two girls left the house and walked into the hills.

They walked a long way that day, over the green hills, with Kate guiding her sister and telling her where to put her feet so that she wouldn't trip. As the sun was low in the sky, they scrambled up to the top of a ridge, and there Kate saw a valley golden in the late light; there was a wood and beyond the wood, fields and in the middle of the fields, a solid stone house, so big you might have called it a castle.

"We'll aim for the house," said Kate, "and ask for a bed for the night."

Kate took Anne by the hand and led her down the hill, stepping carefully over brooks and round boulders. They found a way through the trees and across the fields, until they stood before the great wooden door of the castle.

Now in this castle, as in every castle, there lived a king. The king had two sons. The elder prince was a handsome man, he sat well on his horse with a hawk on his fist and a hound at his heels and everyone thought well of him. But the younger prince was sick, he lay on his bed, tossing and turning, his cheeks flushed with fever and the king could find no cure for his sickness.

The king heard the knocking at the door that evening and he went down himself to open up. He saw two girls standing outside, hand in hand. One had a white cloth covering her head, but the other had bright eyes and she was looking up at him hopefully.

"Have you a bed for the night for me and my sick sister?" said Kate.

"I have indeed," said the king. "Welcome to my home," and he opened the door wide for them.

That night, Kate sat at dinner with the king, and he told her all about his younger son, how he lay all day on his bed tossing and turning, and how they could find no cure for his sickness.

"And it's the strangest thing," said the king, "whenever someone comes to sit at his side and watch over him through the night, well, in the morning they are gone, vanished, disappeared! We never see them again, you know. I'd give a peck of silver to anyone who would watch the night through with my son, but no one will."

"I will," said Kate. "I'll do it tonight."

So Kate sat that night by the side of the youngest prince, looking into his pale face, just his cheeks tinged with the fire of the fever. It grew dark. The hours passed, one by one by one, until the clock on the wall struck midnight and at once, the prince sat bolt upright in his bed and opened his eyes. He didn't seem to see Kate sitting there. He swung his legs out of the bed and pulled on his boots, and then he was out the door and running down the stairs. Well Kate, she jumped up and followed him. She followed him out to the stables, and there the prince saddled a horse and jumped up onto its back. Kate, well, she jumped up behind him and put her arms around him, but he didn't seem to notice her at all.

And then they were off, riding through the fields and out of the fields into the woods. Kate looked around her and saw nuts growing in the tops of the trees, so she reached out and she picked them and put them in her apron pocket. They rode out of the woods and into the hills until there rose before them a great, dark hillside. The prince reined in his horse and called out, "Open up, open up for the prince on his horse!" And Kate called out quickly, "And his lady behind him!"

And before her eyes, the hillside opened up—a dark passageway led into the hill. The prince set his horse to the path and together they rode into the darkness, under the hill.

At last Kate saw a flickering light ahead, and they came out into a hall, an arching vault full of little people dancing. It was the good folk, the fairies, and they were having a dance. There were fairy fiddles and fairy pipes, and the little folk were dancing wildly, 'round and 'round.

When they saw the prince, they pulled him from the horse and made him dance with them, 'round and 'round until he was so dizzy he collapsed. And then they would feed him fairy food and fairy wine and pull him to his feet to dance once more. Kate stood in the shadows and watched everything. Then from far outside the hill, she heard a cock crow, and at that moment, the fairies bundled the prince back onto his horse. Quickly, Kate jumped up behind him, and they rode together out of the green hill, into a dewy dawn.

The prince rode back with his lady behind him, back through the woods and the fields, back to the castle. There he staggered upstairs, pulled off his boots, and collapsed on his bed, flushed with the fairy fever. But Kate took the nuts from her apron pocket and when the king came in, in the morning, there she was, sitting by the fire, roasting her nuts and cracking them open.

The king was amazed.

"If you watch a second night with my son, I'll give you a peck of gold," he said.

"I'll do it," said Kate. "I'll do it tonight."

Well just as before, Kate sat by the prince's bedside as the dark hours went by, one by one. At last, the clock struck midnight, and the prince sat up in bed and opened his eyes. He didn't see Kate. He just pulled on his boots and was out the door quick as the clouds racing across the moon. Kate ran after him, out to the stables, and there she jumped up behind him, but he didn't notice her at all, he just rode away through the fields, away through the woods. As they rode through the woods, Kate picked the nuts from the tops of the trees and put them in her apron pocket. And they came once more to the dark hillside.

"Open up, open up for the prince on his horse!"

"And his lady behind him!" called Kate.

And that dark passage into the hill opened up once more, and in they rode to the fairy halls, to the fairy dance. The fairies pulled the prince from his horse and made him dance with them, and drink with them and dance again, until he could hardly stand. But Kate slipped away through the shadows this time, and she went exploring the dark halls under the hill.

There in a corner, she found a fairy baby, playing with a stick. Kate smiled as she watched and as she smiled, she heard a voice from who knows where saying, "If only they knew, if only they knew, one tap of that little stick would make Kate's sister Anne as well as ever she was!"

Well, when Kate heard that, she had to have the stick. So she took nuts from her pocket and rolled them to the fairy baby. The baby liked the nuts and crawled off after them, gurgling with delight, and he dropped the little stick. Quick as sunlight streaming through the darkness, Kate darted forward and snatched it up, and she put it in her apron pocket.

Then she hurried back to where the prince was dancing, the cock crowed outside the hill, and the fairies lifted the prince onto his horse with Kate behind, and out they rode to the dewy dawn.

Back at the castle, the prince staggered upstairs to his bed, but Kate took the little stick and went to where her sister Anne was sleeping. She unwound the soft white cloth from around her head and tapped the sheep's head with the fairy stick. At once, the horrid head fell off and Anne's own pretty face jumped back on again. And later that day, when the eldest prince came back from his hunting with his hawk on his fist and his hound at his heel, he saw Kate's sister Anne, and he had eyes for no one else.

The king had eyes only for Kate.

"If you watch a third night with my son, I'll give you whatever you desire," he said.

"Well, then," said Kate, "I'll do it tonight."

So Kate sat by the prince's side for a third night. He tossed and turned, but she just sat quietly as it grew darker. The clock ticked and the hours passed, until midnight struck. At once, the prince sat up in bed, swung his legs out, and pulled on his boots. He never saw Kate as she followed him out to the stables and climbed up behind him. And then they were off. Riding through the fields, riding through the woods where the nuts clung to the tops of the trees and where Kate reached out to gather them, riding out onto the dark hills, on and on until they came to that great hillside.

"Open up, open up for the prince on his horse!"

"And his lady behind him!"

And in they rode, to the fairy hill, to the fairy dance. The music was wild, the dancing was dizzy, and soon the prince was caught up in it, dancing until he dropped, drinking until he danced once more. But Kate hurried away through the shadows. She was looking for the fairy baby.

This night, she found him cradling a little bird in his hands, ruffling its feathers and cooing to it. Kate smiled when she saw him, and as she stood and watched, she heard that voice from who knows where, "If only they knew, if only they knew, three bites of that little bird would make the sick prince as well as ever he was!"

Well, Kate had to have the little bird, so once again, she took the nuts from her pocket and rolled them to the baby. The baby saw them rolling like marbles and crawled off to catch them, letting the bird fly free. Kate darted after it and she chased that little bird all through the shadows of the hall under the hill until at last she caught it in her hands. She wrung its neck and put the body in her apron pocket.

Just then, far off, she heard the cock crow in the dawn. She ran back to the prince as fast as she could and just in time, she jumped up on the horse behind him, and they were riding, riding, out of the hill, into the light of a new day.

They rode back through the hills, back through the woods, back through the fields, until they came to the castle. The prince left the horse and staggered upstairs to his bed. But Kate sat down by the fire and took the little fairy bird from her apron pocket. She skewered it on the fairy stick and began to roast it over the fire.

The smell of the bird cooking came to the prince as he lay there, flushed with fever.

"Oh," he murmured, "Oh for a bite of that little bird!" So Kate took a morsel of flesh from the bird and she pressed it between his lips. The prince swallowed it down, and a good color came back into his cheeks.

"Oh," he cried again, "Oh for another bite of that little bird!" So Kate gave him another bite, and he opened his eyes and looked at her.

"Oh, do give me another bite of that little bird!" he said. And Kate gave him the rest of the fairy bird. The prince ate it greedily and sat up in his bed, swung his legs out the side and jumped up, as well as ever he was!

When the king came in the next morning, he found the two of them sitting by the fire, roasting nuts and cracking nuts and cracking jokes and telling tales as if they'd known each other a lifetime.

"Well," said the king, "I don't know what to say! Kate, if it is in my power, you shall have whatever you desire."

"Well," said Kate, "All I really want is to marry the prince." The king smiled.

"I can see from his face that this is all he really wants too, and as for me, well I'd be honored to have you in the family," said the king.

And so there was a wedding. A double wedding, in fact, because, you see, the sick sister married the well prince and the well sister married the sick prince. And as the nut tree blossoms, so did they, and as the leaves fall down, they passed away. But the story of Kate Crackernuts and her sick sister Anne lives as long as there are people with breath in their body and courage in their hearts to tell it to you.

## A Wedding Toast

*Here is to the tree of life*
*Its length is but a span*
*It grows between two stones*
*Upon the Isle of Man*
*And here is to that little bush*
*That would that tree entwine*
*It flowers once a month*
*And bears its fruit in nine*

*—Jack Douglas, Amy's Grandad*

# Molly Whuppie

*A story retold by Dan Keding*

Once upon a time there was a man and wife who had fallen on hard times and could no longer feed their children. They took three of their daughters and left them in the woods.

Now the three girls walked far and wide and never saw a house that might give them the promise of a meal or a bed to rest themselves. At last they came to a house in the woods and knocked upon the door. A woman answered and said, "What do you want, bothering at my door?"

"Could you please let us in and might we have some food?"

The woman shook her head and spoke, "I wish I could, my little ones, but my husband is a giant and his greatest pleasure is eating people. He would eat you all up in three bites if he found you."

The three girls pleaded all the more, "We will only stop to eat a bit, and then we will be gone before he ever comes home."

The giant's wife let them in, sat them down by the fire, and gave them bread and cheese and milk. They had only eaten a few bites when they felt the ground tremble and the earth shake and a voice said,

*Fee, fie, fo, fum*
*I smell the blood of an earthly one.*
*Be they alive or be they dead*
*I'll crush their bones to make my bread.*

"Who have you as guests in our house, wife?"

"Just three little girls lost and hungry in the woods. After they eat they will be on their way, so let them be."

The giant glowered and stared hard at his guests but said nothing. After everyone had eaten, he ordered them to stay the night and share the bed with his own three daughters.

Now the youngest of these three traveling girls was Molly Whuppie, and though she was the youngest, she lacked nothing in brains or courage. She noticed that as the giant kissed each of his daughters good night, he placed a gold chain around their necks. When he kissed Molly and her sisters good night, he placed a rope of straw. Molly took care not to fall asleep but stayed awake and listened and watched. When the giant's daughters were fast asleep, she carefully took off the chains of gold and placed them on herself and her sisters and put the ropes of straw on the giant's girls. In the middle of the night, the giant rose and crept into the dark room feeling for the gold chains and the straw ropes. Whenever he felt a gold chain he patted the head of the girl, but whenever he felt the straw rope he took his club and battered the girl till she was dead.

Molly was pretty sure that she and her sisters had better be off before dawn. They ran till they came to a bridge spanning a deep ravine that seemed to disappear in the darkness. Soon they were running through the forest and didn't stop till the sun came up and they were miles away from the giant's house. As they caught their breath, they saw a beautiful house across the meadow. The house belonged to the king, and he listened with great interest as Molly told her story. He welcomed Molly and her sisters into his home and invited them to stay for dinner. After dinner the king took Molly aside and said, "You are a clever young woman, for I have never heard of anyone besting that giant before. I have an idea that can make us both happy. If you can steal the sword that hangs on the back of the giant's bed, then I shall wed my eldest son to your eldest sister. What do you say, Molly?"

Now Molly was brave and not a girl to refuse a challenge, especially one that could bring her eldest sister some happiness. She had seen how her sister and the oldest prince had smiled at each other over dinner. She agreed to try and steal the giant's sword for the king.

Molly made her way to the giant's house. She quietly crept into the first room and then the next, and finally, while the giant and his wife ate their dinner, she crept into the giant's bedroom and hid beneath the bed. After a huge supper, the giant came to bed, and in a matter of minutes was snoring so loudly that nothing else could be heard for miles. Molly climbed up to the back of the bed and slowly lowered the sword down, but just as she got the sword to the floor and had climbed down herself, it fell and rattled on the stone floor. The giant woke with a start, but Molly was already out the door and running as fast as she could for the bridge. The bridge that crossed the deep ravine was held together by only one human hair. Molly was light enough to cross, but the giant was too heavy and came to a stop, shouting across the ravine at Molly, "Woe to you, Molly Whuppie! Never come to my house again."

Molly turned and laughed at the giant. "I've been here once, I've been here twice, and if I want, I will come again."

When Molly came to the king's house, there was a great celebration. The king hung the giant's sword high above his throne. After they all had dinner, the king took Molly aside and said, "You are a clever young woman, maybe the most clever I have ever known or will know. Now I have a deal to propose to you. If you go back and steal the sack of jewels that lies beneath the giant's pillow, I will wed my middle son to your middle sister."

Now fearless Molly was feeling quite proud of herself and the way she could fool the giant. She also had seen how the middle prince had smiled at her second sister during dinner. She told the king she would try to steal the jewels.

That very night she crept back to the giant's house and once more carefully and quietly made her way to his bedroom and hid beneath the bed. When the giant finally finished his dinner, he came to bed and once more was snoring in a matter of minutes.

Molly slowly climbed the bedpost and gently reached beneath his pillow. Slowly, ever so slowly, she reached further and further till her fingers touched the sack of jewels. Slowly she pulled the sack out from under the pillow and began to climb down the bedpost. As she began to tip toe across the room, one green emerald fell from the sack and dropped to the floor. The giant woke with a start, and seeing Molly, he gave chase. Molly ran as fast as she could for the bridge. She crossed before the giant could catch her and stood smiling as the giant fussed and fumed.

"Woe to you, Molly Whuppie! Never come to my house again!"

"I've been here once, I've been here twice, I've been here thrice, and if I want I will come again." Laughing, Molly ran for the king's house.

When Molly came back with the sack of jewels, no one could believe how brave she was or how bold. They talked about her deeds and sang songs about how she outwitted the giant. Again the king had a great dinner in her honor and again he took her aside after dinner and made another proposition.

"Now Molly I have one last deal to offer you. If you go back and steal the ring off the giant's finger I will wed you to my youngest son."

Now Molly and the youngest prince had been smiling at each other at every meal, and she thought that it was about time she took care of herself, so she agreed. She went that very night to the giant's house, but you know there is a time to press your luck and there is a time to rest your luck. Molly crept into the giant's house and slowly and quietly made her way through the house once more till she could hide under the bed. The giant finished his meal and noisily came into the room. Again within a few minutes he was snoring so loudly that he could keep the dead from their rest. Molly snuck out from beneath the bed and climbed up next to the giant's hand. Slowly she began to take the ring off his finger. Slowly and carefully she inched it off till it was almost off, but then he woke. The giant grabbed Molly before she knew he was even awake. He held her tight and began to dance around the floor.

"I've got you now, Molly Whuppie, I've got you now!" The giant laughed and he laughed. Finally he stopped dancing and held Molly close to his face and said, "Molly Whuppie, you have been a thorn in my side. How shall I punish you, girl?"

Now the giant was big and the giant was strong, but the giant was not too smart and he should never have asked her that question.

"Well, I know that I wouldn't want you to put me in a sack. And I know that I wouldn't want you to put the dog and cat and scissors and needle and thread in there with me. And I know I wouldn't want you to hang that sack on a peg on the wall. And I know I wouldn't want you to go out to the woods and find the biggest tree in the forest and carve it into a club and then beat the sack till I was dead."

"Well since that's what you don't want, that's just what I'll do." The giant took Molly and placed her in a sack and put the dog and cat and scissors and a needle and thread in there with her and hung her on a peg. He left to go carve a club from the tallest tree in the forest.

As soon as he was gone, Molly began to sing, "Oh what do I see? Oh if you only saw what I saw."

Now the giant's wife was close by, and she had no more brains than her husband. "What do you see Molly?"

Molly kept singing, "Oh what do I see. Oh if you saw what I saw."

The giant's wife begged and begged to be let into the sack.

"Do you see stars? Do you see fairies? Do you see other worlds? Oh please let me in so I can see them too."

Molly took the scissors and cut a hole and dropped out of the sack. Then she helped the giant's wife into the sack and sewed it up again. The giant's wife didn't see a thing it was so dark in that sack, and she began to cry out to be let down. Just then the giant came home and began to hit the sack with the club. His wife cried out for him to stop, but he couldn't hear her over the noise of the cat and dog barking and mewing.

Molly came from behind the door and ran as fast as she could for the bridge. The giant gave chase, but Molly was faster.

"Woe to you, Molly Whuppie. Never come to my house again!"

Molly laughed and laughed. "I've been here once, I've been here twice, I've been here thrice, and now I've been here four times and have no need to come again."

Molly laughed and ran back to the king's house and gave him the ring. She married the youngest son and she ruled with wisdom when she was queen because everyone knows a king is only as wise as the queen beside him.

As for the giant, well, after losing his sword and his jewels and his ring, he became a hermit and never bothered anyone again. Soon everyone forgot about him except when they told Molly's story.

# The Glass House

*A story from Sussex and Kent retold by Dave Arthur*

Not so very long ago and not so very far from here there lived a witch. And this witch lived in a large house on the edge of a small village. The house was no ordinary house, not like you or I might live in. No, this house was made of glass. Everything was glass—the floors, the walls, the doors, the ceilings, the furniture —the lot. Everything was glass. Well, you can imagine how dirty a house of glass would get. You just put your finger on a pane of glass and you leave a dirty mark, don't you?

Well, working in this house for the witch was a young princess. Don't ask me how or why, because I don't know, I'm just telling you what I heard. This princess worked her fingers to the bone, from the moment she woke up to the moment she went to bed she was dusting and polishing seven days a week. And all the time the witch would stand behind her and say, "Mind you don't break anything! Mind you don't break anything!"

One day the witch went to the kitchen cupboard, which was, of course, glass, to get something for lunch. Disaster! The cupboard was empty. Nothing. Not a crumb. Not a morsel. There was nothing for it but a trip to the supermarket in the nearby town. Before she left, the witch reminded the girl, "Make sure you don't break anything." She went out climbed into her little car and headed for town.

No sooner was the witch out of the house than the girl switched on the radio, tuned into a local music channel, and started to dance as she dusted. She danced and she dusted, she danced and she dusted, when suddenly she knocked over a glass vase, which fell to the floor and broke into a thousand pieces. Well, actually, it broke into nine hundred and ninety-six pieces, but a thousand sounds better. As it hit the floor the floor cracked, the cracks ran up the wall, across the ceiling, down the doors, across the windows. The whole house was wrecked. All the girl could remember was the witch saying, "Mind you don't break anything! Mind you don't break anything!" She was terrified. She had to escape. She ran into the garden and up to the cherry tree, and she said,

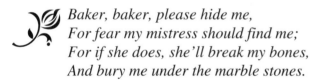

*Cherry tree, cherry tree, please hide me,*
*For fear my mistress should find me;*
*If she does, she'll break my bones,*
*And bury me under the marble stones.*

The cherry tree said, "I'd love to help you, but I daren't. If I helped you and the witch found out, she'd break my branches, she'd tear my leaves. I'm sorry, you'll have to go and ask someone else."

So the poor girl ran out of the garden and down the village street until she came to the butcher's shop. She ran in and said,

*Butcher, butcher, please hide me,*
*For fear my mistress should find me;*
*If she does she'll break my bones,*
*And bury me under the marble stones.*

"I'd love to help you," said the butcher, "but I daren't. If I helped you and the witch found out she'd turn me into a toad. Sorry but you'll have to ask someone else."

So the poor young princess ran past the pond and up the hill until she came to the baker's shop. She ran in and she said,

*Baker, baker, please hide me,*
*For fear my mistress should find me;*
*For if she does, she'll break my bones,*
*And bury me under the marble stones.*

The baker, who was slapping some dough around, making croissants, or buns, or some sort of cake, looked up from his bench and said, "Yes, all right, we'll find somewhere for you to hide."

He looked all around his shop until his eyes fell on the big old wooden flour bin against the back wall.

"Quick," he said, "climb in there and the witch'll never find you."

The girl climbed into the box, and the baker shut the lid and slid the bolt across.

Whilst all this was going on, the witch had come home from her shopping. She parked her car, opened the back and took out the shopping bags, and staggered up the path. As she got near the house, she saw the cracked front door. She pushed it open with her knee, and screeched with rage when she saw that her house had been completely trashed. She dropped the bags onto the floor and ran out into the garden, and up to the cherry tree. She grabbed the tree by a branch and hissed, "Where is the princess?"

The cherry tree was absolutely terrified, every leaf was shaking. "Sh-sh-she was here b-b-b-but I didn't help her."

"Just as well you didn't," said the witch, "or otherwise I'd have ripped your leaves off. I'd have broken your branches. Which way did she go?"

"Th-th-that way," said the cherry tree, pointing a branch toward the village. "To the butcher's."

The witch was out of the garden in two shakes of a lamb's tail, running hell for leather for the butcher's shop. Hair flying, black cloak billowing out behind her, green fingernails clawing the air. She got to the butcher's and rushed in.

"Where's the princess?"

"Oh, she was here," said the butcher, "but I didn't help her. I told her to go away."

"Just as well for you," said the witch, "Or I would have turned you into a toad. Which way did she go?"

"Up the hill toward the baker's," said the butcher.

The witch was out of the door up the hill, running. Hair flying, cloak flying, nose twitching, sniffing for the princess, because in stories witches can smell princesses.

She got to the baker's and kicked open the door with a karate kick she'd learnt in adult education classes.

"Where's the princess?"

The baker looked up at the witch.

"Go away, you bad-tempered old thing, leave the girl alone."

"I won't leave her alone," snarled the witch, "she's wrecked my glass house, and I know she's here somewhere. I can smell her."

With that the witch started to walk around the shop. She walked all around the flour bin and didn't see or smell anything. The only explanation I can think of for that is that the smell of the baking cakes and bread covered up the smell of the princess. The witch went upstairs and looked under the beds, behind the wardrobe. Nothing. She went into the attic, behind the water tank. Nothing. She stomped down the stairs and was just about to walk out of the shop when she heard, "Ahh . . . ahh . . . ahh . . . chooooo!" come from the box. You see, some of the baker's flour had got up the princess's nose and made her sneeze. Well, the witch knew where the princess was then, and she ran across to the box, and with superhuman strength she ripped open the lid, stuck in her arm, grabbed the princess by the scruff of the neck, and hauled her out, saying,

*Aha ha! Oo hoo Hoo!*
*You didn't think I would find you.*
*And now I'm going to break your bones*
*And bury you under those marble stones.*

"Oh no you're not," said the princess, and started to struggle. And they went up and down the shop, struggling and wrestling; the baker dodging and weaving out of their way.

At one side of the shop was a large barrel of water, and in the struggle, they bumped into it, and the water went all over the place. The princess and the witch splished and splashed their way up and down, and 'round and 'round. On the other side of the shop was a large barrel of flour. They bumped into it, and that, too, went over. There was flour and water all over the floor, and the more they wrestled the more the flour and water started to mix. It mixed into a thick, sticky dough, which started to rise up around the witch's ankles, legs, knees, waist, chest, shoulder, and head. At last, all you could see of the witch was the tip of her long hooked nose, the tip of her tall black pointed hat, and her ten green fingernails.

The baker and the princess started to roll the dough up into a giant ball—a hundred times as big as you'd ever get at a pizza house.

They opened the door of the shop and rolled the dough ball out of the door, and off it rolled down the hill, with the witch in the middle, faster and faster, until it came to the pond. Splash! In it went and sank to the bottom. Glub! Glub! Glub! That's the sound a giant dough ball makes as it sinks. Slowly the water dissolved the dough, and the witch swam to the surface, but, because she'd been dunked in water, all her powers were gone. She crawled out of the pond. She had a fish in one ear, a tadpole in the other, and a frog up her nose, and she was covered in green pond weed. She slunk off to her sister's house and told her the whole story.

"Have a cup of tea, dear," said her sister. Which, of course, is all you can do in that sort of situation.

The princess thanked the baker for his help and told him that she was really a very rich princess. Well, this made the baker fall in love with her immediately, and he asked her to marry him.

She agreed, and they wed. Then they had to decide where to live.

You wouldn't expect them to live in a bakery would you? She was, after all, a princess.

No, of course not. The answer would have been the glass house, but she'd trashed it, hadn't she? Well, they thought about this for a while and then went down to town and bought a large—a very large—box of special glue. The sort of glue that sticks anything. And then every night when the bakery closed they went up to the glass house and gradually stuck the whole thing back together. After a few weeks, it was looking as good as new, and you couldn't see a crack anywhere. They moved in and settled down to a happy life. And as far as I know, they're still there to this day.

# The White Cow of Mitchell's Fold

*A story from Shropshire retold by Amy Douglas*

There was once a great drought in Shropshire. A cold dry winter was followed by a cold dry spring and a hot dry summer. The stores were used up, many of the cattle were slaughtered to keep their food for the humans and everyone tightened their belts. Times were hard. Hard though it was, most of the people could survive one failed crop, but that winter was cold and dry, too. They had managed to save seeds to plant in the spring, but still the rains did not come. Many of the seeds did not sprout, and those that did were stunted. As the dry weather continued and summer arrived, they were burnt brown by the sun. The usually green, verdant countryside was brown, the brown of hard-baked mud, the brown of dust on the wind, the brown of tanned, thin bodies. What few cattle survived were nothing but bone, skin and sunken eyes. The eyes of the people became sunken in their sockets too, and the light of hope was slowly fading within them.

However, there was one old woman who managed to keep some flesh on her bones. Not far from Stapeley Hill on the outskirts of Middleton in Chirbury lived the hope of the village, old woman Mitchell, or, more often, Old Witch Mitchell. It was a rare day that someone did not appear at the door, bringing a carefully hoarded little bag of food asking for a charm to bring rain, for the life of their weak children, a charm to bring hope. Old Witch Mitchell always gave a charm, but still the skies stayed clear and the dust swirled in the fields.

There was another who refused to give up hope. A farmer. Every morning and evening he would make the climb up Stapeley Hill and look about him at the wide skies, searching for a cloud, a grey smudge on the horizon, praying for rain. The others laughed at him for wasting his precious energy, but it made no difference—every day, twice a day, he made his pilgrimage. But at last, even he began to give up hope. He had made his weary climb one evening and looked out across the clear skies and the dust swirling in the fields. He looked at the remnants of his own farm, and though he still thought that the rains would come, perhaps it would be after he and his family were long gone. Just as the hope was dying in his eyes and heart, he heard a sound, a cracking of dry twigs. He turned around and coming out from the dry bracken was a cow. But not one of his cows or anyone else's 'round about—this cow had flesh on her bones. A silky well-kept coat, a black glistening nose that made her look as if she had just drunk. While the farmer stood dumbstruck in surprise, the cow, showing no fear, walked over toward him, put her wet nose into his hand, and licked it with her rough tongue.

Hardly daring to believe it, the farmer realized that she was asking to be milked. He turned and ran down the hill. He grabbed a pail, told his wife what had happened, and told her to gather the villagers and lead them up the hill. The cow was still there waiting. She stood still and calm while each person there took a pail of warm creamy milk. One of the villagers said that they should take her down to the village and pen her up, but the farmer said, "No—she is a gift, if we treat her well and with respect, if each takes only as much as they need, a pailful, then she will return—besides, what would we feed her on!?"

Not all of the villagers had come to see the cow, many had laughed at the farmer's wife and claimed that the farmer had gone mad in the sun. But when they saw the line of people coming down the hill with their buckets full of milk, they laughter died and the next day at dawn, they were first up the hill with their pails and vessels—anything they could find.

For several months the cow appeared at dawn and dusk, and she kept the people of Middleton in Chirbury alive. Hope had come back into their lives.

One person, however, was not happy. The people no longer needed to buy hope, and Old Witch Mitchell found that no longer were the villagers bringing her food and respect; she was forgotten now that they had the cow. The flesh dropped off her and her skin hung in wrinkles. She decided to investigate what had happened to all the villagers—surely they couldn't all be dead! Well—when she found out about the cow, she was not happy. Jealousy and rage built up inside until she hatched a plan from bitterness. She stoked up the fire she kept lit even in that hot, hot summer heat. She heated the poker within it until it was glowing red. She took a pail and pushed the poker through the metal bottom, once, twice, three times, as many as she could.

That evening Old Witch Mitchell joined the line of villagers making their way up the hill to the cow. She waited modestly until all the other pails were full and then she took her turn and began to milk the cow into the pail. At first the cow stood patiently, but as the old witch kept milking and still the pail wasn't full, she began to twitch her tail and shift restlessly. Still Old Witch Mitchell kept milking, and the milk drained through the riddle running free on the hard baked ground, a stream of milk flowing down the hill. The milk was coming less freely now. The cow turned her head, and as she saw the milk wasting on the ground, the milk in her teats dried and the witch drew blood from the teats, the drops staining and streaking the white milk. The red color of the blood crept into the soft eyes of the cow, she turned on the witch, kicked the pail flying, turned on her heels and bellowing ran like a mad thing away from Stapeley and its hill.

The witch smiled and made her way home.

Down in the village, the villagers heard the bellowing, and they knew that something must be wrong. Led by the farmer they went running to the hill. Coming down the hill they could see the stream of milk, only now beginning to soak into the dry ground. In fear of what they might find they raced to the top of the hill, where there was nothing to see but a broken pail and a few spots of blood, but then—

"There!" cried the farmer, and there, was trail of damp foot prints. They petered out before they reached the cottage of Old Witch Mitchell, but all could and did guess what had happened.

They trailed up the hill with vain hope the next morning, but as they had feared the cow was not there waiting for them, nor did she ever return.

But neither, when she had gone, did the people return to Old Witch Mitchell. Her rival had gone, but still the cow had won, for none came now for a charm or a blessing. Rather, when they did see her they would avert their eyes and walk in a different direction. But she was still Old Witch Mitchell and none dared cross her.

The drought once again took hold of the villagers, and the first to die from its tightened grasp was Old Witch Mitchell. They found her body lying like a bundle of old sticks in the woods, the ground dead and withered beneath her. They took her to the top of the hill, and there they buried her, but still they were frightened of her, frightened that her spirit would walk again. So around her grave they built a wall of stones. As the circle of stones rounded toward completion, something strange began to happen. A cool breeze began to play around the top of the hill. The clear skies began to haze, and there was a grey smudge on the horizon. Slowly the clouds gathered and as the last stone was heaved into place, they felt the first cool spatterings of rain against their cracked skin. Finally, the drought was over.

Mitchell's Fold is a stone circle on the top of Stapeley Hill in Shropshire. There are fifteen stones left of the circle out of a probable thirty. In Shropshire, a fold is a farmyard and so Mitchell's fold is a pen, a fold in which to keep the witch Mitchell. At one point a local farmer blew up some of the stones and took the pieces to put around his horse pond, but they say that nothing good ever happened to him afterward.

# The Elder Tree Witch

*A story from Somerset retold by Amy Douglas*

There once lived a farmer. He didn't have a large farm, but it was big enough for him to support his family and small enough for them to take care of. They took good care of the farm and had good pasture, so their few cows gave the best milk of any of the cows roundabout. The yard was always swept clean, the dairy was spotless, the cattle and horse had healthy gleaming coats. The fields were bordered by neat thick hedgerows of blackthorn, hazel, holly, and dogrose, but there were no trees in the fields or the hedgerows and no elder. No good farmer allowed elder onto his land at that time or in that place. There were too many stories and too much knowledge.

There came a time when the farm was no longer doing as well as it had done. The yard was still well swept; the hedges, neat and trim; the cattle sleek and the dairy spotless, yet there was little to be done in the dairy, for the cows weren't milking—nothing but drips and dribbles. Since the cattle were still healthy, there was only one explanation—someone else was taking the milk. There must be a thief coming into the pasture at night.

So the farmer put on his warm clothes that night and crept out into the dark. Keeping close to the hedgerows, moving carefully and quietly, he made his way to the field where his cows were pastured. There was only the thin edge of a moon that night, but it was clear and the stars were bright, and slowly his eyes adjusted to the dark. He came to the field with his cows and crouched down at the gate. He saw his cows, peacefully standing and lying . . . and then he saw it. Against the deep velvet of the sky, the black shadow of a tree in the hedgeline. The back of his neck began to prickle and his hands turned cold and clammy as he stood up, opened the gate, and began to drive the cows back toward the farm to the small home pasture next to the farm. He shut the gate as the last cow went through, but where was the iron chain? He couldn't find it and the wind was beginning to rise —he could hear it tapping the branches against one another and the creak of resisting boughs. He shoved a stone against the gate, and picking up his step, he made his way inside and crawled into bed with his wife.

The next morning he told his family what had happened—his wife, his daughter and his mother-in-law. They sat and listened, and then his wife said,

"When the iron chain was gone, did you put a cross in the mud by the gate?" But the farmer hadn't. The daughter got up from the table and went over to the window. As she looked out she held onto the frame, her fingers turning white as she gripped it and she began to tremble.

"What is it?" her mother cried.

"It's there, the tree, in the pasture, with the cows!"

"What tree is it, girl?" asked her grandmother.

"An elder."

The girl, pale-faced, made her way around the house, making sure all the shutters were fastened tight. And old grandmother, she took the old iron coal scuttle and dug into the fire, so that the red coal embers lay on top of it and she stoked the fire up into a blaze.

The farmer, muttering, made his way around the kitchen, picking up this pile here and that pile there until his wife wondered what on earth he was doing.

"I'm looking for the silver button that came off my Sunday jacket."

"Well it's on your Sunday jacket of course—I sewed it back on on Monday!"

Well the farmer's wife had sewed the button back on, but now she took the scissors and she cut it off again.

The girl, she watched her father's preparations, but grandmother watched her fire.

The farmer took his gun from the shelf, the button from his wife, and a deep breath then made his way to the door.

The wife held the door open and the farmer stepped outside, his gun at the ready, but the tree was in the middle of his cows, and he couldn't get a clean shot at it without getting a little closer, a few steps more, a little closer yet—he took aim, but his arm was shaking so much that the gun wasn't steady. He let the shot fly and missed. The tree let out a shriek of rage, a blast of air whistling through the branches. The branches lifted up into the air and began to reach for the farmer as the tree leapt toward him. The farmer, he leapt too, and he ran faster even than he'd chased his wife twenty years earlier, making for the open doorway. He threw himself toward safety, his wife slammed the door behind him, and before the end of his coat had made its way in, she banged the iron bar into place to hold it, just in time before there was a thud and a rattle as the tree flew into the door and her branches slid down its wood.

All over the house there was a rattling and a tapping as the branches felt their way, trying to find a chink or a gap where they could force their way in, and all the time they could hear the creaking of the wood and the screech of the wind between the branches. There was no way for the tree to get in, but there was no way out for them either—and outside stood their livelihood—the cattle, horse, goat, and pig—and no way to protect them.

But the fire was hot. The shovel was ready. Grandmother got up from the hearth, her arms straining beneath the weight of the iron and coal. She nodded her granddaughter toward the back door. Pale and trembling, the girl opened the back door then ran back to stand by her mother. Grandmother stood in the doorway, as straight and tall as she could. The sound of the wind moved around the house, and there was the tree, flying straight toward her, its branches flailing, reaching out to take its victim. The tree was nearly upon her, and then she threw that shovel, red hot coals, iron and all, straight and true amongst the branches. Grandmother stepped back and shut the door. The family watched through the window as the flames took hold. The tree had collapsed onto the ground. The branches writhed in agony, enveloped in flame, until slowly they rested on the floor, moving no more, and crumbled into ashes.

At last they opened the shutters. The front door was unbolted, and the farmer freed. The wind had dropped, but as they made their way outside and looked at the pile of ashes, a gentle breeze gathered. It picked up the ashes and carried them high and far until all that was left was a small piece of bare ground.

The next day they heard the news of Old Sal, who had fallen into her fire, and both she and her house had burned down. Then they knew just who had taken their milk. All the people roundabout breathed a sigh of relief to be rid of Old Sal, and not one shed a tear for her.

From that day on the farm prospered again. Once more the cows gave freely of their rich milk and were safe in the fields, though there was always a new iron chain fast at the gate, just in case.

# Holy Days and Days of Heroes

# The First Simnel Cake

*A Shropshire story retold by Amy Douglas*

A long time ago in Shropshire there lived an old man and old woman called Simon and Nelly. They weren't rich, but they were honest, and though they were poor, they made do. They had lived in their small cottage since the day they were married. They had worked all their lives, but they had good times too, and between them they brought up a whole brood of children.

The children were all grown up and moved into homes of them own, but once a year, every year, they would gather all their family together for an Easter celebration.

And so it was one year. Lent had come to an end, and soon their children would be gathering under their roof, and they wanted to make something special for them. However, there wasn't much in the house. They began scraping together all the bits and pieces of food they had to see what they could make.

They searched through the cupboards and the larder. There was some Lenten dough left over and a little bit of the Christmas plum pudding hoarded away, and they thought if they put the two together, they might just have something worth eating. Simon squished the crumbs and pieces of the rich sweet plum pudding together. Nelly rolled out the Lenten dough and wrapped it around the pudding so that there should be a hard crust on the outside with the sweet surprise hidden inside. Nelly hummed and Simon whistled as the two worked together side by side. But then they had to decide how to cook it.

"What else can we possibly do but bake it?" said Nelly.

"It's a pudding—of course we should boil it like we do the plum pudding," said Simon.

"So that's what you think is it? This is the first time you've ever helped me in the kitchen—you normally just leave me in here, with the heat and the hard work and expect me to get on with it and suddenly you're an expert chef! Well, Simon, my man, I think I know a lot more about cooking than you'll ever know, and I say we're going to bake it so we'll bake it."

"I may not have done a lot of cooking, but I've done plenty of eating, and I don't think it would take much to better *your* cooking!" said Simon.

---

"I see!" screamed Nelly, and she picked up the stool she had been sat on and swiped it at Simon's head.

Simon wasn't going to take any of that, so he grabbed the broom from by the door and started beating at Nelly's ankles.

"Take that you good for nothing husband!" cried Nelly.

"And you can take that right back, woman who's never cooked a decent meal in her life!"

"How dare you!" cried Nelly cracking the stool over Simon's head.

Simon aimed the broom at Nelly's backside, but missed and caught a tray of eggs that they were going to boil and stain with onion dye for Easter.

"Now look what you've done you clumsy oaf!"

Nelly hurled the stool at Simon, but she threw it so hard she threw herself after it and landed on the kitchen tiles with a bump. Simon ducked, fell over the broom, and landed right beside her.

The two of them sat on the floor, catching their breath and rubbing their bruises.

Nelly looked at Simon with the broom leaning on his chest so its bristles looked like a huge great bushy beard. Simon looked at Nelly flat out on the floor with pieces of a broken stool around her and raw egg dripping onto her hair.

The corners of their mouths twitched, they smiled, and soon the two of them were rolling around the floor in helpless laughter.

"Oh dear," said Simon, wiping his eyes with his big spotted handkerchief.

"Oh dear," said Nelly, wiping her eyes with the corner of her apron.

The two of them pulled each other into a big hug, and they decided they would first boil the cake and *then* they would bake it.

They took what was left of the stool and built up the fire and set the pan to boil. They took the pieces of the broom, broke it up, and used it to heat the oven. When they took the cake out of the boiling water, they thought they might as well use up the broken eggs, so they brushed the cake with them and then set the cake to bake. When the cake came out it was glossy with the shine the eggs had given it.

They cleaned up the house, set the cake on the table, and their children said that it was the best cake that they had ever tasted. In fact, they liked it so much that they all wanted the recipe. And everyone else who tasted the cake liked it so much that they wanted the recipe, and it wasn't long before everyone in Shropshire wanted one of those cakes for Easter.

And what did they call the cake? Well of course they called it Simon and Nelly's cake, but (like the cake) that was a bit of a mouthful, so they took the first half of Simon's name and the first half of Nelly's name and called it the Simnel cake. And they still do. And it still tastes as good as it did that very first time!

# *Recipe for Shrewsbury Simnel Cake*

## Introduction

Over the years, the Simnel cake has developed and been elaborated. There are now several different types of cake, including the Devizes Simnel is in the shape of a star and the Bury Simnel, a flat spiced cake, but the Shrewsbury Simnel from Shropshire is still the most popular.

The original Simnel cakes surrounded by Lenten dough, boiled in a cloth, and baked in the way that Simon and Nelly first devised give a very hard cake; there is a story that an old woman used her Simnel cake as a footstool for years! These days the Shrewsbury Simnel has evolved into a rich spiced fruit cake. The Lenten dough used to wrap up the outside has been replaced with almond paste, and there is an extra layer of the paste in the middle for good measure. It is usually decorated with eleven balls of the paste, which represent all the apostles except Judas (who is considered unworthy). Sometimes other Easter symbols are added—nests with chocolate eggs inside, rabbits, chicks—so be plain and simple or go wild—it's up to you!

### Ingredients

| *U.S. Measures* | *English Measures* |
| --- | --- |
| **The Cake** | |
| 1 ⅝ cups mixed fruit | 13 oz mixed fruit |
| 1 cup flour | 8 oz flour |
| 2 level tsp baking powder | 2 level tsp baking powder |
| 1 level tsp ground cinnamon | 1 level tsp ground cinnamon |
| 1 tsp mixed spice | 1 tsp mixed spice |
| ½ cup plus 2 Tbsp cup butter | 5 oz butter |
| ½ cup sugar | 4 oz sugar |
| 3 eggs | 3 eggs |
| **Apricot Sauce** | |
| 4 tbsp apricot jam | 4 tbsp apricot jam |
| 3 oz water | 3 oz water |
| 1 tsp lemon juice | 1 tsp lemon juice |

## Almond Paste

| | |
|---|---|
| 2 cups ground almonds | 1 lb ground almonds |
| 2 cups icing sugar | 1 lb icing sugar |
| 2 eggs | 2 eggs |
| 2 tsp vanilla extract | 2 tsp vanilla extract |
| Juice of 1 lemon | Juice of 1 lemon |

# Method

### *Almond Paste*

Mix the almonds and icing sugar together. Beat the eggs lightly and add to the dry ingredients, together with the vanilla essence and the lemon juice. Mix to a paste and knead well.

Roll out two circles (same diameter as the cake tin), one for the middle and one for the top of the cake. Make eleven small balls, and use the remainder to roll out a long strip to cover the side of the cake.

### *The Cake*

Grease a 7-inch cake tin and line with greaseproof paper, greased on both sides.

Sieve the flour, baking powder, and spices together. In a separate bowl, cream the butter and sugar together until fluffy. Beat the eggs together in another separate container. Add a third of the fruit, a third of the beaten eggs, and a third of the flour to the creamed butter and sugar and fold together. Repeat until all ingredients are used, keeping a fairly stiff mixture throughout, but if necessary add a little milk.

Put half of the mixture into the cake tin, use one of the circles of almond paste and put over the mixture. Press down gently on the almond paste, working your way from one side to the other to make sure there are no air bubbles. Add the rest of the cake mixture on top.

Bake in a slow oven (300°F/150°C, gas mark 2) for about 1 ½ hours until the cake is well risen and firm to the touch. (With this cake, don't rely on inserting a knife or skewer to see if the cake sticks to it; the almond paste will give the impression of an uncooked cake.)

Empty onto a cooling rack and leave until cold.

*Apricot Sauce*

Mix the apricot jam with the water and simmer for five minutes. Add the lemon juice. Strain.

Use this mixture as a glue to hold the almond paste to the cake.

### *Decorating the Cake*

Brush the sides of the cake with the apricot sauce and wrap the almond paste around the outside. Brush the top of the cake with the apricot mixture and apply the second circle of almond paste. Arrange the eleven almond paste balls evenly in a ring around the edge of the top of the cake, using the apricot sauce to help them adhere.

Beat one egg and brush lightly over the cake to glaze.

Put the cake back into the oven at a temperature of 425°F/220°C/gas mark 7 for 5 to10 minutes or until the top of the balls are golden brown.

Applying the paste smoothly and evenly is by far the most difficult part of the recipe. It is most easily achieved by rolling out the almond paste onto a piece of greaseproof paper, pushing onto cake and then peeling the paper away. Icing sugar can be used to prevent the paste from sticking to fingers and the rolling pin.

# Golden Shoes

*A story from London, retold by Helen East*

*When I was a bachelor I lived by myself,*
*And all the bread and cheese I got I put upon the shelf.*
*But the rats and the mice they made such a strife,*
*I had to go to London to find myself a wife.*

*Well, there's some come to London to get themselves a wife,*
*And there's some come to find themselves a better sort of life,*
*Some come to buy, some come to sell,*
*Some come to listen and some come to tell.*

*And some, so they say, once upon a time, came to lose themselves a*
*man—a would-be husband, an unsuitable suitor …*

And where did they do that? Why Old Saint Paul's, of course, at the shrine of the Maid, Saint Uncumber. Some folk had fancier names for her, like Wigefort and Dignefortis, Reginfleid and Liberata. But whatever they called her, she was the one women called on, when they needed a bit of help in unencumbering themselves.

It hadn't been so easy for her of course, way back when ever it was that she'd been young, resisting some persisting pagan prince. She'd had to grow a beard, to put him off, a big bristly, bushy one right down to her knees, and as if that wasn't uncomfortable enough, she was crucified as well. But by the Middle Ages, well, people prided themselves on being a bit more civilized, so all you had to do was to select the right saint and pray. And then, naturally, pay.

Some gave the Maid Uncumber gold, some gave her silver, some gave her wild oats and nightly thanks for ever. It all depended on the size of the purses and the success of the pleas. They must have been successful, by and large, because, by the time my story starts, her effigy was encrusted with coins, her beard studded with silver and her little wooden feet encased in solid gold shoes.

Golden shoes! What a wonderful sight! To most people in London at that time, any kind of shoes was a sign of wealth. Plenty went without, inside and out; cold soles slipping on the cobblestones. And one such a one was a young musician come up to town for Bartholomew's Fair—and did well enough while it was there, but he'd stayed on once it was gone, fiddle under his arm all battered and worn, tunic and hose all tattered and torn, and nothing to keep him going now but the wind at his back and the hope in his heart. If hopes were horses, we'd all ride high! But he was walking; 'round and 'round and 'round. Billingsgate to Bishopsgate, playing for scraps—and fighting for that, too. Then there were the nights snatching brief respite in doorways, with dogs and draughts and one eye always watching for the Watch.*

And this particular day it was just beginning to snow.

Our wandering fiddler lad, wondering where to go, found his bare feet had stopped on the steps of Old Saint Paul's. Inside was dry and dim; infinitely welcoming. Smell of incense in the air, gentle murmuring of prayer. Timidly he tiptoed in. No one seemed to notice him.

In the flicker-light of tapers, shrines of saints stood side by side. The fiddler went to Saint Uncumber's; it seemed to him her face was kind. As he sank down to the ground he saw wild oats piled round her feet and, delirious with hunger, snatched them and began to eat. Only when he'd swallowed them down, did he realize what he'd done. Stealing from a Holy Shrine! Sacrilegious capital crime! On his knees he begged forgiveness, trying to think of ways to pay. All he had to give was music. Would that satisfy the maid?

Gently he took up his fiddle, and with heart and soul he played.

Shoulders hunched, head bowed, he was anxious at first, afraid his sort of music would not be allowed in this awesome, sacred place. But as his fingers stroked the strings, a song of thanks rose up in him, and found its voice in the violin. And as it flowed, the music rose, soared like a bird, and hung, divine, wreathing the statue, filling the shrine. Feeling its strength, the boy stood straight, and for the first time raised his eyes to the saint. Surely she had heard.

He scarcely saw the shining silver of her clothing, nor the gleaming golden shoes. He was looking at her face, carved so carefully out of wood. The eyes, the cheeks, the chin, the lips—they seemed so alive.

And as he looked—yes! He was right! Her forehead wrinkled, one cheek dimpled, and the effigy gave him an answering smile.

---

* The Watch: This was the name for the night watchmen who patrolled the wealthier areas at night. There was no police force until the eighteenth century.

Weak with relief he played a tune so sweet that now he made the lady sigh, and caught a crystal tear from her painted eye. Then with a laugh he bent back to the task, with a lilting, rhythmic courtly dance. And as he did, her body, too, began to quiver and tremble and—so gracefully—to move. Now he drew his bow so fast that the music almost laughed and her toes began to tap and her feet stepped in and out, till she kicked out all at once—and a shoe fell in his lap.

A Golden Shoe! The shoe of a saint! He stared at her. and she seemed to nod, as if to say, "Yes, take it away. A gift—for you." And then she was wood again. And he, in a dream, fiddle under his arm, golden shoe in his hand, turned and walked to the door. Never again would he be poor.

He stepped outside with a cry of delight—and a hand fell on his shoulder and the cry went out.

"Stop thief! Capital crime! Look! The golden shoe from Saint Uncumber's Shrine!"

 *What if you should catch a thief,*
*Catch a thief, catch a thief,*
*What if you should catch a thief,*
*My Fair Lady.*

*Hanged he'll be at Tyburn Tree,*
*Tyburn Tree, Tyburn Tree,*
*Hanged he'll be at Tyburn Tree,*
*My Fair Lady.*

So the fiddler was to be hung, and everyone was well pleased because hangings were famous fun in those days, a free spectacle for all the family and rich pickings for all the ale, eel, and oyster sellers, not to mention the pickpockets, peepshows, and peddlers. Besides, he was a good-looking lad, all the better to sigh and cry over, and he'd stolen from the Maid of Saint Paul's—not your average everyday crime at all.

And best of all, he was a musician, his fiddle cradled in the crook of his arm, so there were high hopes of getting a last good tune out of him and the crowd called out choices as they followed the cart and the condemned from Newgate to Saint Giles and on again after a stop for a drink. (And whether he drank to his own health or not, at least the fiddler did sip something, which, they all did agree was better that the teetotaler who wouldn't and ended up hung the quicker for it—minutes before his pardon came.) "Which all goes to show ..." as the people said, when with even more merriment, noise, and numbers they reeled on right to the end of the town, where Tyburn waited and "the west" began.

And there by the gallows was the place you could stand and say what was on your mind, before you were hanged.** But to the crowd's great pleasure, the young fiddler said, "Nay." Being a musician, he didn't want to talk, he just wanted to play. And what was more, although he said he would play for them all, he asked if it could be beside the Saint's Shrine in Saint Paul's.

The hangman's thoughts could not be heard amongst the crowd's great roars, and the priest's protests were drowned as well in an outburst of applause. The crowd decided it was fair enough, because the lad had stolen her shoe, that reparation—and celebration—should include Saint Uncumber, too. Ignoring the other offenders, who were waiting their turns to swing, they bundled the fiddler onto the cart and back to the city again.

The church had never been so full, with people three deep 'round the walls. But silence fell upon them all when the lad began to play. The sounds he drew out of his fiddle! Low lilting laughter and sweet sobbing sighs; dreams of young maidens and fishmonger's cries; dirges that froze them to stone in their seats; dances that brought the half dead to their feet; the rafters were ringing; the belfry bats singing; fish skipped from the water; pigs jigged at the slaughter; fathers forgot to care who kissed their daughters. Only the lad and the saint seemed unmoved. His face, looking up, was like ice, while she, looking down, was just wood.

So his hopes and his music came to an end, and the fiddler fell to the ground. And the crowd, forgetting its purpose, pulled out purses and threw money down.

The fiddler lay still in a hail of bright coins past caring any more. Until—a gasp of surprise made him open his eyes to see the saint toss her gold shoe to the floor.

Well, you can imagine the flurry and fuss, the relief, and the wild celebration, how the tongues tattled, rumor ran riot, and truth turned to wild speculation.

But the brave fiddler lad, they all do agree, lived healthy and wealthy and well. So there was one who in London town did find a better life.

And did he also find a wife?

That only Uncumber can tell.

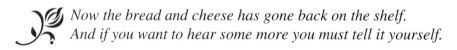 *Now the bread and cheese has gone back on the shelf.*
*And if you want to hear some more you must tell it yourself.*

---

** The place where you have a right to speak exists to this day, on the corner of Hyde Park. We call it Speakers' Corner. Nowadays you don't have to be condemned to be allowed to stand up there and have your say!

# Oranges and Lemons

## Traditional English Rhyme

 *Gay go up and gay go down,*
*To ring the bells of London Town.*

*Oranges and lemons*
*Say the bells of Saint Clement's*

*Bulls eyes and targets*
*Say the bells of Saint Marg'ret's*

*Brickbats and tiles*
*Say the bells of Saint Giles*

*Pancakes and fritters*
*Say the bells of Saint Peter's*

*Shirts, sherry and shawls*
*Say the bells of Saint Paul's*

*You give me the fidgets*
*Say the bells of Saint Bridget's*

*Two sticks and an apple*
*Say the bells at Whitechapel*

*Old Father Baldpate*
*Say the slow bells at Aldgate*

*Maids in white aprons*
*Say the bells at Saint Catherine's*

*Pokers and tongs*
*Say the bells at Saint John's*

*Kettles and pans*
*Say the bells at Saint Anne's*

*You owe me five farthings*
*Say the bells of Saint Martin's*

*When will you pay me?*
*Say the bells at Old Bailey*

*When I grow rich*
*Say the bells at Shoreditch*

*Pray when will that be*
*Say the bells at Stepney*

*I'm sure I don't know*
*Says the great bell at Bow*

*Here comes a candle to light you to bed.*
*Here comes a chopper to chop off your head!*
*Chip chop, chip chop,*
*The last man's dead!*

This traditional rhyme is accompanied by a traditional game. Two children hold hands and make an arch. They decide between themselves which one represents oranges and which one represents lemons without the other children knowing. The other children walk or skip through the arch and tag on to the end of the line so that there is a continuous ring of children dancing through the arch. All the children sing the song. The last four lines are spoken. On "chip" the children's arms making the arch move down to trap a child, then come back up to remake the arch on "chop" and release the child. The arms come down on "last," "man's," and "dead." The child trapped within the arch arms on "dead" is out. The arch children ask the child whether she wants to be an orange or a lemon, and the child whispers back her choice. If she says oranges, she stands behind the arch child who chose oranges at the beginning of the game, if she says lemons, she stands behind the arch child who chose lemons.

The rhyme starts again. When all the children are out and standing behind one or other of the arch children, then there is a tug of war between the oranges and the lemons.

# The Great Bell of Bosham

*A story from Sussex retold by Dan Keding*

In the old days the towns along the coast and up the great rivers of England were always fearful of raids from the Vikings—the Norse raiders from across the sea who plundered the villages and monasteries. One day a boy in Bosham saw strange ships approaching the shore and ran back to the town warning everyone with cries of "The Norsemen are coming! The Norsemen are coming!"

The people took what they could carry, driving their animals before them and fled for the safety of the woods. The monks in the monastery hid their treasures and ran to join the escaping villagers.

When the Norsemen entered the village, they found it deserted. Each house stood empty, every barn bare of the whatever it had held before the raiders arrived. The Norsemen carried away whatever the villagers had left behind and then stormed into the monastery. They sacked the monastery and its church and took anything of value that had been left behind.

Now the church was famous for its seven bells that rang out each Sunday and holy day. The Vikings found the bell ropes, and when they pulled them heard the sound of the great bells. They especially liked the sound of the deepest bell, the largest bell. They imagined how beautiful it would sound back in their village, hung outside their chief's hall in their homeland. They hauled the bell down from the tower, through the village and to the shore. The great bell was loaded on to one of the Viking ships. The timbers of that vessel groaned under the weight of the bell and the other loot from the town.

When the people and the monks returned, they came back to the ruins of what had once been their homes. The monks, hoping to lighten the hearts of the villagers, rang their bells, but the sound of the great, bass bell was gone. They rang the bells again, and this time they were answered by the deep sound of the seventh bell calling to its brothers and sisters from the deck of that Norse ship. Its deep voice boomed across the water. It rang and answered the sound of the other six over and over again, and then it was still. The great weight of the bell and all the other stolen loot was too much for the ship. When the waves of an incoming storm battered its side, it sank to the bottom of the sea with all its cargo and men.

The huge bell lay on the sea's floor for hundreds of years. A wise man finally told the people of the village that if they could find a team of six pure white horses, not a red or brown or black hair among them, then they might be able to bring the bell to shore. The quest was on, and after a long search six white horses were found and brought to the beach. Men dove down to the seventh bell and attached ropes to it. Then the battle began between the sea and the horses of Bosham. The team pulled and pulled and slowly, agonizingly the bell began to move toward the shore. Suddenly the ropes broke and the bell settled down into the bed that had held it all those years in the arms of the sea. As the horses were taken from the beach, one of the men saw that the last horse had one brown hair hidden in the folds of its left ear. The old man's words rang true: "Six pure white horses—not a red or brown or black hair among them."

There the great bell remains on the floor of the ocean. But when the other six bells ring out from the tower, it is said that the seventh one answers them, faintly booming under the sea calling to the bells of Bosham, keeping its place in the music of the bells.

# Brother Jucundus

*A story from York, retold by Amy Douglas*

In the middle of York there were once two monasteries, Saint Leonard's Priory and Saint Mary's Abbey. The monasteries were so close that only one wall separated them. In fact, they had once been a single monastery, but there had been a dispute about just how zealous the Lord would wish his devoted subjects to be, and they at last solved the dispute by building a dividing wall and the monks splitting into two.

In the Saint Leonard's half lived a monk called Brother Jucundus. He was a man who loved to talk, loved to sing, loved stories, and thought that all of these things were helped along by a love of strong beer. Brother Jucundus had been lured into the monastery by the thought of the simple life and by a love of the choir. However, it was not the life of leisure and singing he had anticipated. His bed was hard, and he didn't get to spend nearly enough time in it. The food was plain, all there was to drink was thin ale, and he hadn't been able even to look at a woman in weeks! All in all, he was beginning to wonder why on earth he was there.

These were the thoughts that were going through his mind during the afternoon sleep period. He was trying to make the most of his hour of rest, but there were people going past the monastery outside, laughing and singing and keeping him awake. As he lay there, he realized that he could also hear music in the distance. Suddenly he realized what all the noise was about. Today was fair day!

He could stand it no longer. He climbed out of bed and stole to the door. Looking both ways down the corridor he tiptoed out and along the passageway. All was still and quiet except for the echoes of some of the monks snoring.

The hardest bit was sneaking into the prior's room to take some money from the poor box. After that he sped toward the porter's lodge, carefully lifted the keys, opened the outer door of the monastery, and he was free!

A beaming Brother Jucundus made his way down the street toward the fair. He had the most marvelous afternoon he'd had since he joined the Abbey. He stuffed himself full with roast chestnuts and gingerbread. He went to see all the sideshows, the strong man and the bearded woman, the dwarf, and the giant. He found an inn that served real ale instead of the thin watery stuff he'd been making do on—strong fruity, frothy beer that soothed the tongue and warmed the throat.

Brother Jucundus, out of practice with the strong beer, staggered around the fair, friends with everyone. Looking for a place to sit down he found a seesaw and plonked himself down on one end of it. Now some young lads, seeing the monk on the seesaw, bleary eyed and head drooping, started to laugh and decided to have a game with him. Two of them jumped on the other end, and Brother Jucundus was sent flying up into the air. His eyes opened, he clung to the wood beneath him, he looked about, and then he started to laugh. Up and down, the lads sent Brother Jucundus, up and down, up and down, and Brother Jucundus began to sing.

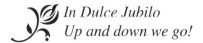

*In Dulce Jubilo*
*Up and down we go!*

And that was where the two monks sent to find the errant Jucundus found him. Their jaws dropped in disbelief to see one of their brethren being launched up and down in the air, his habit swirling around him. The young men looked up to see the stern faces of the two very sober monks, lowered Brother Jucundus to the floor, tipped their fingers to their caps, and went off to explore the rest of the fair. The two monks hoisted Brother Jucundus to his feet and dragged him back to the priory to face the prior.

The prior looked over his desk at the unkempt monk before him, his nose wrinkling at the strong smell of alcohol exuding from him. He listened to the catalogue of Brother Jucundus's misdemeanors, shaking his head as the whole terrible story unfolded.

"Have you anything to say, Brother Jucundus? Can there be any excuse for your behavior? Or do you at least repent of what you have done?"

Brother Jucundus raised his head and looked into the eyes of the Prior. A broad smile lit up his face.

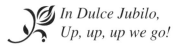

*In Dulce Jubilo,*
*Up, up, up we go!*

The prior sighed.

"There's no help for it. Such a crime deserves the severest punishment. Take him to the cellar."

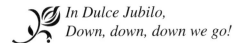 *In Dulce Jubilo,*
*Down, down, down we go!*

Brother Jucundus, still singing, was dragged out of the prior's office, and true enough to the song, it was down, down, down they went into the cellar.

Brother Jucundus's eyes lit up when he saws the barrels of beer and wine, but that wasn't why they were there. Soon all the monks from the priory were squashed into the cellar.

Stones were fetched and the mortar was mixed. Brother Jucundus was pushed up against the cellar wall with a fresh loaf of bread and a jug of water while the wall around him began to rise.

Brother Jucundus's only comment was that he was sure they'd enjoy their work more if they sang while they did it, and he carried on singing,

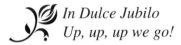 *In Dulce Jubilo*
*Up, up, up we go!*

Before the wall was finished, Brother Jucundus was lying on his back snoring. But the monks carried on until every crack and cranny was filled and Brother Jucundus was soundly walled in. With somber faces they left the cellar and left Brother Jucundus to his fate.

It was some time later that Brother Jucundus finally woke up. His head felt fuzzy, but he stretched and opened his eyes. It didn't make any difference—it was still dark.

He turned to swing his legs off his bunk and stand up, but he wasn't on his bunk, he was lying on the floor—and a hard stone floor at that. Brother Jucundus pulled himself up into a sitting position and leaned back on the wall to deliberate his situation. But as he leaned back, so did the wall! It gave way beneath his weight, and Brother Jucundus tumbled through the wall to land in a sprawled heap on a cellar floor. Brother Jucundus hauled himself to his feet, dusted off his habit, and climbed up the cellar stairs.

Nothing was familiar. He was still in a monastery. There were monks all around him, but he knew none of their faces. The layout of the monastery was similar, but corridors would turn in a different direction from the one he expected. And when he tried to ask anybody where he was, they looked at him in horror and put their fingers to their lips.

It wasn't until late that night, lying on the bunk, that one of the monks had led him to, that Brother Jucundus worked out what had happened. He had been punished for going to the fair by being walled up in the cellar of Saint Leonard's, and then when he woke up, he had fallen through the wall into Saint Mary's! And Saint Mary's was much stricter than Saint Leonard's! If he thought life was tough in Saint Leonard's, then now he really was in a pickle! For a start, it was a silent order—nobody was allowed to speak except on Easter Day. The beds were harder, there was less food, and the ale was even weaker!

But Brother Jucundus made the best of it. He had no choice. The monks were not allowed out of Saint Mary's; the gate was kept locked, and the porter kept a good hold of the keys at all times.

Brother Jucundus was made welcome at Saint Mary's, the monks all assuming that he had joined the order in the normal way instead of through the cellar, and indeed he was given a job—as cellarer. Every mealtime it was Brother Jucundus who went down into the cellar to fetch up the ale to go with the meal. And so a whole year went by until one day Brother Jucundus was kneeling in prayers and he could hear music filtering in through the walls. Not the deep resonant chanting he was used to, but a fiddle, a whistle and voices singing loud and free. As he listened harder, he heard shouts of joy and laughter. Brother Jucundus realized that once again fair day had come around. But Brother Jucundus was trapped, unable to escape to the fair and the misery of his plight almost brought him to tears.

Such was his mood when he made his way down to the cellar to fetch the ale to go with the lunchtime meal. As he stood in the cellar a thought crossed his mind—he couldn't physically go to the fair, but here he was in the cellar, he could at least drink a toast to the fair day. Brother Jucundus opened a new barrel, not of the weak ale that the monks drank every day but instead a barrel of wine saved for guests. It tasted good. Smooth, rich, and warm as it flowed down his throat. One glass disappeared without his realizing, but in a second it was full again. Brother Jucundus sat and reminisced about the marvels of the fair, he could almost smell the hot roasted chestnuts, hear the music playing, and the seesaw—the seesaw had been so much fun. Brother Jucundus began to hum to himself,

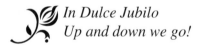
*In Dulce Jubilo*
*Up and down we go!*

Up above in the dining hall, the monks were getting restless. The food had arrived, but there was no sign of the beer. They shuffled their feet and cleared their throats, but there was no sign of the cellarer. Soon all eyes were resting on the abbot, waiting for him to do something. The abbot was staring at the doorway though which the cellarer should be appearing. The doorway was empty. The abbot sighed, rose to his feet, and went to investigate.

He was not amused to find the cellarer splayed out on the cellar floor, sloshing a large tankard of the finest wine from side to side in time with,

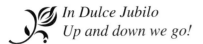
*In Dulce Jubilo*
*Up and down we go!*

This was an emergency that called for the necessity of speech.

"Brother Cellarer, what is the meaning of this!"

And Brother Jucundus said, "All together now:

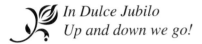
*In Dulce Jubilo*
*Up and down we go!*

The abbot stood white-faced, open mouthed, and furious. In all his days in the abbey, he had never had to deal with such disobedience and flagrant disrespect for the rules of the order.

The other monks tiptoed down the stairs to see what could possibly be happening.

The abbot turned to them.

"There's nothing we can do with such a sinner as this. We must give him the most severe punishment. We'll wall him up and leave God to deal with him."

And so it was. A group of monks went off to mix up some mortar. A loaf of fresh bread and a jug of water were brought. There were some handy stones lying around and an alcove that was just the right size and the work commenced.

Once again Brother Jucundus was walled in, and once again he accepted it with good grace and continued to sing while the walls went up, and indeed for some time afterward.

The monks from Saint Mary's took some ale from the cellar, went upstairs, ate their meal, and, having got rid of Brother Jucundus, went back to their quiet ways.

On the other side of the wall at Saint Leonard's, however, life was in upheaval. The old prior was dead, and the monks were struggling to agree on who his successor should be.

The cellarer of Saint Leonard's was dwelling on the succession as he slowly made his way down the stairs to fetch the ale for the evening meal. But as he came into the cellar, he stopped in his tracks. The jugs he was holding dropped to the floor. The cellarer raced up to the refectory his hands empty. All the monks turned to look at him as he stood in the doorway.

"Brother Jucundus, he's still alive! He's down in the cellar singing!"

The monks looked at the cellarer in disbelief, but he stuck to his story and the monks made their way down the steps. They couldn't believe their ears as all of them heard Brother Jucundus's deep, resonant voice bellowing out,

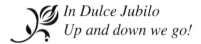
*In Dulce Jubilo*
*Up and down we go!*

They fetched pickaxes and chisels; they chipped away at the mortar and pulled away the stones to reveal Brother Jucundus.

"It's a miracle!" they cried.

There he sat, a little thinner perhaps, but his eyes bright. The loaf of bread was still warm from the oven and the water still fresh.

"It's a sign!" cried one of the monks.

The monks agreed—God had chosen a prior for them.

"Prior Jucundus, Prior Jucundus," all the monks took up the chant.

And so it was. Brother Jucundus became the prior of Saint Leonard's, and all agreed he did a fine job of it. The priory was always ringing with music in praise of the Lord, there was always plenty of good food and strong beer on feast days and once a year on fair day, all the monks left the priory to go to the fair and to spread the word of the Lord.

# Little John and the Nottingham Fair

*A story from Nottingham retold by Dan Keding*

Autumn had come to the forest and with it the cool winds that brought the clear days. The harvest was in, the apples ripe and young and old were getting ready for the long nights and short days of winter. With the fall came the great fair in Nottingham Town that gathered people far and wide to its stalls and entertainment and contests. There would be jugglers and singers, dancers and storytellers, food and drink of all sorts, and contests. The most famous contest would be archery, but also there would be wrestling and quarterstaff, feats of strength and races of both man and beast. Now Robin Hood was not tempted to go to the fair this year. He had already rubbed the sheriff's nose in his own stupidity by winning the archery contest the year before and had no need to do so again. But Little John had other thoughts.

"I have heard that the sheriff has offered such a small prize this year for the archery contest so we would not come to town and claim it for ourselves. I think that I would like to go and test my skill and bring that prize, though small, back to our forest."

"If you must go, John, disguise yourself well for your size and hairy head are well known to the sheriff and his men."

So Little John took off his Lincoln green and dressed himself in scarlet with a deep red jacket and hood to hide his long brown hair and beard and off he went to Nottingham Town.

John walked among the booths and the brightly colored tents at the fair. At every turn there was something new to delight the eye, tents filled with music and dancing, others serving ale and sweet cakes, some filled with minstrels singing ballads and telling stories, others serving sausages and fresh baked bread still warm from the oven. John walked among the tents, his great bow and a quiver of arrows slung over his shoulder. John stood almost a head taller than the tallest man, and his shoulders were broader than any there; many folks cast an eye at his great size, and many a young lady smiled at the handsome youth.

First John stopped to quench his thirst with some brown ale, and he treated all within earshot to a pint. Then he went dancing, leaping high and turning in midair, delighting all who watched. He danced with several young ladies till they could dance no more and everyone declared him a fine man and a great comrade with whom to share a day at the fair.

There was a great crowd at the quarterstaff competition, and John made his way there, for he loved to play at the quarterstaff and was known as the master of that martial art. When John reached the ring, he noticed that no one was fighting. Instead, one man was walking up and down and laughing at the men in the crowd, trying to bully them into trying their luck against him. This was Eric of Lincoln, the quarterstaff champion, celebrated in ballad and story for his skill.

"Now is there no man here who will cross staffs with me? No one here who will fight for the love of his lass and prove his courage? I was right to believe that the men of Nottingham are feeble and weak-kneed when compared to those of us from Lincoln."

Eric smirked and pranced around the ring like a rooster while all the men of Nottingham avoided his gaze and stared at their feet. The few who had tried their luck in the ring were nursing sore heads and bruised bodies.

Eric spied John in the crowd and saw that he was head and shoulders above the others.

"You, the long-legged fellow in scarlet, are you afraid to cross staffs with me today? Your shoulders are broad, but is your head hard enough to take a blow from my staff? Are you like the rest of these faint-hearted men of Nottingham, or will you give me a fight?"

Little John stared at Eric of Lincoln for a moment, but it seemed to last a lifetime. Finally he spoke.

"Yes, I'll give you a match. I wish I had my own good staff here and it would sing through the air like an arrow as it journeyed toward your head, but I'm sure that there's a fine man here who will lend me his own quarterstaff so I can teach you a lesson in humility."

Several men held out their staffs, and John examined each till he found one that came close to his liking.

"It's more like a splinter of wood in my hands, but it will do for this fellow."

Eric of Lincoln laughed and said, "Well spoken—for a man soon to be beaten."

John vaulted the railing that surrounded the ring and landed lightly on his feet. He seemed almost too quick for a man of his size. Each man walked slowly around the other sizing him up and looking for a weakness in his defense.

"Watch closely, men of Nottingham, as I carve up your hero."

Eric moved quickly and struck. Though he was skillful his blow was easily turned aside. Once, twice, and three times he attacked Little John, but the strikes were turned aside first to the left then the right as if John were giving a lesson rather than engaged in a duel.

Then almost in a blink of an eye, he backhanded Eric beneath his guard and rapped him on the head, sending him reeling backwards.

As Eric stopped to gather his wits, a shout went up from the people of Nottingham. As Eric came back toward the center of the ring, he was more cautious and kept out of John's considerable range. But the longer they fought the more angry Eric of Lincoln became, and soon he began to strike at John so quickly that it sounded like rain pounding on the roof. But each blow was turned aside, and with each parry Eric became even angrier and more daring till John saw his opening. He rapped Eric on the head once, then twice, then slipping his left hand down the staff, he swung it in a huge arc. It landed on Eric's head, and he crumpled to the ground. John bent down and whispered something in his ear, and to the cheers of the audience he left the ring, handed the staff back to its owner, and melted into the crowd of fairgoers.

Several folk helped Eric to his feet. Eric looked as if he'd seen a ghost.

"What did he say to you when you fell?" one man asked.

"He told me there was no shame in being beaten by Little John."

The people looked for their hero, but he had left his red jacket and hood hanging from a tree and had disappeared into the green woods once more.

# Robin Hood and the Monk

*A story from Nottingham, retold by Michael Dacre*

*In somer when the shawes be sheyne*  
*And leves be large and long*  
*Hit is full mery in fayre foreste*  
*To here the foulys song*

*To se the dere draw to the dale*  
*And leve the hilles hee*  
*And shadow hem in the leves grene*  
*Under the grene-wode tre.*

*In Summer when the bushes shine*  
*And leaves be large and long*  
*It is full merry in fair forest*  
*To hear the birds song*

*To see the deer draw to the dale*  
*And leave the hills high,*  
*And leave the hills high,*  
*And shadow them in the leaves green*

It befell one Whitsuntide, early in a May morning, when the sun was up and shining and the birds were singing merrily, that Little John turned to Robin Hood as they stood at the edge of a forest glade.

"Oh what a beautiful morning!" cried Little John. "By him that died on the tree there is no happier man than I in the whole of Christendom!" But Robin Hood was in a terrible mood and made no answer.

"Buck up master!" said Little John. "Open your eyes to the beauty of this May morning."

"Aye, may be," said Robin, "but one thing grieves my heart—that I may not go openly to mass nor matins. It's more than a fortnight since I went to church to seek my Savior. Well, stuff the sheriff and his men! I'm going into Nottingham today to hear mass in Saint Mary's Church and may the might of mild Mary go with me!"

"If I were you," said Much the Miller's Son, "I'd take twelve strong men with you as well as the might of mild Mary. I mean, anyone might have a go at you on your own, but there are not many as would take on twelve."

"By my faith!" cried Robin. "I go to worship, not to war! Look, of all my merry men, I'll take none but Little John here and he can carry my bow."

"You can carry your own bow, master," said Little John, "and I'll carry mine—but look, we'd better have some practice before we go. Let's shoot for a penny under the trees here."

"Shoot for a penny!" cried Robin Hood. "With the greatest archer in the world? I'll tell you, Little John, for every penny you put down, I'll hold up three!" And so they started shooting at a stand of saplings on the other side of the glade and such was Robin's mood that morning, he couldn't shoot for toffee and Little John won five shillings from him. Then a strange quarrel fell between them as they went on their way. Little John insisting he'd won the five shillings and Robin Hood striding ahead, saying, "No!" until Little John grasped him by the shoulder and roared, "Give me my five bob, you flipping little footpad!" whereupon Robin Hood turned on Little John and, jumping up, hit the big man in the mouth. Little John got quite cross and pulled out his sword.

"If I didn't love you," he said, "I'd hit you—very hard. As it is, you can get some other fool to be your serf." And he strode back into Sherwood Forest, leaving Robin to go on into Nottingham on his own.

As he slipped in through the gates, he prayed to Mary the Mother of God to bring him safe out again, as well he might, for such was his mood that morning, he refused to wear a disguise; so when he entered Saint Mary's Church and knelt before the altar, everyone saw that it was Robin Hood, with his hair and beard of bright red curls, his hood and hose of Lincoln green, his bow and arrows on his back. Right behind him stood a burly monk with a big head and a black habit and he knew Robin at once; so as soon as he could, he sidled off out of a side door and ran, as fast as his bulk would allow, to the sheriff.

"Bar the gates!" he cried. "That false outlaw Robin Hood is kneeling at mass in Saint Mary's Church. Rise up, sheriff, and take him! He robbed me once of eight hundred pounds and I can never forget it!"

"Huh! He's done worse things to me I'll never forget," growled the sheriff, and he rose and gave orders to bar all the gates. Then he armed himself and made off to the church with many a mother's son, well-armed and white-faced, rattling along beside him through the dusty, crowded streets. In at the church doors they thronged, swords in hand, baying for the blood of Robin Hood, heedless of the sanctity of the church and the screaming of the women and children.

"Oh dear," muttered Robin to an old woman kneeling next to him. "I'm beginning to miss Little John." But he drew his sword, for he would not use his bow in the crowded church, and ran straight to where the sheriff and his men stood thickest. Three times he ran through them, swinging his great sword like a madman and many a mother's son was horribly mutilated that day and six of them died screaming of their wounds that evening; but then his sword broke in two against the stronger steel of the sheriff's helmet, and he was weaponless—so they closed upon him and, because they wanted him alive, they beat him bloody and senseless with the hilts of their swords and threw him into a dark and narrow dungeon deep down under Nottingham castle.

The sheriff received the big-headed monk in the public courtroom and thanked him dryly for giving the outlaw away.

"Now go—oh my head!" he said, "and bring this good news to the king, for he alone can decide what to do with Robin Hood." He offered the monk an escort of soldiers but the monk refused, thinking to get all the glory to himself, saying

"I'll go alone with only my little pageboy for company and so escape notice."

But Robin Hood had many friends in the town, and word spread like a forest fire that the black monk had betrayed the outlaw and was now on his way to the king in London. So, faster than the wind, a messenger sped to Sherwood and brought the news to the merry men. Then they were not so merry. Some of them wept and wailed and some just sat and stared, but all at once Little John was out of the trees and stood among them.

"Let up your wailing!" said Little John. "For God's sake, you're a gang of outlaws, not a flock of nellies! Robin's been in worse scrapes than this and got away with it. He's served Our Lady many a day, and I trust her not to let him die a wicked death. So stop your puling! I shall take this monk in hand by the might of mild Mary. No, just me and Much will go. The rest of you stay here by the trysting tree and prepare a feast for our return."

Then away ran Much and Little John through the forest, until they came to an old, tumbledown house overlooking the London road. There they hid, Little John keeping watch at a broken window. Soon they heard a clattering of hooves and here came the monk riding over the hill, his great black habit billowing in the wind, his little pageboy riding behind.

"That's the one," said John. "I know him by his wide black hood. It's a shame about the boy, though." The two yeomen stepped out into the highway, humbly and courteously, tugging their forelocks and addressing the monk in friendly tones.

"Beg pardon, good father," said Little John, "but have you any news of that flipping little footpad, Robin Hood? He robbed me of five shillings only this morning, but I hear the good for nothing thief's been taken, thank God."

"Ha-hah! He robbed me too," said the monk, "of eight hundred pound and more, but it was I that laid hands on him so you can thank me for it."

"I pray God thank you," said Little John, "and we will when we may—but look, by your leave, we'll go with you for a while, for Robin Hood leads many a wild fellow in these parts and if they knew you were riding this way, they'd slaughter you like sheep."

So as they went on their way, the monk and Little John talking and laughing together like old friends, John held on to the horse's reins, while Much kept an eye on the little pageboy.

All of a sudden John reached up and caught hold of the monk's hood and pulled him off his horse, heedless that the wretch fell on his head; for Little John was in a terrible mood and he wrenched out his sword and raised it high above his head. Then the monk saw that he would soon be dead and cried and wept for mercy in a loud, shrill voice.

"He was my master that you have brought to grief," said John, "but never shall you tell your tales unto the king."

And John delayed no longer but sliced off the monk's head with one great blow, and Much pulled the little pageboy off the horse and cut off his head too, for fear that he would tell. They buried them both right there, under the moss and the ling and then rode to London on the monk's horse, bearing with them the sheriff's letter. That got them into the king's presence, where Little John went down on one knee, crying boldly, "God save you, my liege!" and handing him the letter.

The king unfolded it and read it and said, "So might I thrive, there is no man in England I longed more to see than you—but where is the monk that should have brought this letter?"

"Ah," said John, "he was killed on the way in an ambush by Robin Hood's men. Only us two got away alive. But his death was worthy of him, I'll swear to that."

"Indeed, yes, well," said the king, "we'll have him buried with due honor in Westminster Abbey."

The king then gave Much and Little John twenty pounds a piece, made them yeomen of the crown with livery to boot, and bade them go straight back to the sheriff with sealed orders to bring the famous outlaw alive before the king himself. They took their leave and, on fresh mounts without even stopping for a cup of tea, rode like the wind back to Nottingham, where they found all the gates locked. John called up to the porter, "Why are all the gates locked?"

"Because Robin Hood is here in prison and his outlaws attack us every day, shooting at our men upon the walls!"

"Daft buggers," muttered Little John, then called up, "So let us in, you gormless noddy! Don't you recognize the king's livery? We have sealed orders from the king himself concerning Robin Hood!"

The porter hastily let them in, and it wasn't long before they were standing face to face with the sheriff of Nottingham, who doffed his hood as he opened the king's seal and read the letter. Suddenly he said, "Where is the monk who bore my letter?"

"Ah," said John, "the king is so fond of him, he's given him a place in Westminster Abbey."

That satisfied the sheriff, and that evening he gave them both a slap-up meal, with the best wine and ale in his cellar, during which the sheriff said, "We'll take him to London tomorrow, with three hundred knights and men-at-arms."

And that night, in their quarters, John said to Much, "We can't hope to rescue him tomorrow. We'll have to do it tonight."

And as soon as the sheriff was fast asleep, dead drunk as usual on his own wine and ale, the two outlaws made their way openly down into the dungeons. The soldiers on guard recognized the livery of the king and let them through and they came at last to Robin's cell.

"Gaoler," whispered Little John, "we have secret orders from the king to slit Robin Hood's throat right now, before he escapes from your incompetent sheriff. You can watch if you like—it'd be something to tell your grandchildren."

But as soon as the gaoler opened the outer door, Little John was upon him and had him pinned to the door by a knife through his throat. John took his keys and opened the inner door and stooped down into the narrow, foul-smelling cell, where they found Robin chained to the wall, lying in filthy, sodden straw. Little John unchained him, and great was their joy at seeing each other, though Robin could not stand. They cleaned him up as best they could and dressed him in the gaoler's clothes and helped him back up the stairs, John grunting, "Change of gaolers— this one drinks too much—almost as much as the sheriff!"

The soldiers roared with laughter and the three outlaws made their way up onto the walls, where they let themselves down by a good strong rope that Much had found in the dungeons; and so they slipped away, in the misty, grey, predawn light, back into the greenwood.

And so it was, when the cock began to crow and the day began to break, the sheriff's men found the gaoler dead and Robin Hood gone. Eeeeh, the sheriff *was* upset. He wept and wailed and tore out his hair and ground his teeth to splinters.

"I will never dare come before the king again!" he cried, "for if I do, he will surely hang me!"

But when the word came to the king, he said, "Little John fooled the sheriff but, in faith, he fooled me too, else I should have hanged the sheriff. Little John is true to his master and Robin Hood is bound to him for ever but let us speak no more of this, for Little John has fooled us all."

But Robin Hood was in merry Sherwood, as light as leaf on tree; and Little John turned to him and said, "The king has paid me the money you owed me, with interest, God bless him. And I have paid you a good turn for an evil one and brought you back under the greenwood tree. You can pay me when you feel like it. Now fare you well and have a good day." And he turned to go.

"Nay, by my truth!" cried Robin Hood. "So shall this never be! I make you the master, here and now, of all my men and me!"

"Nay, by my truth!" said Little John. "So shall that never be! Your good fellow and your friend—no other shall I be."

Then they embraced and kissed and wept on each other's shoulders; and then they made merry under the fine-spun leaves, feasting on venison pasties with ale and wine and they were glad.

| | |
|---|---|
| *Thus endys the talkyng of the munke,* | *Thus ends the talking of the monk,* |
| *And Robyn Hode i-wysse.* | *And Robin Hood likewise.* |
| *And God that is euer oure on trew kyng,* | *And God that is ever our own true king,* |
| *Bryng vs all to his blisse.* | *Bring us all to his bliss.* |

# Sir Gawain and Dame Ragnall

*An Arthurian legend retold by Dan Keding*

It was wintertime, when adventures are common and the veil between this world and the next becomes thin, that Arthur was hunting with his warriors for the New Year's feast. The king had ventured far from his knights and found himself quite alone in a clearing when he heard a voice.

"Arthur Pendragon! I have you in my grasp and I will not let go!"

Arthur turned at the call and saw a huge knight. Moss and leaves clung to the knight and his armor, once black now resembled an old tree that had grown comfortable in the forest. In fact, if he had not called out and moved, Arthur would have walked past him as part of the woods. But there was no denying the malice in his voice or the enormous war club that he held lightly in his hand.

"Sir you have me at a disadvantage. I do not know your name nor why you have a grievance against me."

"My name is unimportant. I am the knight cursed to roam these wilds. Now that I have the king of the Britons in my power, he shall not leave these woods alive."

The giant raised his club and was about to strike at Arthur. Arthur held up his hand and cried, "What manner of man would strike down another who is defenseless against him? You are armored and have sword and club, while I am dressed for hunting with nothing but a long knife and a bow and arrow. You will be held a coward for this act."

The knight laughed and replied, "I do not conduct myself by the rules of your company but by the enchantment that has laid me low. Still, I shall give you a chance, Arthur. I propose a riddle, and if you can bring me the answer one year from now, then I will spare your life, but if you fail you will bow your head to my sword. Are you willing?"

"I will answer your riddle or suffer your sword. What is the riddle to which you seek an answer?"

"What is it that every woman desires? You have one year Arthur."

Laughing, the knight turned away and melted into the forest.

Arthur rode back to his castle confident that he could solve the riddle. He would ask his queen, Guinevere, and she would know what every woman desires.

As soon as he returned, he sought out his queen and told her of the day's strange events and the riddle that he had to solve.

"The answer is simple, my lord. Every woman desires a husband just like you."

That was the answer Arthur was looking for all the time. It not only made him happy that the riddle was solved but that his queen thought so much of him.

One of her ladies in waiting smiled and spoke, "That is only true for some women. I think women want youth more than anything."

Another lady spoke and said, "I think they want beauty."

As word spread about the riddle, more and more answers came to the king's ear.

"A good husband that stays at home."

"A husband that leaves often."

"Gold and wealth."

"Jewels and silks."

And so it went on and on so that by the time one year had passed, Arthur had almost as many answers for his riddle as there were women in his kingdom. The day approached for Arthur to reunite with the giant warrior, and he was no closer to an answer. He rode out to meet his fate, deep in thought as he wove his way through the forest to that clearing. He was almost there when he heard someone call his name.

"Arthur. Arthur Pendragon, king of the Britons."

"Who calls out to me in this lonely place?"

"I do."

Arthur looked down, and there he saw a sight that froze his blood. If it were not for the human voice that escaped those lips and the fine silken dress that draped over that hideous shape, he would have thought that some monster, some creature of his worst nightmares, had come to life. She sat on a fallen tree. Her monstrous shape seemed to fill his eyes. Her face was twisted, and instead of teeth she had tusks like a wild boar. Her hair was filthy and matted and filled with insects. Her nose and eyes ran with puss, and her ears were little more than holes in the side of her head. Her hands were twisted, and instead of nails she had broken claws, filthy and ragged. Arthur had not seen nor imagined a more horrible sight.

"Madam, what would you have of me?"

"Arthur, it's not what I would have of you, but you of me. You see, my king, I know the answer to your riddle."

"The answer, please!" he cried. " I am not a hundred paces from my death."

"There is a price for everything Arthur, even the answer to such a simple riddle as this one."

"I will give you anything," cried Arthur.

"I knew you'd say that. I am Dame Ragnall, and I will hold you to that promise. The answer to your riddle is sovereignty. Women want the right to make their own choices."

Arthur stood there dumbfounded. How could he have been so stupid not to know. He spurred his horse forward till he came to the clearing. The dark knight was waiting.

"Do you have the answer?" The giant held his sword high above his head.

"Sovereignty." Arthur held his breath.

The giant warrior slowly lowered his sword. "So you have spoken to my sister Dame Ragnall. I hope the price will not prove too steep."

With those words, he turned and walked into the woods blending into the forest like an old tree.

Ragnall was also gone, nowhere to be found.

Arthur returned to his castle, and his queen and his knights and their ladies rejoiced at his safety. The next day, a great feast of thanksgiving was held, and there were stories told and songs sung and food and drink for all.

Suddenly the hall grew silent, and a cold wind passed through the company. The doors opened, and there stood Dame Ragnall. Everyone held their breath as she slowly made her way though the tables to the king's seat. The dogs hid beneath their masters' chairs, the hawks flew to the top rafters and remained silent, and even the singers and storytellers had no words.

"Welcome, Dame Ragnall. Will you join us for this feast? For without your help there would be no celebration."

"I thank you, though I have not come to feast, but to receive my payment."

"Of course," said Arthur. "What would you have of me?"

"I want the hand in marriage of your fairest knight."

The hall grew more silent as each man stared down at the table before him and for the first time wished they were not the best or fairest of Arthur's warriors.

Arthur had no choice, for the word of a king is law.

"Choose your husband, my lady."

Ragnall slowly walked through the hall passing behind each warrior. She stopped at Sir Kay, whispered in his ear and he turned white as a ghost. She stopped at Galahad who blushed violently. Finally, she stopped behind Sir Gawain.

"This is the one I want for my husband."

There was a hue and cry, especially from the ladies of the court.

"Not Gawain. He is the fairest and most brave."

"Don't I deserve such a man?" snarled Ragnall.

Gawain stood and faced Ragnall.

"I am my king's man and so am bound by his promise. Lady, will you honor me and be my bride?"

Ragnall consented and the celebration became a wedding feast. Ragnall stuffed food into her mouth till there was no room left and it oozed out between her coarse lips. She tore the meat apart with her claw-like hands and drank wine till it ran down onto the table. All of the company watched in horror, knowing Gawain's fate.

Soon the feast was over, and Ragnall and Gawain retired to their wedding chamber.

"Kiss me, Gawain." Ragnall stood there, waiting for his embrace.

Gawain hesitated for a moment.

"So this is the way you treat your bride, is it? Perhaps there is no honor in the court of Arthur."

"I am your true husband," said Gawain and he walked to her, cupped her face in his hands, and he kissed her.

"Turn your back and wait over there while I dress for bed."

Gawain waited as he was told, but then he heard a voice. It was not the hard, strangled croak of Ragnall, but a voice sweet with tenderness and love.

"Gawain, you can turn now."

The woman who stood before him was beautiful, her eyes radiant like a spring sun and her face full of life and joy.

"Where is my bride?" cried Gawain, as his hand reached for his sword.

"I am Ragnall," said the lady. "I was imprisoned in that body by a wicked wizard and cursed as was my brother, the giant who challenged Arthur. I could not break the curse till some man accepted me as his bride and kissed me of his own free will. You have broken the curse, Gawain, but only part of it. You see, now I can be beautiful for you when we come to bed each night and cursed and loathsome during the day or beautiful during the day and bewitched and pitiful at night. Will you be mocked by your friends on account of your bride or will you find me horrid and repulsive each night? The choice is yours."

Gawain spoke without hesitation.

"No, it's not. My lady, the choice is yours. If there is pain or shame, it will be yours and so should the decision. You choose."

Dame Ragnall laughed and her laughter sparkled through the room.

"You have broken the curse completely, for you have given me my sovereignty."

The next morning Arthur and his court were stunned to meet the real Ragnall and hear her story. Her brother was sent for, and he joined that company of knights. Gawain and Ragnall lived together in love and joy.

# The Alderley Legend

*A Cheshire story retold by Nick Hennessey*

There was once a farmer on his way to sell his mare at Macclesfield market. He had risen early and set out when the flat fields were still clagged with cold mist. But as he climbed the road where it ran steep over the hill at Alderley Edge, the sun rose too, broadening the day. The cathedral of beech trees that domed above resounded in a choir of autumn color. Red, yellow, gold, and green the leaves shone like treasure. And by the time the farmer reached the top and stood on Castle Rock, his chest rasping from the climb, the clods of mist on the plain beneath him had already begun to dissolve at the touch of the early sun. He took a moment for himself, to catch his breath and enjoy the view. And what a view it was! To the west the land glided off to the grey sea, to the north gathered the distant outline of Winter Hill and to the East the Pennines, stretching north to south like a great giant sleeping beneath a blanket of forest, field and moor.

"Now that," said the farmer, "is real wealth! What a sight, eh?" The horse tossed its head and thumped the ground with a hoof. "As my old man used to say, them's that don't know the land, don't know themselves."

The farmer looked out again, narrowing his gaze, glancing this way and that across the landscape that lay before him.

"Riches indeed. But we've still a ways to go on the road, you and me," he said as he heaved a leg up over the horse's broad back and settled in. "And views won't feed a hungry belly. Come on girl." He pulled on the rope halter, and the horse turned and gently clopped on down the track.

Enjoying the autumn colors in the trees, the farmer began to whistle, a tune that soon fell in time with the soft thud of hooves on the ground. He felt good about the day. Even though he was fond of his old mare and he knew he would be returning alone on foot, he felt in good spirits.

He was lost in his tune when the road passed Thieves' Hole.

"That's a fine horse!" came a voice. The horse started, throwing up its head. The farmer snapped out of his tune, pulled the horse to rest, and looked to the roadside. Sitting on the roots of a tree beneath a low spread of golden leaves was an old man, a crooked stick in his hands.

"Er ... Er ... Ta very much!" he stammered, still a little surprised.

The old man stood up, hunched on his stick, and shuffled closer.

"You wouldn't be selling her by any chance, would you?"

"Actually I would. I'm on me way to market right now."

The old man's eyes shone a little and his withered mouth curled in a half smile.

"I'll give you ten pieces of silver," he said, drawing up close to the horse and running his hands down its strong neck.

"Well, that'd save us a journey, wouldn't it, girl?" the farmer muttered. But a cold wind blustered through the trees reminding him of the long winter ahead and his meager harvest.

"Thanks for the offer, old man," he said, "but ten pieces of silver is a fairer price for buying than it is for selling. And it's a fine day for a market, so I'll be on me way."

But as the farmer set off once more down the track, the old man called out behind him, "You'll find no sale at the market today! And I'll be waiting for your return!"

The farmer shut his ears to the old man's words and set his eyes on the road ahead.

Well, the sun was high like a crown in the sky, when the farmer and his horse wandered in to Macclesfield. The streets were thick with folk speaking in all manner of tongues. There were people from as far away as Derby, Matlock, and even Chester. There was so much excitement, so much bustle and barter, with the smell of spit roast and wood smoke in the air. Children running, lambs bleating, pigs squealing in the pens and the busy nod and shake of trade.

The farmer found himself a pitch, tied off his horse, and stood by waiting for the first keen eyed bidder to pass by. But he waited and he waited and he waited and he waited. All around him money passed from hand to hand, the market thrived, but not a single person stopped even to cast an eye over his beast. He tried calling out, "Horse for sale!" But no one turned, no one looked. It was as if he wasn't even there.

By late afternoon when the crowds were gone and only a few drunks stumbled in the dirt, the farmer had had enough. He climbed up on the back of his horse and with a heavy heart began the long journey home. He didn't understand it. It had been a good day in the market, but no one had paid any interest to him at all.

The sun was lying its head in the west as the farmer once more passed Thieves' Hole.

"I'll give you ten pieces of silver." The farmer looked up and in the deepening shadows saw the old man hunched at the roadside.

"Fourteen and you've a deal!" said the farmer, trying not to sound desperate.

The old man stood up and smiled, "Then follow me," he said, and cut off from the road through the trees and the farmer followed behind. And they went from Thieves' Hole to Seven Firs, from Seven Firs to Golden Stone, from Golden Stone to Stormy Point and Saddlebole and there they came to a hard face of rock. Like a blind man the old stranger ran his hands across the gnarled rock, muttering words under his breath. All of sudden there came a crack of thunder, a deep shudder in the ground, and the rock cleaved in two revealing a passageway that led down into the belly of the earth.

"Follow me. And mind your way," said the stranger. So with the halter rope in his hand, and his heart in his mouth, the farmer followed down into the hillside. Down and down and down they went. Deeper and deeper and deeper. The farmer steadied himself against the cold stone wall, and the mare pushed up close behind.

The path led down, steeply at first but then leveled out until they came to two great iron gates that clanked and wheeled open as they stepped through into a great cavern with a high doming roof. The farmer looked in amazement. On the ground lay armed warriors with shields and spears at their sides. And in the middle raised up higher than the rest, lay a man with a crown on his breast. The farmer gawped.

"Are they . . . dead?"

"Dead? No," said the stranger, "they are sleeping. They are dreaming. They are waiting for a time when the call will come and they will rise and ride once more through the land. For more years than I can tell I have searched for a horse for the king, he that lies above the rest. And now I have found it. That horse is yours, and for that you will be paid well indeed." He raised a thin finger toward a corner of the cave where there lay a heap of glimmering treasure.

"Take only coins and only what you need."

The farmer let loose his hold on the halter rope and stepped carefully over the sleeping warriors. He stooped to his knees in front of the glinting hoard. He had never seen such wealth. There were not only coins, but all manner of things. A cauldron made of burning gold with a rim of pearls. A kind of chessboard of gold with pieces of silver. A sword and a sheath that flashed like moonlight on the mere. The farmer ran his hands through the pile, fingering piece after piece, his eyes glancing this way and that over the harvest of wealth that lay before him.

"Riches indeed," he muttered, wondering what to take. But he remembered the old man's words and so reaching down and took a handful of gold, crammed it into one pocket, and then a handful of silver and crammed it into another. He stood up and stepped carefully over the sleeping men.

"You have taken wisely," said the old stranger, "but before you go remember this: as one day your horse will carry the king through the land, so too must you bear what you have seen, and though it is a mystery it should never be a secret. You must tell all those that have the ears to listen, though few that may be. And now you must leave."

So the farmer turned his back on the old man, the sleeping king, his mare, and the gold, and as the iron gates clanked shut, he made his way back up the passageway. Up and up and up he climbed, higher and higher until at last he was out on the hillside with the hard rock behind him and night breeze on his face.

And the sun was just rising up bright over Shining Tor in the east when the farmer, his chest rasping with the climb, stood once more on Castle Rock. He looked out across the Cheshire Plain, as the early light fingered the wealth of fields and forests below him. He put his hands to his pockets and felt the coins.

"As my old man used to say, them's that don't know the land don't know themselves." He turned and left.

# Stories for When the Sun Sets

# A Rhyme

*A rhyme from Newcastle retold by Jack Douglas*
*(Amy's Granddad)*

*There was a man of double deed,*
*Who sowed his garden full of seed;*
*And when the seed began to grow,*
*It was like a garden full of snow;*
*And when the snow began to fall,*
*It was like a bird upon a wall;*
*And when the bird away did fly,*
*It was like an eagle in the sky;*
*And when the sky began to roar,*
*It was like a lion at the door;*
*And when the door began to crack,*
*It was like a stick across your back;*
*And when your back begins to smart,*
*It's like a knife stabbed in your heart;*
*And when your heart begins to bleed,*
*You're dead, you're dead, you're dead indeed!*

# Teeny Tiny

*A story retold by Amy Douglas*

*Note to the storyteller: This story really only works when read aloud. Suitable for five to eight year olds, it is an old English version of the classic jump story. The tension should be built throughout the story, and the last paragraph should be slow and quiet, the children wondering what the teeny tiny woman is going to do with the courage she has plucked up, before shouting "TAKE IT!"*

Once upon a time there was a teeny tiny woman who lived in a teeny tiny house in a teeny tiny village.

One day the teeny tiny woman decided to go for a teeny tiny walk. She put on her teeny tiny bonnet, then her teeny tiny coat and went out of her teeny tiny door.

She walked down a teeny tiny road until she came to a teeny tiny gate. She went through the teeny tiny gate and on the other side was a teeny tiny path. She walked along the teeny tiny path to the top of a teeny tiny hill. At the top of the teeny tiny hill was a teeny tiny church with a teeny tiny churchyard. In the teeny tiny churchyard she saw a teeny tiny bone on a teeny tiny grave. Now the teeny tiny woman thought to her teeny tiny self,

"That teeny tiny bone will just make a teeny tiny bit of soup for my teeny tiny tea." So she picked up the teeny tiny bone and went home to her teeny tiny house.

When she got home, she felt a teeny tiny bit tired. So, she went up her teeny tiny stairs to her teeny tiny bed. She put the teeny tiny bone into a teeny tiny cupboard and went to sleep.

When she had been asleep for a teeny tiny time, she was woken up by a teeny tiny voice saying,

*"Give me back my bone!"*

At this, the teeny tiny woman was a teeny tiny bit frightened so she hid her teeny tiny head under the teeny tiny bedclothes. After a teeny tiny time, she stopped shaking and went back to sleep.

But after she had been asleep for a teeny tiny time, she was woken up again by the teeny tiny voice from the teeny tiny cupboard, but this time it was a teeny tiny bit louder,

*"Give me back my bone!"*

At this the teeny tiny woman was a teeny tiny bit more frightened so she hid her teeny tiny head a teeny tiny bit further under the bed clothes. This time she lay shaking for a teeny tiny bit longer until she went back to sleep.

But when she had been asleep for a teeny tiny time she was woken up by the teeny tiny voice form the teeny tiny cupboard, this time a teeny tiny bit louder than before,

## *"Give me back my bone!"*

At this the teeny tiny woman was a teeny tiny bit more frightened still, so she hid her teeny tiny head even further under the bed clothes, so that her toes were sticking out the end and she picked up the teeny tiny pillow and put it over her head. And this time shc lay there shaking for a quite a long time before she went back to sleep.

But when she had been asleep for a teeny tiny time, she was woken up by the teeny tiny voice from the teeny tiny cupboard and this time it was a teeny tiny bit louder still,

## *"Give me back my bone!"*

At this the teeny tiny woman was terribly frightened, but she plucked up all of her teeny tiny courage, took a deep breath, and stuck her teeny tiny head out of the teeny tiny bed clothes and in her loudest teeny tiny voice said,

## *"TAKE IT!"*

# The Dead Moon

*A story from Lincolnshire retold by Dan Keding*

Long ago the marshes and wetlands of Lincolnshire were a dangerous place to walk when the Moon did not shine. When her bright light was hidden, then the bogles and the dead things and those horrors that crawl along the ground and through the imaginations of men and women waited in the darkness and in the bogs for those that chanced to stray from the path. These monsters crept through the wasteland and through the villages causing harm to the folks who lived near the fens.

At length the Moon came to hear that the people of the fens were hounded by these horrors and she decided to come down from the sky and see what she could do to help keep her people safe. When the Moon had come to the time of the month when she normally turned her back on the Earth, she stepped down and walked through the marshlands. She wore a long black cloak with black hood to hide her radiant face and her shining hair. She walked through the bogs, and it was a fearful place even for her. There were dark pools of water at every turn, twisted branches that reached out for her cloak, and quaking mud that seemed to announce her presence. Everywhere there was darkness except for the small pool of light that streamed from her shoes as she walked. As she walked deeper into the bogs, she knew she was not alone. Witches rode past her on huge black cats grinning at her as they passed by. The evil eye stared at her at every turn. The will-o'-the-wykes danced around her their lanterns swinging on their backs. Dead folks rose from the depths of the marshes, their faces chalk white, their eyes red, their flesh hanging on their bones as they beckoned her and reached for her as she passed. The Moon now saw what the people of the fens feared, and she feared it too, but she was determined to see it all and so she walked on.

As she turned a bend in the path her foot slipped on a rock and she reached out to catch her balance, but the snag she reached for twisted and caught her wrist and held her fast. A root caught her ankle and then another and another till she was held fast and in the power of those who hated her. She stretched and pulled and fought, but it was no use. She was caught. As she stood in the dark and battled her enemies, she heard a voice crying out in the night. It was a man. Lost in the bogs, he had left the path and followed the will-o'-the-wykes' light unaware of their dangers. As he plunged through the bogs the dead rose to meet him and the witches laughing in chorus rode past him. The roots of the dead trees caught him and began to pull him down. He was doomed.

The Moon was so angry that another would fall to the darkness right before her very eyes that she struggled and though she could not free her hands she threw her hood off her face and her light shone like a beacon across the bogs. The creatures of the night shrank from that radiance and the man, free of their hold, saw the safety of the path and ran from those terrors as fast as his legs would take him.

The Moon was so weary from her struggles that she fell forward into the deep, dark pools of the bogs, her hood covering her light once more. Once the darkness came back, her enemies taunted her even more, striking at her and driving her deeper into the black water and oozing mud. The dead folk held her fast, angry that her light had kept them in their graves all those years. The bogles brought a huge stone and placed it over her to keep her prisoner in the murky waters. The witches laughed and sang and knew that now their spells would have no rival and those they preyed upon no champion. Two will-o'-the-wykes kept guard above her watery grave and delighted that their false light was the only light left in the darkness of the bogs. When the morning came, the Moon was buried deep and no one knew where to look or how to find her.

Days passed and nights passed and the people of the marsh looked forward to the new moon and the safety and comfort her light would bring.

But the Moon never came back. Instead the bogles and the witches, the dark things that crawl along the edge of the bogs and the dead that rise with the darkness all became bolder. Now every night they were the rulers of the marshlands and now they ventured down the roads and into the villages. Scratching at the doors of the bog folk, trying their latches and their windows, screaming out in the night so that no one could rest and the night was filled with fear and terror. Sorrow gripped the land with a cold hand of darkness. No one could travel at night, no one was safe at night, and no one could sleep except in the realm of nightmares.

The days turned into a week and the weeks turned into a month and still the Moon was hidden from the night. Each day the villagers talked of what they could do until they decided to visit the wise old woman that lived near the old mill.

"Please, lady, could you help us find the Moon? Her light has left us and the darkness is everywhere. We fear that the bogles and witches, that those who are dead but walk at night will become bolder, and that there will be no safety at all."

The wisewoman looked into her mirror and into her bowl of water and into her book, but all was dark and no answer came to her.

"Everything is dark and dead and I have no answer for you. Tonight set straw and salt and a button on your door step to keep the horrors away. If you hear any news at all, come back to me and I will search again."

The people did as they were told, but still each night was too long and each day too short. The people talked of nothing else. The folks talked in their homes, they talked in their shops, they talked at the inn—always about the Moon. They thought she had abandoned them.

One day at the inn as they talked about the Moon, a man from another village on the far side of the bogs overheard their conversation. Suddenly he jumped up and shouted, "In my terror I'd forgotten, but I reckon that I know where the Moon is alright. I was lost on the bogs, the night creatures all around me when suddenly a light shone so bright they were driven off, and I found the path again and returned home safely. I think I remember a shining face and white, white hair that filled the night. The woman was standing near a black snag in the water. As I raced along the path toward home, the light disappeared again and all was dark. Could it have been her?"

The people of the village took this news to the wise old woman. She looked in her mirror and into her bowl of water and into her book, and she saw a shred of light.

"What you must do is this: go into the bogs tonight. Go together and stay together. Put a small stone in your mouth, take a hazel stick in your hand, and don't say a word till you are all home safely. Walk together and do not be afraid. Make your way into the heart of the marsh and keep looking till you find a candle, a cross, and a coffin. You will be close to her then."

The next night the villagers came together and without a word all put a small stone in their mouths and held a hazel stick in their hands. Together they walked deep into the bogs. As they walked they heard whispers all around them and the sounds of the night pressing closer and closer. Slimy hands reached out and touched them but shrank back from the hazel wands the villagers held. The dead and the bogles, the witches and the creatures of the night all watched as the people of the fens walked deep into the heart of the bogs.

Suddenly they saw what seemed like a faint candle glowing in the night. It was a will-o'-the-wyke sitting on a black snag, the snag's bare arms outstretched every bit like a cross. Below the snag they saw the great rock, part of it sticking out of the black water, shaped like a huge coffin. They all fell to their knees and all said the Lord's Prayer to themselves—forward for the cross and then backward to keep the bogles and the witches and dead away. They all took hold of the stone and pushed and heaved till it moved. For a moment they saw the most beautiful, radiant face looking up at them with such hope and such gratitude. Then the light shot through the night up toward the sky and the creatures of darkness screamed in pain from the light. The next moment the Moon was back in the sky shining down with all her glory onto the bogs. The path home was as safe and as clear as the day.

Since that day the Moon shines her brightest light over the bogs and the fens, for she knows all the evil that is hidden there and all the terror that it can bring. She also remembers the courage of the marsh folk and how they walked into the darkness to search for her when she was buried and dead and lost to the night.

# The Golden Ball

*A story from Yorkshire, transcribed from the
telling of Richard Walker*

A long time ago in Halifax in Yorkshire there were two sisters. And you know how it is with sisters. Generally one is a little bit tidier than the other, one tends to get things right a bit more often than the other. One's just got the edge, know what I mean? Well these two sisters were like that, but they loved each other dearly and they used to go around together quite a lot.

When they were fairly young they went to a fair that came to Halifax and on the way back from the fair they met with a man. This man was all in gold. All his clothes were gold, his hair was gold, his skin almost shone with gold. He was a golden man and in each hand he had a golden ball. He was throwing them up in the air and as the sisters came up to him he said, "These are for you. These are a present for you." And to each of the sisters he gave one golden ball. He said, "You can keep these balls as long as you want—play with them, do what you will with them, but if you should lose them, then you would surely hang and die, because the penalty for losing the golden ball is death."

So the two sisters took the balls home and they became their favorite playthings. They played with them constantly and had a wonderful time with them. They grew up, but still they played with their golden balls. Until one day, neither lost her golden ball, and on that day this is how it happened.

One of the sisters—remember I told you that one of them wasn't quite so clever as the other? Well, *that* one was playing with her golden ball, and she was playing with it by the railings that surrounded an old house in Halifax. Now this house was a bit strange, a bit spooky, a bit haunted. Nobody went near it, nobody liked it at all, and it had been empty a long time. She was throwing her ball up into the air and catching it when it was as though it took a mind to itself. Over the railings it sailed and into the long damp grass on the other side. Then, as she watched, it sort of rolled along to some bushes and then it rolled between them, and she could see it on a dirty old path. And so it was lost from sight and she'd lost her golden ball!

She went back and confessed, and oh, it was terrible! She was seized and put into prison to be hung by the neck until dead, because the penalty still had to be enforced and nobody would get the ball back, save her boyfriend. Because she was lucky, she had a boyfriend who was young and loyal and as fine a lad as ever you've met. This lad said, "I'll get your ball back!" But he'd got nothing. He got a little bit of food together, put it in a bag, and tied it to his belt.

And then he thought, "I'd better have a weapon to go into that house." But he didn't have a sword or anything like that. He took a rusty old ploughshare, cleaned it up as best he could with a bit of damp grass, stuffed it in his belt, and away he went at night. He climbed over the railings that surrounded the haunted, horrible, dank, dark, dreary, dismal house. And as he landed on the other side, up popped a witch. And she looked at him and pointed and in a creaky old voice she said, "Ahhhh … you've come, have you? You've come for the golden ball, have you? Well, my lad, maybe you'll get it and maybe you won't. You must spend three nights in the house, but in the daytime you'll sleep, because you won't sleep at night. Hee hee hee hee …" and she vanished.

Well the lad didn't know what was going on, but he made his way to the big house and to the door in front of it. He pushed it, and it opened creakily by his push. He made his way inside, and it was just getting dark. He made his way upstairs thinking he'd better find himself a bedroom, somewhere to settle down if he was to spend some time there. So he went upstairs and found a bedroom, and he settled down and was just lying down, thinking about some sleep, when he heard a slipping and a slithering down below. He went to the window and the window looked out on a courtyard. As he watched, the paving stones of the courtyard slithered away and out of them crept all the ghosties and ghoulies, the greenies, the kerbobbolins, all the nasties from down, down, deep in the bowels of the Earth.

And they crept up and they were crackling and crunching and playing, and they were playing with the golden ball and one was yelling, "Give it to me, give it to me, I want a go, give it to me, go on!"

And they yelled and they yelled and they played and they played with the golden ball, and then suddenly they said, "Give us a giant! Give us a giant!" They pointed to the lad who was looking through the window.

"Hey you!" they said, "We want a giant."

And the lad thought, "A giant?"

And then he heard outside the door the footfall, the heavy, deep, footfall, of a giant. Quick as a wink the lad hid behind the door, and in came the most horrible giant you've ever seen, with long, lank hair down to his waist, boots as big as the average man. He bowed his head to get in, and he looked around the room. And he looked for the lad and the lad was hiding behind the door, so he went over to the window and pulled up the window as far as he could. And he looked down to where all the nasties were below. And as he looked down the lad went up, and he grabbed his ploughshare, the blade that he was using as a sword, and with the most almighty thwack he could do, he chopped the giant in half. And the top half fell down below where all the nasties picked it up and were playing with it and then the lad with all his strength picked up the bottom half and heaved it down below. So they grabbed the giant in his two halves and they slipped and slithered with him down, down through the cracks, through the holes in the pavings. They pulled him and they pulled him and took him down, down below the Earth.

And *that* was the *first* night.

Well, the lad slept through the second day. He had to make his food last, but he had a little bit of it, and he was just waking up on the second night when once again he heard the slithering and the sliding of the pavers down below. He looked down below and out of all the cracks and the crannies, the holes came all the ghosties and the ghoulies, the toboosties and the nasties—all the nasty creatures you can think of came and once again they were playing with the golden ball. They were playing with the ball for an hour or more and then they looked up at the lad and said, "Hey! Give us another giant, maybe you'll win your ball back yet, we want another giant, we want another giant!"

And as the lad listened, he heard coming up the stairs the footfall of an even bigger, even uglier, even more horrible giant—at least that's what he thought it was. And he was right. This time he didn't hide behind the door because he thought the giant might know. So this time he hid behind the bed. The door opened and in came a two-headed giant, the most horrible of two-headed giants, with green lanky hair, a green lanky beard, and horrible bloodshot eyes. He looked behind the door.

"Right, you're not there," he said. "I thought you'd be there," he said, "Cos that's where you got my brother. Ooh, where are you?" And he looked around the room and he went over to the window and he looked through the window, and the lad quaked in his corner. And then he went to the chimney breast. Now it was a big chimney, one of those you could climb right into and look right the way up the chimney. The giant looked up the chimney. "Are you up there," he said, "hiding?"

And as he did that, the lad leapt out, and he raised his plough blade and he chopped and he chopped and he chopped, the hardest he could, and he chopped that giant in half, too. Well, with the top half, by the arms, the giant pulled himself up, up, up, up, up the chimney all the way up. And then one arm reached down and a leg was climbing up and he grabbed the leg from the lower half. And then the two halves of the giant as best they could made their way along the roof, but they slipped and they slithered and they fell down below. Down into the court-yard where all the ghosties and the boosties, the gowdies and tobogoblins and the nasties were waiting and they held him and they grabbed him and then they disappeared down, down, down into the depths with the two halves of this second and most horrible giant.

And *that* was the *second* night.

Well the lad slept through the next day, and when he woke up, he heard all the creaking and all the groaning of the nasties and kerbogglies, but he didn't hear where they'd come from and he didn't know where they were. Because they seemed closer. They seemed as if they were under the very bed he was lying on. And sure enough they were, because they were playing with the ball under the bed. All laughing and whispering and saying, "He'll never find us here! We'll get him, we'll get him."

All of a sudden a wrinkled hand with long fingernails came round the corner and onto the bed, and the lad snicked with his plough blade and chopped it off. And it fell, but then another hand came, and he snicked and chopped and all night long hands came round reaching for him and all night long he chopped with his blade. He chopped at feet and he chopped at heads that came round and he chopped and he chopped and he chopped …

But did he get the golden ball?

The next day the girl was to be hung. She was at the gallows tree and a noose had been hung from the highest and the strongest branch of that tree and she was standing on an old stool—the noose to be put around her neck and then to be pushed off the stool so that she was to throttle or break her neck if she was lucky.

She was standing there and the hangman was with her.

"Right, me dear, have you made your will? Have you done all you need to do?"

And she said, "J—j—just a minute, look, LOOK!" And in the distance she saw someone coming and she said, "Look, look—I see my father coming. Oh father, have you brought my golden ball and come to set me free?"

But her father said, "Nay, lass, I've not brought thy golden ball nor come to set thee free, but I have come to see thee hung upon this gallows tree."

And then she looked and she looked and further, she saw somebody else coming and she said, "Wait, wait hangman, I see my mother coming, Mother, have you brought my golden ball and come to set me free?"

But her mother said, "Nay lass, I've not brought thy golden ball nor come to set thee free, for I have come to see thee hung upon this gallows tree."

Well the next to come was her sister and she said, "Sister, sister, have you brought my golden ball and come to set me free?"

And her sister said, "Nay lass, I've not brought thy golden ball nor come to set thee free, for I have come to see thee hung upon this gallows tree."

And the next was her grandmother, and so it went through the whole family and the hangman was getting more and more impatient, until he said, "Stop lass, no more. No more, my girl, now you must hang."

He put the coarse rope noose around her neck and he pulled it tight and got it just right. And she said, "No, just a minute, wait, wait, WAIT!"

And she saw her lover, her boyfriend, coming and she said, "Boyfriend, lover, have you brought my golden ball and come to set me free?"

And he said, "YES, lass! I've brought thy golden ball and I've come to set thee free, for I will *not* see thee hang upon this gallows tree!"

 *And it's one for sorrow, two for joy,*
*Three for a girl, four for a boy,*
*Five for England, six for France,*
*Play us a tune, let's have us a dance.*

# Jenny Greenteeth

*A story from Lancashire retold by Des Charnley*

In the county of Lancashire in northwest England, there is a town called Clitheroe. A pleasant country town guarded by a castle. The River Ribble flows by the town. At a small village called Waddington, the road crosses over the river. The wise traveler remains on the road—and so should you. Let me explain why.

Many, many years ago, there lived in a wood close to Waddington a young woman called Jenny Greenteeth. She lived on her own in a tidy little cottage. Every Wednesday she would go to the market in Clitheroe. When buying at the stalls, people would turn to look at her, for she was very beautiful. Is it any wonder, then, that she was seen by the son of the local lord. He immediately fell in love with her, and very soon they were walking out together. People were saying it wouldn't be long before they were wed. They seemed to be such a happy pair.

In fact, this son did propose, and Jenny accepted him. The lord of the castle agreed that Jenny should become one of the family. Arrangements were made for the wedding. Then came tragedy. I do not know what happened. All I know is that Jenny got a letter saying that the wedding was off and that the son was bound for a new life in London. There was no place for Jenny in this new life. This news came to Jenny just twenty-four hours before the wedding was due to take place.

Jenny changed after that. From being a sweet, loving, carefree beautiful girl she became a plain, wizened old maid. She never more came into Clitheroe. The company of humans was loathsome to her. Her little cottage in the wood was the only place she wanted to be. Now she despised beauty. The lovely spring flowers, she would trample underfoot. Mushrooms would be kicked until they weren't worth picking. Birds' nests would be shaken from the trees. The berries that the birds needed to feed on in the winter, Jenny would crush between her cruel fingers.

That part of the wood where Jenny lived, well, it always seemed to be raining there. Nature was mourning for the hurt that was being suffered by her children. But nature does not forget or forgive an injury. She was just biding her time.

One morning Jenny went to draw water from the well. There was wet moss around the well, and Jenny's boots slipped. She reached forward to grip the rope that lowered the bucket down into the well, thinking it would prevent her from falling down, down, down, into the well. When the bucket reached the level of the water, far down the well it stopped. Jenny was still holding the rope, but the hem of her skirt was saturated. Her boots were soaked through, and she could not get a grip on the smooth walls of the well. There was no way that she could pull herself up. Jenny called and called for help. Her voice became hoarse from shouting, but nobody came to help her. Jenny died in the well.

But that is not the end of my story. For Jenny still appears on the banks of the River Ribble at Waddington. Either as weeds, or thick nettles, or brambles. She is a shape shifter. Every seven years, someone dies in that river, drowned by cruel Jenny Greenteeth. So take my advice and never, never go anywhere near that river.

# The Standing Stones

*A story from Cornwall retold by Dan Keding
(one of his gifts from England, from Mike Rust)*

A long, long time ago, but not so long that we can't remember, there was a king in Britain named Arthur, and he had a magician, a wizard named Merlin. Now Merlin had three sons, and to call them ugly would be an insult to ugly people. But he was their father and he couldn't see the truth. So Merlin chose three of the most beautiful young women in the whole land to be their brides. But when the young ladies saw them they refused, and Merlin became enraged. He had his soldiers take the ladies to a cliff that looked out across the sea. And there he turned them into three standing stones to look out across the sea and be battered by the wind and the mist for all times. Now Merlin was a great wizard, but he didn't get this spell just right, and each Midsummer Night's Eve the three standing stones turned back into young women. Then they would walk into the sea and they would scrub and scrub and try to wash the stone from out of their flesh, and when dawn came in the east, they would hurry back to the cliff and once again turn into standing stones. The story has it that if you see them move, you'll surely die.

Now the generations passed and the centuries with them, and a man returned to the village by the sea by the standing stones. He returned after the death of his wife so that he could raise his son in the village where he had grown up so the boy could know his grandparents and hear the stories that his father had heard. One Midsummer Night's Eve, the family sat round the hearth and talked, and the talk turned to the ladies of stone.

"There's nothing to it," said the man. "It's just one of those stories that the storytellers like to tell, and who can believe a storyteller? I'll go there this very night and prove they're just stones."

His mother begged, his father pleaded, but he only gave in when his son asked him not to go.

"All right, I won't go, but you all know I'm right," he said, and with that they went to bed.

Just before dawn the boy awoke, and he awoke with feeling that something was wrong. He dressed quickly and went to his father's room, but his father was gone, and the boy knew. He ran to the cliff and got there just as the sun was coming up in the sky. The boy turned toward the stones, and he watched in horror as one of them slowly moved back to where it belonged. He ran down to the beach, and it was he who found the father, dead in the water. The police said he had been caught by the undertow as he swam, but the people of the village knew better. When the boy told his grandparents what he'd seen, they sent him away.

He went to live far from the sea in a small town. He went to the university and eventually taught there. But at night he dreamed of the sea.

When he was an old man and ready to retire, he thought to himself, "I would enjoy living by the sea again. Did I really see what I thought I saw? It was so long ago. Perhaps it is just an old story the storytellers tell, and who can believe a storyteller? Who indeed?"

He found a catalogue, and in it he found a house in Mexico by the sea. He sent his belongings across the water, and he followed. He took a train across America and down into Mexico, and there he found the village. The people were friendly.

"Señor, you will love your hacienda. It is a beautiful house with a great veranda, a porch that faces the garden. And on the far side of the garden, behind a row of bushes, the Pacific washes against your shore."

The old man walked down the road and with each step he felt younger. He found the house, and it was beautiful. His belongings were waiting inside. He walked through to the veranda and gazed at the lovely garden. He could hear the ocean beating against the beach. He walked to the hedge and parted it to gaze at the water and fell back for there at the water's edge were three standing stones.

It couldn't be. It must be a mistake, a coincidence. He almost ran back to the house. He made himself some tea and started to unpack. When he glanced out the window again, the stones were inside the garden. He closed his eyes and kept saying that it was not happening. He ate his lunch, his back to the window. When he finally looked out, they were in the middle of the garden.

The old man poured himself a drink, sat on the veranda, and watched the stones. He fell asleep and when he woke, they were next to the porch railing. He stood and leaned over to look at them, and when he did one of the stones touched him.

They say that in a village in Mexico, there is a story told by the storytellers about a standing stone on a veranda of a beautiful house. And the story goes that each Midsummer Night's Eve, it turns into an old man who walks into the ocean and tries to scrub the stone from out of his flesh, and if you see him he will surely kill you.

# The Girl and the Anorak

*A story from Birmingham retold by Graham Langley*

When I grew up in Birmingham, I had a mate whose dad was a bus driver. His dad's name was Jock Miller. He was from Scotland, and lots of men from Scotland get called Jock. He drove the Midland Red buses, which means that he didn't drive around the city, but he drove out of the city and into the countryside round about. Now his route took him out to the west of Birmingham, into Worcestershire and Shropshire.

One day he was leaving Digbeth Bus Station and heading off through town. It was a lovely sunny day, and the bus was half full of people. He drove through town and out along the Hagley Road, heading west. He got to Quinton and headed for Halesowen down Mucklows Hill, which in those days was a narrow, steep, winding road.

As he drove down the hill, the clouds came over, the wind started to blow, and the rain came down so hard that by the time he was driving out into the countryside on the other side of Halesowen, he was driving through a major storm. His windscreen wipers were throwing themselves backward and forward trying to wash away the rivers of rain that ran down the screen.

When he was out there in the countryside, driving along the little lanes, a young woman got to get off the bus, and all she was wearing was a light summer frock that she had been wearing downtown.

"My Goodness," said Jock, "You can't get off the bus dressed like that. You'll catch your death of cold. It's not fit for a dog out there. Here, you'd better borrow my anorak." And he lent her the old anorak that he kept in the cab in case he needed it.

Well, she thanked him very much and she said, "You must call and collect it from me," and she showed him the little lane where she lived and described the house and everything to him. So he said he would.

Now a few weeks later, he was up there in his car and he thought, "Oh I'll just nip in and get my coat." So he found the lane, and sure enough there was the house just as she'd described it. He pulled up and parked. He went up the path and knocked on the door.

An old woman came to the door, and Jock said, "Can I speak to the young woman who lives here, please?"

"Oh, there's no young woman lives here, and there hasn't been for many years now."

"That's strange," says Jock. "A few weeks ago I lent my anorak to a young woman on my bus. She was about nineteen years of age, and she had long black hair. She said she lived in this house."

Now at this the woman got very upset. "I don't know who you are or who it is that sent you, but you've no right coming here with such tales upsetting old folks. Go away. Go away and leave us alone."

Well Jock was real surprised. He had no idea what he could possibly have said that would have upset the old woman, and he began to apologize.

"I'm dreadfully sorry, I must have made a mistake."

Then an old man came to the door, and again Jock apologized for his mistake.

"Perhaps there's another house nearby just the same?" But he was told that no, there wasn't.

Then just as he was about to leave, he passed them, and there on the piano was a photograph.

"Oh, excuse me," he said, "That picture. That picture on the piano. That's the young woman. That's the young woman I lent my anorak to."

Well, at this the woman got even more upset and was fit to burst into tears.

"You're a horrible man. You're a horrible man. Go away. Go away and leave us in peace."

The man calmed the woman down, then he turned to Jock.

"I think you should know, that's a photograph of our daughter, and she was killed on the road down here many years ago. I think you should come with me."

They walked down the garden path and along the lane to the church. They walked across the graveyard and there, hanging on their daughter's gravestone, was Jock's anorak.

# Mr. Fox

*A story retold by Dan Keding*

A man came to our town, his name was Fox, Mr. Fox. You could tell by the clothes he wore and his carriage and the horses that pulled it that he was a man of wealth. He visited the young ladies in the town and had breakfast with one, tea with another, and supper with a third, and as was the custom of the day, there would be an old grandmother or aunt sitting in the corner reading or sewing, chaperoning the two young people. He became very fond of one girl, Mary.

One day as they were talking, she asked him where he lived and what his house was like.

"Oh Mary," he said, "I live in a beautiful house. The king himself would be jealous of my home."

"You shouldn't boast," said Mary.

"Boast? You come visit me sometime. Follow the river road to the forest, then follow the old wood road to the pasture, cross the pasture and on the other side of the willows, the weeping willows, you'll find my house. Come visit, we'll see who's bragging."

They both laughed and talked of other things.

The next day Mary was walking near the river, and she thought to herself that she could go that very day and visit Fox and see if his house was truly that magnificent. They could have tea, and he could take her home in his fine carriage. She thought she'd like that.

She followed the river road, and as she did the waters lapped against the shore and whispered, *"Go back … go back."* But Mary didn't listen.

She came to the forest and followed the old wood road, and the leaves rustled and pleaded, *"Go back Mary … go back."* But Mary didn't listen.

She came to the pasture and the wind rushed through the tall grass and begged her one last time, *"Go back!"* But Mary didn't go back.

She stooped under the willow trees, and as she did the birds stopped singing and even the wind died down. Mary saw a beautiful house with a long front porch and marble columns rising to the second floor. The front door was so wide three men could walk through side by side and not touch the frame. In the middle of the door there was a golden door knocker in the shape of a fox's head. Mary knocked, but there was no answer. She went to a window and looked in but saw no one. She tried to knock one last time and as she stood in front of the door, she looked up and carved above the door were the words, "Be bold, be bold."

"That must be his family motto," thought Mary. Well I can be bold, too. And she took hold of the latch. The door opened, and she stepped in. The house was truly magnificent. There were oil paintings on the wall and Persian carpets on the floors. Every book in the library was bound with leather embossed in gold. The dining room table sat fifty people, and each place setting was solid gold. The stairway that led to the second floor was so wide that Mary could stretch out both arms and not touch either side. At the top there was a picture window that looked out over the lawn. To her right a dozen doors, each locked. To her left a dozen more, each locked except the last, and carved in this door were the words, "Be bold, be bold, but not too bold."

Mary walked in. It was a man's bedroom with a four-poster bed and dressers of teak and mahogany. Even the combs on the dresser were gold. She was just about to leave, when she saw another door, half hidden by a curtain.

This must be his closet, she thought. She just wanted to take a quick look at his fine clothes, so she pulled the curtain back. What she saw was a short, squat iron door and scratched into the rust were the words, "Be bold, be bold, but not too bold less your heart's blood run cold."

The room was as black as night.

As her eyes became used to the dark, Mary saw three huge barrels in the middle room. She put her hand in the first one, and it was filled with bones. She went to the second, and it was filled with skin and hair. She dipped her fingers into the third, and it was filled to the brim with blood. Then she saw the butcher table and the knives and axes. Then her eyes glanced up, and was it the light, or did she really see those hooks with the bodies of young women and young men hanging from them. She ran.

When she got to the top of the stairs she looked out, and there was Fox dragging a young woman toward the house. There was no place to run, no place to hide. Mary ran down the steps and turned and pressed herself against the wall of the staircase hoping he would not see her. The door burst open, and in strode Fox and the woman. She was struggling, but she might as well have been a child for all his strength. They started up the stairs, but in one last desperate move the woman took hold of the banister and held on with all her strength. Before your heart could beat, before your eyes could blink, his sword danced from his scabbard, and he cut off her hand. It flew through the air and landed at Mary's feet. She heard the first door slam then the clank of the iron door. For some unexplainable reason, she picked up the severed hand and ran home.

The next day who should come to visit but Fox. He walked into the family library where Mary waited alone. The room was dim, lit only by a few candles. The drapes that hung from the ceiling to the floor were shut tight.

Fox smiled, the candle glinted off his teeth.

"Mary, I've given this a great deal of thought, and I want you to be my wife. Say yes, Mary, and we'll visit my house this afternoon. Just the two of us."

Mary smiled faintly and replied, "I'll marry you but before we go can I tell you about a dream I had last night."

Fox smiled and sat down in a chair next to a small table. "Tell me about your dream, Mary. I'm very good at interpreting dreams."

"I dreamt that I was walking through the woods and across the pastures and I came upon a beautiful house and carved into the front door were the words, 'Be bold, be bold.'"

The smiled slipped from Fox's lips, and he whispered, "It was not so, it is not so."

Mary smiled, "It was just a dream."

Mary continued, "I went inside and there was a second door, a man's bedroom and carved in this door were the words, 'Be bold, be bold, but not too bold.'"

Fox clenched his fists, "It was not so, it is not so."

Mary replied, "It was just a dream."

And then she said, "There was a third door and scratched into the rust on this iron door were the words, 'Be bold, be bold, but not too bold, lest your heart's blood run cold.'"

"I found horrors in that room I can't begin to tell, and I ran. When I got to the top of the stairs, I looked out the window, and I saw you in my dream dragging a woman behind you. I hid by the stairwell and in my dream, you cut off her hand."

Fox's fists smashed the table before him, and slowly he rose.

"It was not so, it is not so, and I pray to God it shall not be so."

Mary, the smile gone from her lips, stared into his eyes, "But it was so, and it is so, and for the rest of my life I will pray to God it was not so."

And she took the severed hand from her desk drawer and threw it at his feet.

Fox smiled and slowly drew his sword, "Ah Mary, you shall never live to tell a soul."

But Mary, smiling again, reached for the drapery cord and drew the drapes back, and standing behind them were her six older brothers, each a sword in his hand. They fell upon Fox and dragged him out to the courtyard where he screamed and begged and prayed to whatever God a man like that can pray to. The brothers tied one arm to one horse, the other to another horse and his legs to others and they sent Fox to the four winds.

# Gytha of the Mill

*A story from North Yorkshire retold by Amy Douglas*

It was in the days when the Danes had come to Britain. They had swept across the land and the Saxons were defeated—not yet entirely conquered, but defeated. Alfred was still their king, and he had many supporters, but the war was won.

Julian was one of the leading Danes, a great warrior who had fought by the side of his king, and in return he had been give the whole of the Vale of Eskindale. He looked around his land and smiled a great beaming smile of victory, and then he got to work. He chose a high place for his castle, near the village of Goathland, and he began to build his castle. It was going to be one of the greatest castles ever built—a tribute to his own greatness—and perhaps more important, a stronghold should the Saxons ever rise again. All was well and Julian was enjoying the peace and the pickings of war. Until one day. The mason in charge of his castle came to him and said it that the foundations were set, the walls were rising, and it was time to put in the sacrifice to wall in some spirit to protect the castle. What creature was it to be?

Julian looked in surprise at the small man standing in front of him.

"What creature?" he bellowed, "What creature? What creature could it possibly be? What creature could Thor and Odin possibly want more than a woman, a ripe, sweet woman to sooth the needs that even the Gods themselves have."

The mason turned a little pale.

"A w-w-woman? The … er … custom is more a dog, or maybe a wolf."

The mason ducked as a tankard went flying past his ear

"A dog?! A dog! Thor would rain down thunder and lightning upon us and the castle would be doomed. Maybe that's what you want, cur!"

This time the pot caught the mason full on the side of the head and he sank to his knees.

Julian leaned back and thought for a moment.

"Bring me Gytha of the mill." There was silence. The mason staggered to his feet.

"But Gytha … she's her father's only child and besides … Gytha …"

Gytha was the most beautiful girl in Goathland. Men's eyes could not help but follow wherever she swayed past. Her hair was the color of ripe corn in the summer, her lips that of blood on the snow and her eyes, her eyes were like a clear sunny day full of the promise of spring.

"Gytha will please my gods well," smiled Julian. His henchmen were called, and soon they were on the way down the hill to the mill.

Gytha was the first thing they saw as they arrived. She sat outside by the mill pond singing as she span, working her drop spindle, dropping and winding, dropping and winding.

She looked up, gave them a cautious smile as they approached and gestured to the barn where the sacks of flour were stacked, thinking that once again they had come to take the supplies that they needed, leaving little for the Saxon people. But this time was not like the others. This time they made their way straight to her, for they had come not for the corn or flour, or at least they had come for a flower of a different kind. She screamed as they grabbed her, her spindle still clenched in her hand. Her father came running at the sound, his two huge fists swept one Dane to the ground, then a second, another followed shortly after, but a well-aimed stone found its mark against the side of his head, and he crumpled to the ground.

Gytha was brought before Julian, who sat there, a cold thin smile on his lips, as he told her why she had been brought there. Now Gytha was young, but war had taught her many things. She had expected harsh treatment, but by a man of flesh, not beyond the grave by a god. She fell at Julian's feet, grabbing his mantle, pleading, promising all manner of sweet things, but Julian swept her to one side with a blow of his fist and she lay there, still.

Word spread like wildfire around the village, shockwaves rippling throughout the country until the event came to the ears of King Alfred himself. But while Alfred bided his time in hiding, many others came to Julian to beg for the life of the lovely Gytha. Her father was one of the first. Force had not worked, and now, for the first time in his life, he resorted to begging. Julian watched as the strong miller groveled on the floor, and sensing his silence the miller's words drew to a halt, thinking that he may have managed to soften that hard heart. But as Julian spoke, it was not with words of freedom, but a voice full of a well-planned joke that the miller should be the one to wall her in. The miller gave a great cry and threw himself at Julian, but the Danes caught him before he could touch Julian, and he was carried away to learn some manners.

The youths came, all those who had hoped Gytha might one day warm their hearths, even the old hermit of Eskindale came to talk of Christian kindness and to turn away from these harsh gods that called for such a sacrifice, but Julian laughed at them all and the hole was built into the wall. A small hole, with room for a bench and a girl, a jug of water and a loaf of bread.

Some kind spirit had allowed Gytha to remain unconscious from her blow during the two days as the hole was built, but she came to as they carried her across the yard and forced her into the hole. She saw the light disappear as stone upon stone blocked the last rays of sunlight. She saw her father, a lifeless husk of a man lifting small pebbles, all that his diminished strength would allow him, until her light was gone for ever. And then the screaming began. She screamed and wailed and everyone who heard that sound felt their blood run cold. In that keening animal sound, they heard the voices that live only in the dark, they felt the cold hands of night around their hearts, they sensed the wings of death's ravens brushing against their souls.

The screaming lasted for three days, growing steadily weaker until at last it stopped, and it seemed as if the walls themselves breathed a sigh of relief.

The walls grew steadily higher and after a year, the building was growing to completion. There was room for Julian to move out of his temporary hut and into the stone walls, and the memory of Gytha faded as the life had faded gently out of her father.

One night, Julian was asleep in his bed when something awoke him. His head still drugged with sleep, he tried to rise in the bed and found that he couldn't. He realized what had woken him—he could hear a wailing from below. He relaxed, it wasn't unusual for his henchmen to bring back a sometimes unwilling girl from the village, but then he realized the sound was getting closer. With a shock of recognition, the blood froze in his veins. He saw the door open and there in the doorway was Gytha, still as beautiful as ever, her yellow hair hanging in a thick rope to her waist, her spindle in her hand. Julian tried again to move, but his body was locked rigid. Gytha came to the bottom of his bed, and she stood there, still crying the wail of a trapped animal as she passed the spindle from hand to hand over his feet. Slowly she made her way upward to his ankles and then she turned and walked away out of the room until Julian could no longer hear her, and he sank back into a troubled sleep.

When Julian awoke in the morning, the dream was still with him, but the sun streaked the room bright with daylight, and he smiled at himself. He swung himself over the side of the bed to find that his feet were full of cramp, and he flinched from the floor. He bent down, trying to massage the life back into them, but it was of no use. As the day passed Julian was reduced to shuffling like an old man about the castle.

The next year, Julian was not asleep on the anniversary of Gytha's death, and so when he heard the sound of her wailing, he knew that it was not a dream. He lay sweating as the sound grew louder, the door was pushed open, and she walked in.

In death, she was still as beautiful as in life, yet now her eyes were not those of a spring day, but a harsh winter—bleak and cold they stared from their sockets. She stood at the foot of the bed, her spindle in her hand, and while Julian lay helpless, unable so much as to lift a finger, she began to pass the spindle from hand to hand above his ankles gradually rocking her way higher until she reached his knees. Finally she stopped, turned, and slowly left the room, her cries becoming fainter until at last he could hear them no more. Julian pushed the rugs aside and swung his legs out of bed. As he tried to put his weight upon them, he crashed to the floor, sharp pains lancing up his legs, and from that day Julian walked no more. Gytha still came to visit him though, every year, and every year Julian lay awake at night in fear. He called upon his gods, Odin and Thor, pleading for their help. Asking them again and again why they had forsaken him, Julian, their most staunch and devout believer, asking them what he should do. There was no reply.

The hermit of Eskindale heard of Julian's rantings, how he railed against his own gods through the night and once again he tried his luck. He came bearing tidings of the white Christ and his mercy, and this time the man who had laughed, listened. Julian turned away from his old gods, he did penance, and he built a church to the white Christ. But it seemed that the Christ was as deaf as Thor and Odin, for Gytha still came each year, and a few weeks after the church was completed, she took the last of his life from him. Julian was the first to be buried in the new churchyard.

Though Julian was dead, the story isn't over. A villager arrived home one night with a strange disease—there was sweat on his forehead, his eyes were wide and staring. He was delirious, the words tumbling out of his mouth and seeming to make no sense, about a great black shape, a dog or a goat, with red sparking eyes and feet, feet that made almost no sound, just a pad, pad, pad, like bare human feet, the shape rushing past him and then nothing but swirling darkness. They might have taken less notice, but the man had walked home past the churchyard, the churchyard with only one grave. The next day the man was dead. He wasn't the last. The phantom took many of the villagers' lives, most of them young girls and soon the villagers were careful to be in their homes by nightfall for anyone who was overtaken by that dark shape would not last long. Some called it Gytrash, others Padfoot. Whatever the name, fear hung over Goathland like a blanket, and Julian's reign was more absolute than ever it had been during his life.

Something had to be done.

The village called a council to decide what to do. Yoef was elected the leader. They sat, they talked, they drank, they scratched their heads, they drank, they argued, they fell over.

So they called another council meeting. In the end they reached the decision that all knew they would finally come to but had been avoiding. They were going to have to go to the Speywife of Fylingdale. The Speywife was the one who knew all there was for a mortal to know about these things—she knew all the herbs, the healing chants, the old wisdom.

However, there was one problem. The year before, the villagers had tried to burn her, and to be honest, she hadn't taken too kindly to the whole affair.

The Speywife was not a pretty sight. Her hair hung about her shoulders in long, grey tangles. Her face was covered in warts (all those warts you remove from one person have to go somewhere you know). And her eyes—her eyes sliced out of her face like bright beady gimlets—that saw rather more than you'd care to have anyone see.

Yeof took his courage in his hands and made his way to her door. He timidly reached up and gently tapped. There was no answer. Taking a deep breath he raised his hand again and knocked a little louder. The door remained firmly shut. Breathing a deep sigh of relief, he turned to go and walked straight into her. He leapt backward and slammed against the door, which finally opened and he fell on to the floor of her hut.

"Umm … I brought you some eggs?" he said. He held out the cloth bag, which was now dripping from one corner. She looked at him with her head cocked slightly to one side.

"Humpf."

Yeof scrambled to his feet and stood up to let her pass. She walked past him and once again the door was shut in his face.

Yeof sighed and walked home.

The next day he tried again. Armed with a bag of produce collected from everyone in the village, he set off. This time he was ready for her suddenly appearing act, but the door swung open, and he stepped over the threshold into the dark smoky atmosphere of the hut, then the door shut behind. Plants he had never seen before hung drying from the roof. He peered about and there, there he caught the glint of her eyes boring into him. He cleared his throat.

"Look, I umm, I'm really sorry about the … errr … bad … errrr … feeling between us in the past, but I … er …, wondered if you … err … might see your way clear to … just giving us a little bit of help.

Silence.

"I … err … brought some cabbages."

There was a muffled sound that could have been a cough or a laugh.

The old woman stood up and walked toward him. She came so close that he could smell her stale breath and feel the warmth of it against his neck as she put her arm around him and whispered, "How much do you need my help, Yeof?"

Yeof gave a smothered yelp, his knees gave way, and he keeled to the floor.

Suddenly the smoke disappeared and Yeof found himself flat on his back outside the hut with laughter ringing in his ears.

"Tane to tither … the one to the other—if you work it out I might help you."

Yeof began the journey home, his knees still weak with relief.

The council met again the next day, but still no one could make any sense of the Speywife's message.

The subject wandered and the chat started, and talk began of other strange things. Someone mentioned Julian's old keep, already falling into ruins, yet Gytha was still spinning, her sobs still echoing around the deserted courtyard.

Yeof sprang to his feet. Inspiration hammered into his head—one to the other—the two spirits put against one another.

Yeof sank to the ground again—the elation drained out of him. He was going to have to go back to the Speywife. This time he took a chaperone.

The Speywife nodded as he stuttered the answer.

"You must make a trail from the keep to the moors. Make it with honey and salt and corn. You must dig a grave and hold a funeral. Take the corn dolly from the last of the crop and wrap it in a shroud as if it were the body of a young girl. As you hold the funeral procession, grieve for all those you lost to Padfoot. When the evening gathers, find a place to watch and see what happens."

All was done as the Speywife ordered, and as evening came, the villagers gathered on the far side of the grave so that Padfoot could not overtake them. They sat as the dark gathered and night spread its fingers over the moors and chilled the people as they sat, waiting.

Then they saw it. The dark shadow slinking over the moors, its red eyes flashing as it turned its head, each person sure that it was looking at them, that it would leave the grave and come for the living souls gathered on the ridge. But the shadow quickened its step and flung itself onto the grave, tearing out the freshly dug earth, burying its way down to sink its teeth into the neck of the dead girl. But then they looked up.

There was a glimmering in the keep, a blue light, following the trail, coming down across the moor. As the figure got closer, it resolved into Gytha—Gytha as they remembered her. Still with the slim beauty of the fifteen year old, her spindle in her hand, cloaked in an ancient sorrow, but her face calm. Finally Gytha had stopped screaming.

The Gytrash was burying deeper now. Soon its teeth would close on nothing but the corn, and it would know that it had been tricked. But Gytha was there, standing at the foot of the grave, passing her spindle from hand to hand, moving her way up the grave. The dark spirit began to howl. They saw its red eyes flash and its gaping maw heading for Gytha before she made the last pass with the spindle, and the earth collapsed into the grave. Gytha stood alone on the bare patch of earth. She looked up, and the dark cloud that had covered the moon drifted away. She smiled and then was gone.

The villagers let out the breath they didn't know they had been holding. They smiled and a ripple of joyous laughter rang out across the moors before they stood up, dusted themselves off, and walked home, arm in arm, safe in the moonlight.

# Riddles

## 1

*I washed my face in water*
*That neither rained nor run*
*I dried my face on a towel*
*That was neither wove nor spun*

## 2

*What man loves more than life*
*Fears more than death or mortal strife*
*That which a contented man desires*
*The poor possess, the rich requires*
*The miser spends, the spendthrift saves*
*And all men carry to their graves*

## 3

*Clink clank down the bank*
*ten against the four*

## 4

*What has hands but no arms*
*A face, but no head?*

## 5

*What has a mouth but no face*
*Always running, always in one place?*

## 6

*Two legs sat on 3 legs eating 0 legs.*
*In came 4 legs, picked up 0 legs and ran off with it.*
*Up stood 2 legs, picked up 3 legs*
    *and threw it after 4 legs.*
*4 legs dropped no legs and ran away.*

## 7

*What God never sees*
*What the Queen seldom sees*
*What we see every day*
*Read this riddle, I pray*

## 8

*What runs round a field, but does not move?*

## 9

*We have a horse*
*Without any head*
*And all dressed up*
*Not living or dead*

## 10

*It's long and slim and works in the light
Has but one eye and an awful bite*

## 11

*Riddle me, riddle me, what is that
Over the head and under the hat?*

## 12

*What goes upstairs without moving?*

## 13

*Behind the bush, behind the thorn
I heard a stout man blow his horn
He was booted and spurred and stood with pride
With golden feathers by his side
His beard was flesh and his mouth was horn
I'm sure such a man could never have been born*

## 14

*What has six arms
Can cover farms
And one day might make a man?*

# Answers to Riddles

1   I washed my face in the morning dew and dried my face in the sun

2   Nothing

3   A person milking a cow

4   A clock

5   A river

6   A person on a stool, eating a fish.  In comes the cat, picks up the fish and runs away with it. Up steps the person, picks up the stool and throws it after the cat. The cat drops the fish and the person gets it back. (We don't know if they ate it or not, though!)

7   An equal

8   A hedge

9   A clotheshorse

10   A needle

11   Hair

12   The carpet

13   A cockerel

14   Snow

# A Parting Song

*Traditional English*

Merry are the bells and merry would they ring,
Merry was myself and merry would I sing,
With a merry ding dong, happy, gay and free,
And a merry sing song, happy let us be.

Waddle goes your gate and hollow is your hose,
Noddle goes your pate and purple is your nose,
Merry is your sing song, happy, gay and free,
And a merry ding dong, happy let us be.

Merry have we met and merry we have we been,
Merry let us part and merry meet again;
With a merry ding dong, happy, gay and free,
And a merry sing song, happy let us be.

# Notes on the Stories

The stories gathered together in this collection represent many of the tale types present in English folklore. They reflect the morality, beliefs, and sense of humor of the English people. Most of these beliefs have parallels in cultures across the world, but here they have a distinctive English twist. Some of the stories are found throughout England (these are not listed on the map at the front of the book), and some are from a very specific English locale.

## The Fool

The fool plays a central role in any oral culture. Many cultures have a physical fool—a jester or a clown; the fool in stories plays the same role. The fool holds up a mirror to society, reflecting and exaggerating situations, personalities, and trends to show how absurd they really are. The fool has licence to make the remarks that no one else dares to make but that need to be said.

Most cultures have a hero who is a fool but also wise—for example, Nasrudin, Coyote; in England, as in the Appalachian mountains, Jack is our hero—sometimes he is a straightforward brave hero, but in other stories, he takes the part of the wise fool, as in Jack Turnip. In these stories, the fool aspect of the archetype is on the ascendant!

We have also included a selection of so-called noodle stories. These are stories that let us laugh at the ridiculous side of human nature, that examine the stupidity present in us all and take it to extremes. Sometimes there is a warning, or a moral, but these stories are to be enjoyed at face value—they do say that laughter is the best medicine.

While Start and Finish look like they will be noodles, they are the ones who have the last laugh—and laughter will sort out most differences. If we all had the ability to laugh at ourselves, this world would be a much easier and more lenient place in which to live.

The Farmer and the Cheeses is an out-and-out noodle story. Just as in the schoolyard there is always someone people like to tease, every culture has a group of people they like to make fun of. In England, the Irish are often the butt of our jokes (though that definitely works in the other direction as well!). There is a town called Gotham, and there are many stories about "The Wise Men of Gotham"—all of them setting out to prove just how little they deserve the name.

In Shropshire where I (Amy Douglas) live, the town of Madeley is on the receiving end—they once tried to hold on to summer by fencing in a cuckoo—of course when the cuckoo was ready to leave, it flew over the fence leaving the citizens of Madeley to face the cold (the story is not quite the same if you live in Madeley!).

We all have a little of the fool inside to help keep us sane, and we are all filled with foolish dreams. In "The Mare's Egg," we may see a hare running from a smashed pumpkin, but the people watching saw their dream hatch and take flight for them across the fields.

## Dragons

Say the word "dragon," and most people's minds turn to either Wales or China, but there are plenty in England. Mostly they come from the North Country, and they are to be found in the wild places, moors, and mountains where farming is difficult and living is hard. They devour, go on rampages, and take the fat of the land—all that the people need most to live, their carefully tended livestock and the young maidens. Where life is short and childbearing is hard, potential mothers are cherished most of all.

The dragons are creatures to be feared—a plague on the land—and their passing much to be celebrated. The dragons of England are worms, hungry serpents. They do not always breath fire; sometimes instead they have poisonous breath and venom dripping from their fangs. Their bodies are scaled, sometimes with wings and sometimes without.

## The Devil

In English folklore, the Devil appears in three main guises:

1.  An earth-moving clumsy giant

2.  A tempter that can be outwitted

3.  The terrifying Devil, a punisher of wrongdoers

The stories that incorporate the Devil as a giant are probably the oldest. As Christianity swept through England, many of the characters from existing stories were replaced with Christian figures. The bright gods of Asgard from Norse mythology (the stories of the Vikings) were constantly battling the Ice Giants. The Ice Giants were the beings of the frozen wastes, trying to enfold Midgard, the world in which we live, in their icy grasp. It is reasonable to connect the movements and unstoppable forces of wind, snow, ice, and glaciers—strong forces in the lives of the Norse—with the Ice Giants. It is conceivable that a story such as "The Devil and the Stiperstones" has evolved and developed from ideas and stories brought with the Vikings.

The Devil as a tempter is a dangerous adversary. He will promise you your heart's desire, but there is always a price. The fun for the Devil, however, is in the chase. Like a cat, he ensnares his mouse and likes to watch it squirm. When he makes his bargain, he will always give his victims an opportunity to keep their soul—but the task they have to accomplish is impossible. These stories celebrate the common people. They demonstrate that with quick wits, a good heart, and a lot of pluck, we can make possible the impossible and win free from the Devil's clutches.

In the "Devil and the Coracle," once more Jack escapes from the Devil, but Jack knows—and we know—that Jack will have to keep on his toes, for the Devil will be watching for him!

In "The Devil in Wem," the lads summoning the Devil were extremely lucky to survive their encounter. They had the time and the good fortune to find a holy man who could exorcise the Devil. There are plenty of similar stories that end with piles of ash where the lads were standing and a scorch mark on the floor. Witches who have sold their soul to the Devil may live long lives, but in the end the Devil will come for them and claim his prize. In "The Elder Tree Witch," you can be sure the Devil was standing ready to catch old Sal when she fell into the fire. In other stories, witches have repented at the end and tried to rob the Devil of their souls by having their coffins bound with iron chains, but all is to no avail, and their family and religious helpers stand by helpless as the witch is carried away screaming by a fearsome powerful Devil on his black charger.

## Fairies

Fairies are present throughout England. They come in many guises, shapes, and sizes. Generically they are called the fairies, the fair folk, the little people, or the good people, though there are many, many specific types. They are called the good people as a mark of respect and caution. Fairies are not always good—they mirror the personalities of the humans with whom they mix. If you are kind and respectful in your dealings with the fair folk, then you will be well rewarded, but if you are rude and selfish, then you are sure to merit the same treatment.

Fairies are known for their beauty. There are many stories of mortal men falling for fairy women and marrying them. There are a few examples of mortal women marrying fairy men, but it is much less common. Sadly, these matches are usually doomed for disaster. The marriage is always founded on a condition: in "Wild Edric," he must not reproach her with her background; in other stories, it might be that he must never hit her or touch her with cold iron. Whatever condition is imposed, the mortal man at some point breaks his promise and loses his wife.

As mortals we are drawn to fairy kind. Their integral magic and otherworldliness makes us long for a glimpse of them, to bring a little of their magic into our own world. But beware! As a rule they are best left alone, and it is a wise idea to take precautions against them. If you step into a fairy ring, lured by their beauty and the entrancing music, then you may never come back to the mortal world—and if you do, though you may believe you have only danced a single night, decades may have passed in our time. If you do find your way into fairyland, then do not eat any of the food they offer you, else you will be held in their power for ever.

Fairies seem to feel the same draw to us as we do to them. They have a weakness for human babies. There are many stories in which sweet-natured babies suddenly change character. Their faces grow old and wizened; they cry constantly and eat with an enormous appetite. In such cases, the fairies have stolen a human baby and replaced the child with a changeling. The only known ways to retrieve the stolen baby are either to endanger the changeling's life or to surprise the changeling into revealing its identity. Fairies will also take cattle, leaving nothing but an empty husk behind, with a glamour cast over it so that the farmer will not know the cow has been stolen. But the replacement is just a shadow of the real beast and will soon sicken and die.

These are just a few tricks for which the fairies are known. If you wish to protect yourself from their enchantment, then carry a piece of rowan or iron in your pocket. Hang up a bunch of rowan at each door and window to prevent fairies from entering your house, or again use iron, perhaps a horseshoe nailed to the door. If you are walking in a familiar place and suddenly all seems strange and you cannot find your way home, then probably you have been pixie led. Take off your coat or jumper, turn it inside out, and put it on again. This will ward off the spell. If you can find one, a four-leafed clover will let you see through any fairy glamour.

# Witches

There are two types of witch, and you should meddle with neither. The first is made up of the wisewomen—henwives, hedgewitches, and white witches. These are women who have the sight. They have inherited it through their family, gained it from being born at a particular time on a certain night, or been given the gift by the fairies. Generally they use their gift, together with a lifetime of research into plants and medicines and a good dollop of common sense, to help people. However, their view of how to make the best of a situation may not be the same as the person who came to them for help!

The second type consists of the out-and-out bad witches. They are women who have sold their soul to the Devil in exchange for power. They demand respect and to be well treated. They enjoy wielding their power to create fear and cause pain. Common powers they command are the ability to change shape, most often into a hare; to project a presence over distance, for example, appearing as an elder tree in "The Elder Tree Witch"; and to lay hexes on people. Witches are usually female, but their male counterparts do exist.

As with the fairies, rowan is a good protection against witches. Silver is thought of as a pure metal. Unlike fairies, iron will not harm witches, but the pureness of silver will cut through their protections.

To protect yourself from hexes, you must closely guard your possessions. A witch needs something personal for her spell, such as a piece of clothing, a bit of hair, or nail clippings.

In these stories, it is up to you to decide which sort of witch appears. A bad witch is never called a witch to her face (not unless you want to be turned into a toad) and so might be referred to as a henwife. A strange old crone on the edge of town is likely to be called a witch as an insult, though she may have a heart of gold.

# *Heroes*

There are many heroes in English Folklore, but the two greatest, the two most renowned of them all, must surely be King Arthur and Robin Hood. Both are great, both are heroes, and yet they are entirely different, or perhaps they are different sides of the same coin.

King Arthur stands for all that is good, peaceful, harmonious, and beautiful. He is the true king who unites the land and reigns as its protector. He brings order and beauty to replace fear and strife.

Robin Hood, on the other hand, is the lord of disorder, the creator of chaos. He is the voice of dissent, doing his best to bring the system down. He has no respect for position or wealth. He robs from the rich and gives to the poor and to those who are still loyal to the true king and are being victimized by Prince John.

What gives both these characters their hero status and enduring appeal are their values. Both are religious men. King Arthur's court and creed are dedicated to Christian values. All the good deeds that Robin Hood does are in the name of the Virgin Mary and most of the times that Robin is captured, as in *Robin Hood and the Monk*, it is due to his attempting to get to Mass. Both men are driven to create a better England for all; they fight for a land where everyone is valued, a land of peace ruled by justice and mercy.

To this day, these two heroes are so greatly valued in England that every county, town, and village wants to claim them for its own. We all know that Robin Hood was based in Sherwood Forest, but that was only for the summer. When the leaves fell from the trees, Robin and his men would disband for the winter and find places to shelter until spring; according to local legends, there are few places that he did not travel to during those cold months.

Folklorists and historians mostly agree that there was an Arthur, but none can prove where he lived, and there are endless theories to support this county or that region. All counties claim to have King Arthur sleeping within their boundaries, though Alderley Edge is one of the best-known sites.

Wherever you travel in England you will find rocks, hills, wells, and trees named after King Arthur and Robin Hood—from Robin Hood's Bay near Whitby where he defeated pirates, to Robin Hood's Butts in Herefordshire; from Arthur's stone in Herefordshire, the gravestone of a giant killed by the king, to King Arthur's Castle (also known as Cadbury Castle) near Yeovil in Somerset.

## *Ghost Stories*

Everyone likes a spooky story—stories of the unexplained, of monsters, demons, ghosts, and creatures of the night. Somehow, when the sun sets and darkness reigns, there is more room for the otherworld than in the daytime. The night is filled with all our uncertainties and fears. In the night, anything is possible.

Once the sun sets, England is full of things that go bump in the night. There are ghosts, bogles, will-o'-the-wykes, witches, and monsters—even the Devil himself prowls the land.

These are stories to make your skin crawl, stories to chill your bones so that you pull the blankets close. We hope you enjoy them. But remember, when you come to England, if someone tells you not to stray from the path, then don't; don't go into churchyards after midnight, even if it is the shortcut home; don't go too near the edge of a lonely pool, and if all else fails, carry a handful of salt in your pocket.

# Glossary

**Anorak**  A waterproof jacket

**Bogle**  An evil or mischievous spirit

**Bonnet**  Metal cover over a car engine ("boot" is the trunk)

**Brawn**  An enormous wild boar

**Cellarer**  Monastic officer in charge of looking after the beer and wine

**Chin Wag**  A good long chat, usually of a gossipy variety

**Chummy**  A shepherd's felt hat, reputedly made of dog's hair

**Clog Dancing**  Traditional English folk dance

**Coracle**  A small oval boat with a wooden frame and covered in cured skin or oiled cloth light enough to be carried by one person; it is steered and maneuvered with one paddle

**Corn Dolly**  Dolls made out of plaited corn (Small corn dollies are made for decoration and luck, but *the* corn dolly is made from the last of the corn gathered and is kept to watch over the next crop and protect it. It is then ritually burned, and a new doll made to house the corn spirit.)

**Cricket**  An English sport using a ball, a bat, and wickets, with rules similar to baseball

**Dame**  A title of honor given to women in England

**Drop Spindle**  A tool used for spinning before the advent of the spinning wheel (The spindle is twisted and dropped at the same time, to pull the wool or flax into thread.)

**Esq.**  Abbreviation of esquire, derived from "squire," a person who was the armor bearer or attendant on a knight; now this is a title appended onto a man's surname when no other title or qualifications are used and is used in formal letters

**Fens**  A flat, marshy, or flooded area of ground (In England, the Fens are the flat, low-lying areas around Cambridgeshire, Lincolnshire, and Norfolk. These areas were marsh and bog until they were fully drained in the seventeenth century, but they retain the name.)

**Fey**  Belonging to the fairy world

**Fold**  A farmyard or animal enclosure

| | |
|---|---|
| **Gimlet** | A small tool for boring holes; "eyes like gimlets" implies hard eyes boring deep into their subject |
| **Gypsy** | A member of a nomadic race, the Romany people |
| **Gytrash** | A ghost or specter usually appearing in the form of a black dog, also known as Padfoot |
| **Hag** | A witch or ugly old woman |
| **Hart** | A stag or male deer |
| **Henchmen** | Attendants (often armed attendants) |
| **Henwife** | A woman who takes care of the chickens, sometimes used to identify a wisewoman or a white witch |
| **Jabbering** | Fast, unintelligible speech |
| **Kiddleywink** | Cornish term for a brewery pub with a licence to sell beer and wine, but not spirits |
| **Lenten Dough** | Dough to make a form of unleavened bread eaten during Lent |
| **Magistrate** | A judge |
| **Manor** | The land over which the lord of the manor presides—his manor house and its grounds, hunting lands, and the lands rented out to tenant farmers; a manor house may be shortened to simply the term "manor" |
| **Mercenaries** | Professional fighters who fight for money and have no allegiance to the cause they are fighting for |
| **M.P.** | Member of Parliament, a regionally elected politician who has a seat in Parliament |
| **Odin** | The Allfather, king of the Norse gods, famous for his great wisdom obtained by sacrificing one eye |
| **Order** | (As used in Brother Jucundus) A fraternity of monks or friars who are bound together by a common rule of life and set of beliefs |
| **Padfoot** | A specter, usually in the form of a black dog with red eyes, its feet sound like bare human feet padding on the ground |
| **Ploughshare** | The sharp piece of metal on a plough that cuts through the earth |
| **Pottle** | A pot or tankard for carrying food or liquid |
| **Pub** | A public house where food and drink are served |
| **Quarterstaff** | A thick, straight stick, six to eight feet long |

| | |
|---|---|
| **Romany** | Language and ethnicity of the Gypsies, also used to describe anything pertaining to Gypsies |
| **Rowan** | A mountain ash; this tree is known for its ability to ward off supernatural powers, particularly the spells of fairies and witches |
| **Scabbard** | A sheath for a sword, often buckled to belt |
| **Snick** | To make a small cut |
| **Sorted** | All sorted out, taken care of |
| **Speywife** | Another word for henwife |
| **Started** | To disturb an animal, force it to break free from cover |
| **Stepping** | Step dancing; in England this usually refers to a skillful form of clog dancing |
| **Stotty** | A round flat bread found in the northeast of England |
| **Ta** | Thank you |
| **Tankard** | A drinking vessel, usually made of pewter (If someone loves the tankard, it implies that he or she loves beer.) |
| **Tappets** | A piece of machinery used to give intermittent motion—in "Old Lightowler," the term refers to part of the boat's engine |
| **Thor** | Norse god of thunder and war |
| **Traveller** | A member of a nomadic people of unspecific descent; Gypsies are Travellers, but Travellers are not necessarily Gypsies |
| **Weirding** | A web of spells |
| **Widdershins** | Counterclockwise |
| **Will-o'-the-Wykes** | Strange lights that often appear in marshy ground or graveyards that lure unsuspecting travelers off the path |
| **Wise Woman** | See Henwife |
| **Worm** | A dragon or serpent |

Errata Sheet

# ADDITIONAL READING

**Myths & Legends of the British Isles**; Richard Barber, Boydell Press, ISBN 0-85115-748-3

**East Anglian Folklore & Other Tales**; W.H.Barrett & R.P. Garrod, Routledge & Kegan Paul, ISBN 0-7100-8300-9

**Tales From the Fens**; W.H.Barrett; Routledge & Kegan Paul

**English Myths & Legends**; Henry Bett, Dorset Press, ISBN0-88029-731-X

**British Folktales**; Kathcrine Briggs, Pantheon Books, ISBN 0-394-41589-2

**A Dictionary of British Folktales in the English Language, Parts A & B**; Katherine Briggs, Routledge Publishing, ISBN 0-415-06696-4 (for the 2 volume set)

**Folktales of England;** edited by Katherine Briggs & Ruth L. Tongue, University of Chicago Press, 1965

**Round About and Long Ago: Tales from the English Counties;** Eileen Colwell, Houghton Mifflin Co., ISBN 0-395-18515-7

**Folktales of the British Isles**; edited by Kevin Crossley-Holland, Pantheon Books, ISBN 0-394-75553-7

**The Dead Moon**; Kevin Crossley-Holland, Faber & Faber, ISBN 0-571-13879-9

**A Chronicle of Folk Customs; Brian Day, Hamlyn, ISBN 0-600-59595-1**

**Ghosts & Witches: Haunted Tales from the British Isles**; J.Wentworth Day, Dorset Press, ISBN 0-88029-730-1

**Folk Tales of the British Isles**; edited by Michael Foss, Book Club Associates, London, 1977

**Book of British Fairy Tales**; Alan Garner, Delacorte Press, ISBN 0-385-29425-5

**Folk Tales of the West Midlands**; Frederick Grice, Thomson Nelson and Sons Ltd, Edinburgh, 1952

**English Fairy & Folk Tales**; edited by Edwin Sydney Hartland, Dover Books, ISBN 0-486-41135-4

**Somerset Legends**; Berta Lawrence, David & Charles Publishers, ISBN 0-7153-6185-6

**West Country Folk Tales**; Llywelyn W. Maddock, James Brodie Ltd.

**Le Morte D'Arthur**; Thomas Mallory, edited by R.M. Lumiansky, Collier Books, ISBN 0-02022560-1

**Everyman's Book of English Folktales**; Sybil Marshall, J.M.Dent & Sons, ISBN 0-460-04472-9 Reprinted as English Folk Tales; Sybil Marshall, Phoenix, ISBN 1 85799 439 6

**Tales of Old Devon**; Sally Norris, Countryside Books, ISBN 1-85306-142-5

**The Oxford Nursery Rhyme Book**; Iona and Peter Opie, Clarendon Press, 1955

**Oral Folk Tales of Wessex**; Kingsley Palmer, David & Charles Publishers, ISBN0-7153-5905-3

**The Folklore of Leicestershire & Rutland**; Roy Palmer, Sycamore Press Ltd., ISBN 0-905837-22-3

**The Penguin Book of English Folktales;** Neil Philip, Penguin Books, ISBN 0-14-013976-1

**The Little People's Pageant of Cornish Legends**; Eric Quayle, Simon &
Schuster Inc., ISBN 0-671-663580-8

**English Fables & Fairy Stories**; James Reeves, Oxford University Press, ISBN 0-19-274101-2

**Folktales of the British Isles**; James Riorden, Raduga Publishers, ISBN 5-05-001005-5

**English Fairy Tales**; Flora Annie Steel, MacMillan & Company, ISBN 0-8317-2925-2

**Folk Stories from the Yorkshire Dales;** Peter N. Walker, Robert Hale Publishers, ISBN 0-7090-4486-0

**Folk Tales from York & the Wolds**; Peter N. Walker, Robert Hale Publishers, ISBN 0-7090-4763-0

**Albion; A Guide to Legendary Britain**; Jennifer Westwood, Grafton (An imprint of HarperCollins*Publishers*), ISBN 0 586 08416 9

**Folklore, Myths, & Legends of Britain**; Published by Reader's Digest Association Ltd., London, 1973

# Index

Alderley Edge, 165–8, 212
Alfred, King, 4, 192–3
American Revolution, 10
Angles, 3
Anglo-Saxon, 3–6
*Anglo-Saxon Chronicle, The,* 4
Anne, Queen, 10
Arthur, King, xv, 2–3, 160–4, 184

Ball, John, 7
Battle of Hastings, 5
Birmingham, 99, 186–7
Bishop Auckland, 75–6
Black Country, 99–101
Black Death, 7
Boar. *See* Brawn.
Boats, 5, 53, 79–82
Bogs, 173–6, 213
Bosham, 143–4
Brawn, 75–6
Bridgnorth, 80–2

Canute, King, 4
Caractacus, 2
Charles I, 9
Charles II, 9, 10
Cheshire, 165–8
Church of England, 9
Claudius, 2
Clitheroe, 182–3
Clog dancing, 53. *See also* Stepping
Clun, 102
Coracle, 79–82
Corn dolly, 197, 213
Cornwall, 61, 62–4, 92–4, 184–5
Cromwell, Oliver, 9–10

Cromwell, Richard, 10

Dame Ragnell, 160–4
Dancing, 53, 56–58
Danes, 3, 4, 192–8
Dartmoor, 98–101
Devil, 79–82, 83–4, 85–87, 208–9, 211
Devil's Chair, 80–82
Domesday Book, 6
Dragons, 66–70, 71–4, 208
Dudley, 99–101
Durham, 66, 75–6

Easter, 132–6
Edward the Confessor, 4–6
Elizabeth I, 9
Elizabeth of York, 8
Eric of Lincoln, 152–3

Fair folk. *See* Fairies
Fairies, 94–97, 98, 99–101, 102–4, 108–13, 209–10
Fens. *See* Bogs
Festival at the Edge, xv, xvi
Folk of the Hill. *See* Fairies
Fools, 15–43, 207–8

Games, 10, 141–2
Gawain, 160–4
Geoffrey of Monmouth, 12
George I, 11
George II, 11
George III, 11
George IV, 11
Ghost stories, 212

Giants, 115–19
Gloucester, 81–2
Goathland, 192–7
God, 43–5
Godda, 103–4
Good people. *See* Fairies
Goole, 53
Great Reform Act, 11
Gregory, Pope, 3
Guinevere, 161
Gytha, 192–8
Gytrash, 195–8

Hadrian's Wall, 2
Halifax, 177–81
Hallowe'en, 62
Hampshire, 55
Henry VII, 7
Henry VIII, 7
Henwife, 20–5, 108–9, 210–11, 214
Heroes, 211–12
*History of the Kings of Britain, A,* 12
House of Commons, 8, 11
House of Lords, 11

Ice Age, 1

Kate Crackernuts, 108–13
Kent, 55

Jack, 20–25, 26, 27–34, 60–1
James II, 10
Jenny Greenteeth, 182–3
John, King, 6
Jucundus, 145–50
Julius Caesar, 1

Laidly Worm, 71–4
Lakeland Storytelling Festival, xv
Lambton Worm, 66–70
Lancashire, 182–3

Lent, 132–3
Lightowler, 53
Lincolnshire, 16–17, 20–5, 173–6
Little John, 151–3, 154–7
Little people. *See* Fairies
London, 7, 40–42, 137–40

Macclesfield, 165
Magna Carta, 6
Mary, Queen, 8–9
Merlin, 184
mermaid, 92–4
Midsummer Night, 184–5
Mitchell's Ford, 1, 125–7
Molly Whuppie, 115–19

National Storytelling Festival, xi
Newcastle, 170
Normans, 4–6
Norsemen, 3, 4
Nottingham, 18–19, 143–4, 151–3,
    154–7

Odin, 192, 195, 214
Offa's Dyke, 3

Padfoot, 195–8, 214
Parliament, 9, 11–12
Parliament Act, 11–12
People's Charter, 11
Pixies. *See* Fairies
Plague. *See* Black Death
Poll tax, 7
Pollard, 75–6
Prince Bishop, 75–6

Ribble River, 182, 183
Richard I, 7
Richard II, 7, 8
Riddles, 191–203
Robin Hood, xv, 151, 154–7

Roman Catholic Church, 8–9, 10
Romans, 1–2, 3

Saxons, 2, 3, 192
Severn River, 82
shepherd, 60–1
Shrewsbury, 84
Shropshire, 79, 83–4, 85–7, 90–1,
    102–4, 125–7, 134
Society for Storytelling, xv
Somerset, 40–2, 128–30
South Downs, 60
Speywife, 196–8, 215. *See also*
    Witches
Stapeley Hill, 125–7
Stepping (step dancing), 53, 56–8
Stiperstones, 8–7
Stone Age, 1
Stonehenge, 1
Stuart, James, 9
Suffolk, 55
Sussex, 54–9, 60–1, 120–4, 143–4

Tattercoats, 105–7
Thor, 192, 195
Travellers, 54–59, 215
Trent River, 18

Victoria, Queen, 10–11
Voting, 11

Wars of the Roses, 8
Wear River, 66
Wem, 83–4
West Country Storytelling Festival,
    xv
Wild Edric, 102–4
William the Conqueror, 4, 102, 104
William IV, 10
William of Orange, 10
Wisewomen, 68–69, 174. *See also*
    Witches
Witches, 90–1, 210–11, 120–4,
    125–7, 128–9, 210–11
Wolf, 43–5
Wolverhampton, 99
Worm, 66–70, 71–4, 215

Vikings, 153

York, 19, 145–50
Yorkshire, xv, 71–4, 177–81, 192–8

Zennor, 92–4

# About the Editors

## Dan Keding

Dan grew up in Chicago surrounded by stories told by his maternal grandmother. He has a master's degree in folklore and has written a storytelling column for *Sing Out: The Folk Music Magazine* for almost twenty years. He has been a professional storyteller and ballad singer for thirty years and has traveled throughout the United States and England telling tales at festivals, concert halls, schools, libraries, and coffeehouses. He has performed at the National Storytelling Festival in Jonesborough, Tennessee; the Festival at the Edge in Much Wenlock,  England; and more than two hundred other festivals. His recordings have won numerous awards including, the American Library Association Notable Recording for Children and Storytelling World Winner and Honor Awards. In 2000, he was inducted into the National Storytelling Network Circle of Excellence. He lives in Urbana, Illinois, with his wife Tandy Lacy, director of education at the Spurlock Museum at the University of Illinois, and their two Australian Shepherds, Jack and Maeve. His other book is *Stories of Spirit and Hope: Folktales from Eastern Europe,* winner of the Anne Izard Storyteller's Choice Award, published by August House.

For more details about Dan's work and award-winning recordings, please visit his Web site: www.dankeding.com.

# Amy Douglas

Amy Douglas is a young Englishwoman with a passion for traditional stories and riddles. Although only twenty-nine at the time of this writing, she already has fourteen years of experience working in diverse venues and with all ages: from nursery tales and schools to year-long reminiscence projects; from arts centers to arts consultancy. She has performed at storytelling, literature, and folk festivals throughout Britain, Canada, and the United States.

Amy has been at the forefront of promoting the English storytelling scene for the past decade and a half. She was the first West Midlands Arts Storytelling Apprentice and spent a year studying with professional storytellers throughout Britain and America. She is a founder member of Tales at the Edge, one of the first modern-day storytelling clubs in England and the associated Festival at the Edge, the first storytelling festival of its kind, as well as having served two years on the board of the Society for Storytelling.

For more details about her work and publications, please visit Amy's Web site: www.amydouglas.com.

# About the Storytellers

**Storyteller Helen East in Hyde Park**

**Storytellers Dan Keding, Amy Douglas, Taffy Thomas, and Hugh Lupton
at the Sidmouth International Folk Festival**

**Dez Quarrél in the doorway of
Mythstories museum**

**Mike Rust with his coracle on the banks
of the River Severn in Ironbridge**

# Dave Arthur

Dave Arthur has been a professional storyteller, musician, and folklorist for more than twenty years. His deep-rooted understanding of English tradition and culture is respected throughout the world, and he has toured in Europe, the Americas, Russia, Asia, and Africa. In 2003, he was awarded the Gold Badge of the English Folk Dance and Song Society as a tribute to his wide-ranging accomplishments and dedication across the spectrum of English tradition. With his ex-wife, Toni Arthur, he spent a large amount of time collecting stories and folklore from Gypsies in Sussex and Kent; "The Hole Stone" and "The Glass House" are based on this material. Details of Dave Arthur's many recordings and publications are available on his Web site: www.davearthur.net. Contact: storyart@aol.com.

# Katy Cawkwell

Katy Cawkwell has developed a reputation for clear, powerful storytelling performances, drawing especially on British and Norse traditions. Since 1996, she has performed in a wide range of venues, from a tale of Loki in a burial chamber on Anglesey, to a twenty-minute version of *The Ring of the Nibelung* at the Barbican. She is particularly well known for her version of *Rhiannon* from the Welsh *Mabinogion,* which she has retold across Britain, including at Festival at the Edge and the Beyond the Border International Storytelling Festival. Contact: www.katycawkwell.co.uk and katycawkwell@email.com.

# Peter Chand

Peter Chand is a British-born Indian, living in Wolverhampton, whose parents came from the Punjab region of India in the 1950s. Peter is well known for his humorous tales that exploit the funny side of cultural misunderstandings. In 2002, Peter won the coveted title of the Biggest Liar in Shropshire, competing against a wild assortment of jokers, liars, and tall-tale tellers. Contact: chandstory@tiscali.co.uk.

## Des Charnley

Des Charnley has been telling folktales and legends since 1993. He has a wide repertoire, drawing on stories from all over the world as well as England. For more than the past decade, he has been a regular contributor to the English storytelling magazine, *Facts and Fiction.* Publications: Any Time Tales (CD, May 2004-08-10). Contact: 2 Lake View Villas, Bowness-on-Windermere, Cumbria, LA23 3BP.

## Viv Corringham

Viv Corringham has been a professional storyteller and vocalist since the mid-eighties. She has a master's degree in sonic art and combines storytelling with improvisation, low-tech electronics, eastern Mediterranean music, and soundscapes. She is passionate about creativity in education, her solo projects creating celebratory and stimulating environments where students actively participate in story and music making. Viv works both as a solo artist and with her company, Blue Camel Projects. Her storytelling and music have been celebrated throughout England, Australia, and Canada. Contact: vivdc@aol.com.

## Jamie Crawford

It was while working as a teacher that Jamie Crawford discovered the power of story, at first with his students, then slowly expanding to audiences of all ages. His natural talent and enthusiasm for the stories created such a demand for his work that three years ago he finally gave up teaching and became a full-time storyteller. Jamie works with traditional material, from jokes and anecdotes to extended wonder tales and myths, but draws freely on the genres of film, dance, poetry, and stand-up to create his unique compelling style. Contact: stories@jamiecrawford.co.uk.

## Michael Dacre

Michael has long been recognized as one of Britain's most articulate, witty, and lively storytellers. He tells traditional tales in a powerful literary style that is entertaining and well researched, embracing a love of language and strong narrative, which is sometimes scary, often hilarious, and usually both. Michael is a trained teacher, playwright, and aural historian. He has performed throughout Britain and Europe at arts centers, heritage sites, literature and storytelling festivals, Steiner schools, forests, and castles. Michael works as a solo artist; with his wife, Wendy, a traditional singer; or with Raventales, a group combining song, story, and bagpipe music. He has several recordings available through the Society for Storytelling, www.sfs.org. Contact: raventales@macunlimited.net and www.tellingtales.com/Storytellers/Tellers/Michael_Dacre-Raventales.htm.

## Helen East

Helen East works with stories—written, spoken, sung, and sewn; ancient legend to urban myth, universal tale types to intimate personal stories. Born in Sri Lanka, Helen is widely traveled—east to west, south to north (she counts Iceland a second home). Helen is interested in common lore, diversity of voice, and the meeting point between real and imagined worlds. Her many publications include international bestseller *The Singing Sack* and most recently *Spirit of the Forest*. Contact: www.eastorywilsound.co.uk, heltell@hotmail.com.

## Jim Eldon

Jim Eldon, from Hull in East Yorkshire, was born in 1947. For most of his working life, he has been on the boats as a fiddler, singer, and storyteller. His albums have been championed by BBC radio's foremost World Music DJ, Dr. Andy Kershaw. Discography: The Brid Fiddler (SDCD 003), Jim & Lynette Eldon (SDCD 008), Fiddle & Song (SDCD 009), Home From Se (SDCD 010). Available direct from Jim Eldon or from Veteran (www.veteran.co.uk). Contact: 21 Corona Drive, Hull, HU8 0HH, tel 44 (0) 1482 703261.

# Kelvin Hall

Kelvin Hall has told every kind of tale in every type of venue for twenty years. Storytelling is his passion, which he combines with his skills as a psycho-therapist, consultant, and trainer. He is storyteller in residence at the Ruskin Mill Centre, where he has developed a program of therapeutic storytelling for younger people with special needs. Publications include *Beyond the Forest: The Story of Parsifal and the Grail*. Contact: kelvinghall@ hotmail.com.

# Nick Hennessey

A harper and wordsmith with a love of stories, ballads, and music, Nick is a powerful and passionate performer forging and twisting together the song, the poem, the note, and the spoken word into a bridge broad enough for all. Nick has performed throughout the United Kingdom in venues such as the Albert Hall, the South Bank, and the Lowry in Manchester and across the world, with forthcoming tours in the Yukon and return visits to Japan and Finland planned. He has two solo CDs of harp, songs, and ballads: *Of Fire, Wind and Silver Stream* and *Pebble and Bone*. Contact: www.nickhennessey.co.uk.

# Katrice Horsley

Katrice is an inspirational performer and facilitator who has performed across the globe. She has a range of specific one-woman shows as well as a reper-toire of more than three hundred traditional stories. Katrice has used narrative in education, in community development, as a therapeutic tool, in anger manage-ment and conflict resolution, and in motivational work. She has worked as a per-former, specialist, and consultant for a variety of organizations including UNHCR (the United Nations' refugee agency), Education Action Zones, the UK Department for International Development, the Children's Fund, and many others. Contact: Katalysttales@aol.com/www.katalysttales.co.uk.

# Graham Langley

Graham Langley was born and brought up in the industrial city of Birmingham where he heard and told his first traditional stories when he ran a folk club in the city. His energy and enthusiasm for traditional stories has led him to become a much sought after storyteller in England and overseas. He is a director of the Traditional Arts Team and a major promoter of storytelling events in the United Kingdom. The *Times* calls him "A storyteller for the 21st century." Contact: graham@storytelling.uk.net/www.storytelling.uk.net.

# Hugh Lupton

A true wordsmith with more than twenty years of professional experience, Hugh Lupton is one of Britain's leading storytellers. He has steeped himself in the British narrative tradition, telling (among other things) *Beowulf, Gawain and the Green Knight, The Tain,* and many English folktales and ballads. He has toured throughout the world, often for the British Council. Hugh celebrates language in all its varied forms with epics, talk, riddles, jokes, stories, and music from venues such as the Symphony Space Theatre in New York to his local primary school. Details of Hugh's many publications and recordings are available on his Web site: www.hughlupton.com. Contact: hughlupton@aol.com.

# Mike O'Connor

Mike O'Connor is a musician and storyteller who works throughout England. He writes extensively on musical topics and is the author of *Ilow Kernow,* the definitive book on Cornish instrumental music. In 2002, was honored as Bard of the Gorsedd of Cornwall. Mike has a fine repertoire of seal or selkie legends and Cornish tales. Full details of his many recordings and publications are available on his Web site: www.lyngham.co.uk. Contact: moconnor@ision.co.uk.

# Dez Quarréll

Dez Quarréll has worked within the arts for thirty years as a musician, fine artist, writer and storyteller, project facilitator, and promoter. He has been the instigator of many innovative and original projects, one of which was setting up the world's first story museum, Mythstories, in Shropshire in 1998. A Registered Charity, Mythstories promotes storytelling, literacy, and literature in enjoyable and innovative ways for everyone. It forms part of the curriculum content of the British National Grid for Learning. Visit its Web site: www.mythstories.com.

# Mike Rust

Mike Rust has spent most of his life living in the Welsh Marches, the English lands that border Wales. He has always had a love of stories, jokes, anecdotes, and tales of the strange and the magical. Throughout his life he has collected stories from farmhands and landowners, gamekeepers and publicans. He is a founder member of Tales at the Edge, one of the first modern-day storytelling clubs in England, and the associated Festival at the Edge, as well as a founder member of the Society for Storytelling, a binational body that promotes stories and storytelling in England and Wales.

# Taffy Thomas

Taffy Thomas has been an integral part of the traditional arts in England for more than twenty years, a fact recognized and celebrated when he was awarded the Member of the British Empire for services to storytelling and charity in the New Year Honors List 2001. Taffy tells tales of place and tradition and is dedicated to his role as a link in the chain, holding stories in trust for the next generation. He is famous for his tale coat, embroidered with many beautiful pictures with each picture holding at least one story. Both he and his tale coat have toured throughout the world, including performances at the American National Storytelling Festival in Tennessee. Contact: www.taffythomas.co.uk/admin@taffythomas.co.uk.

# Sally Tonge

Sally Tonge lives in Shropshire and works all over the United Kingdom using stories as a tool for literature, community, and arts development. She tells stories from places she has visited and lived and from the people she has met along the way. "Living and working in Cornwall for eight years made a big impact on me, and I still tell friends who go on holiday to Cornwall to look out as they walk along the beach, for if they see a heart washed up, they should give it a stroke—it could well be mine!" Contact: saltonge@coronationcottages.fsnet.co.uk.

# Richard Walker

Sadly no longer with us, Richard Walker was an inspirational storyteller deeply involved in the English storytelling scene. He was a founder member of one of the first modern storytelling clubs in England, Tales at the Edge, and its associated Festival at the Edge. He also served as a director on the board of the Society for Storytelling (SfS). He was widely traveled and an ambassador for English storytelling. Publications include *My Very First Book of Pirates* (ISBN 1 901223 50 7) and *The Barefoot Book of Trickster Tales* (ISBN 1 901223 83 3). Many of his recordings are available from the Society for Storytelling: www.sfs.org.